T0358186

A Century of
Federal Reserve
Monetary Policy
Issues and Implications for the Future

A CENTURY OF FEDERAL RESERVE MONETARY POLICY

Issues and Implications for the Future

THOMAS R SAVING

Texas A&M University, USA

World Scientific

NEW JERSEY · LONDON · SINGAPORE · BEIJING · SHANGHAI · HONG KONG · TAIPEI · CHENNAI · TOKYO

Published by

World Scientific Publishing Co. Pte. Ltd.

5 Toh Tuck Link, Singapore 596224

USA office: 27 Warren Street, Suite 401-402, Hackensack, NJ 07601

UK office: 57 Shelton Street, Covent Garden, London WC2H 9HE

Library of Congress Cataloging-in-Publication Data

Names: Saving, Thomas Robert, 1933– author.

Title: A century of Federal Reserve monetary policy : issues and implications for the future /
Thomas R Saving (Texas A&M University, USA).

Description: New Jersey : World Scientific, [2019] | Includes bibliographical references and index.

Identifiers: LCCN 2019018763 | ISBN 9789811201776

Subjects: LCSH: United States. Federal Reserve Board--History. | United States--
Economic policy--History. | Monetary policy--United States--History.

Classification: LCC HG2563 .S34 2019 | DDC 339.530973--dc23

LC record available at https://lccn.loc.gov/2019018763

British Library Cataloguing-in-Publication Data

A catalogue record for this book is available from the British Library.

For any available supplementary material, please visit
https://www.worldscientific.com/worldscibooks/10.1142/11319#t=suppl

Desk Editor: Shreya Gopi

Typeset by Stallion Press
Email: enquiries@stallionpress.com

Printed in Singapore

Contents

About the Author

Thomas R. Saving is Director Emeritus, *Private Enterprise Research Center* and University Distinguished Professor of Economics Emeritus, Texas A&M University. He has been elected to the post of President of the Western Economics Association, the Southern Economics Association and the Association of Private Enterprise Education.

Saving received his Ph.D. from the University of Chicago in 1960. Prior to joining the economics faculty at Texas A&M University in 1968, he was on the faculty at University of Washington in Seattle and Michigan State University. He attained the rank of full professor at Michigan State University in 1966, six years after the award of this Ph.D. in 1960.

In 2000, President Clinton appointed him as a Public Trustee of the Social Security and Medicare Trust Funds. On May 2, 2001, President Bush named him to the bipartisan President's Commission to Strengthen Social Security. On April 19, 2006, President Bush appointed him to an unprecedented second term as a Public Trustee of the Social Security and Medicare Trust Funds which expired in December 2007.

His early research was on Monetary Theory and Policy. During that time, he co-authored two books with fellow colleague Boris P. Pesek, *Money, Wealth and Economic Theory*, Macmillan, 1967 and *Foundations of Money and Banking*, Macmillan, 1968 and published 20 monetary theory articles in major journals. After a period of research on the benefit of markets in solving the pressing issues in health care and Social Security when he was a co-editor of *Medicare Reform: Issues and Answers*, University of Chicago Press, 1999, the co-author of *The Economics of Medicare Reform*, W.E. Upjohn Institute, 2000 and *The*

Diagnosis and Treatment of Medicare, AEI Press, 2007, he returned to his first love, monetary economics. He has served on the editorial board of the *American Economic Review*, the *Journal of Money, Credit and Banking* and was a co-editor of *Economic Inquiry*. He has published editorials in the *New York Times*, the *LA Times*, the *Washington Post* and the *Wall Street Journal*.

Part I

The Federal Reserve: A Century of Monetary Policy

Chapter 1

The Advent of Central Banking in the United States

Introduction

The debate concerning the wisdom of an independent central bank has been with us virtually since the founding of the republic. Among the powers delegated to Congress in Section 8 of Article 1 of the Constitution of the United States is the power "to coin money, regulate the Value thereof, ...". Thus, to the extent that a central bank can do the equivalent of coining money and by the rate at which it does this, regulate the value thereof, it would appear that the Constitution precludes us from having a truly independent central bank.

That said, however, Congress can delegate powers to agencies and as a result can establish a central bank and give it the power to coin money and regulate the value thereof. This delegation of the right to coin money and regulate the value thereof meant little during the period of our history where we were on a metallic standard. During that period, the value of domestically coined money was determined by the world price of gold and the rate of exchange between the dollar and gold as determined by Congress.

Except for those periods where the free exchange of money for gold was curtailed, the value of domestically produced money was determined by Congress in its setting of the exchange rate for gold or silver or both. One such period of the suspension of free exchange of money for gold was the greenback era during and following the Civil War. During this period, both gold coins and greenbacks circulated with continuously changing

3

exchange rates reflecting the course of the war. Since Congress authorized the printing of greenbacks and by the extent of the issue it regulated the value thereof, it was certainly within its Constitutional right. In contrast, the amount of gold coinage was outside the ability of Congress to regulate.

It could be argued that the issues involving the establishment of an independent central bank that could do the equivalent of coining money and regulate that value thereof would only be relevant in a world without a metallic standard. Thus, even though the Federal Reserve System began operation as a central bank in 1914, as long as the United States remained on the gold standard, it was limited in its power to coin money and regulate its value. However, for the question of an independent central bank, the past is irrelevant. For all practical purposes, once the nation eliminated the rights of citizens to exchange currency for gold in the 1930s, we left the gold standard. Without the discipline of the gold standard, the Federal Reserve would seem to have all the makings of a central bank that has the ability to coin money and regulate the value thereof.

A Brief History of Pre-Federal Reserve United States Central Banking

In the United States, central banking began with the "First Bank of the United States", chartered in 1791 for 20 years. The First Bank of the United States had a national charter but was essentially a private bank with private citizens owning 80% of the ownership shares. The bank was the fiscal agent for the government, collected tax revenues and paid government bills.[1] To ensure the bank's independence from the Treasury, the First Bank of the United States was forbidden from purchasing government bonds.[2] This prohibition on buying government debt is not surprising as the founding fathers had a mistrust of central banks. This mistrust

---

[1] See "The First Bank of the United States: A Chapter in the History of Central Banking," Federal Reserve Bank of Philadelphia. https://www.philadelphiafed.org/-/media/publications/economic-education/first-bank.pdf.

[2] Interestingly, when the European Union began and the European Central Bank was established, it was also prohibited from buying the sovereign debt of member countries. This prohibition has since been rescinded, as will be discussed in later chapters.

was due in no small part to their experience with the Bank of England, a nationally chartered but privately owned bank, and its role in financing British wars. The First Bank was allowed to die in 1811 after the expiration of its 20-year charter.

The First Bank was succeeded in 1816 by the "Bank of the United States" that operated much like a central bank. Unlike the Bank of England that was entirely privately owned, the federal government owned 20% of the Bank of the United States. At the time, the nation's paper currency was issued by private banks and was convertible into specie, i.e., gold or silver coinage. This convertibility was what controlled the issue since if a bank increased its issue of paper money, the increased issue would find its way back to the bank of issue to be exchanged for specie.

A principal role played by the Bank of the United States was to expedite the return of any specific bank-issued currency to the bank of issue for specie. This practice expedited return of currency and reduced what used to be called float, defined as currency in the process of being returned for conversion. It is not surprising that the banks whose profitability was most affected by the reduction of float were opposed to the Bank of the United States. While Congress reauthorized the Second Bank of the United States, President Jackson vetoed the legislation. Since Congress was unable to override President Jackson's veto, the Second Bank died, leaving the United States without a central bank from 1836 until the Federal Reserve went into operation in 1914.

The primary goal of both the First and Second Banks of the United States was to control the issue of paper money that was, without them, the sole province of private state banks. In one sense, however, the Banks were unnecessary since privately issued paper money would not circulate without the promise of convertibility into specie.

While banks of this period are often referred to as "wildcat" banks, no bank's notes would circulate if their notes could not be redeemed. In fact, notes issued by the various state-chartered banks when spent at locations distant from the issuing bank were discounted. The discount was related to the time required to return the notes to the issuing bank in exchange for specie. In fact, the reality was that a bank located in a remote location in order to make its notes difficult to return would quickly fail, as its notes would be unacceptable by all.

The requirement by users of the notes that they be convertible into specie served to control the issue at each of the independent issuing banks. The Second Bank was especially involved in speeding up the process of submitting currency to issuing private banks for conversion into specie. The effect of this accelerated note redemption ultimately led to the bank's demise as the Jackson Administration ran for re-election on this issue.

Until the Civil War, the nation was essentially on a metallic standard as the value of a dollar was defined by an Act of Congress. Specifically, Congress set the dollar price of an ounce of silver or gold. This bimetallic standard led to the exodus of one or the other metal as the relative world gold–silver price changed. As a result of this, which was essentially a shifting metal standard, Congress adopted in 1833 a one-metal standard, gold.

For all practical purposes, the United States had no national paper currency until the Civil War when "greenbacks" were issued as a national currency to aid in financing the war.[3] These greenbacks were not convertible into gold, but were legal tender so that taxes could be paid with them. Thus, at least for all domestic purposes, the gold standard was abandoned. In addition to greenbacks, the Civil War saw the establishment of the National Banking System to help finance the mounting federal debt.[4] By the close of the war, the only paper currencies still in circulation were greenbacks and national bank notes as the notes issued by state banks were taxed out of existence.

From the demise of the Second Bank of the United States in 1836 until the Federal Reserve Act of 1913 that authorized the establishment of the Federal Reserve System, the nation had no central bank. This period was one of relatively stable prices, with the exception of the Civil War period's inflation and subsequent deflation from 1867 to 1879 when the greenback price of gold was once again fixed. Interestingly, the post-Civil War period was one of declining prices, or deflation, but was also a period of rapid economic growth.

---

[3] On June 22, 1775 the Continental Congress issued $2 million in currency that became known as "Continentals" and were ultimately famous in the term "not worth a continental".
[4] The national banks were allowed to issue banknotes up to 90% of the value of their holdings of government bonds. While the national banks were not central banks, they still played the role of financing a war just as a feared central bank might have done. Indeed, the same ploy, suspension of convertibility, used by the Bank of England to finance wars was imposed by Congress.

Subsequent to the immediate post-Civil War period of growth and declining price levels — the period from 1897 to the opening of the Federal Reserve in 1914 — there was a period of rising price levels. This period of price rises was primarily the result of gold discoveries in South Africa, Alaska and Colorado that led to rapid increases in the world's gold stock. Given that the United States was on the gold standard, the Treasury stood ready to buy gold at the official price. As a result, the increase in the stock of gold corresponded to an increase in the money stock and prices.

Why a Central Bank?

Considering the long history of prosperity in the United States without a central bank, what led to the establishment of our first real central bank? One reason was the increasing complexity of the financial system including the rise of the importance of near banks, the loan and trust companies, what we now refer to as shadow banks. The expanded financial sector opened financial markets to small asset individuals. These financial institutions, for simplicity we shall categorize all of them as banks, take in small deposits and collect them into larger bundles and make loans. This activity allows the banks to pay small depositors for their deposits and make income on the difference between payments to depositors and income from loans.

It is fractional reserve banking that makes all this possible. Banks borrow short, that is, they take in deposits that are available to depositors on demand. Then banks use these funds to lend long, that is, make loans that are not payable on demand. As a result, banks must keep currency as reserves for the contingency that depositor withdrawals exceed additions.

But fractional reserve banking can also be the cause of financial distress. The financial distress comes when the public wants to change the form of their money from deposits at banks to currency. While the banks in one sense are solvent, meaning that their assets are greater than or equal to their liabilities, they hold very little currency. So, when many more depositors than usual want to convert to currency, the bank must find currency. When bank customers cannot get currency now the result can lead to a "run" on the bank and if other banks are similarly affected, it can result in a liquidity crisis.

Such liquidity crises are when a central bank that has the ability to essentially costlessly print currency can come into play. The central bank can then use this freshly printed currency to make short-term purchases of bank assets, called repos, and when the public's desire for more currency passes, they can sell the assets back to the banks.

The cause of this form of liquidity crisis is the fact that in a fractional reserve banking system, deposits become loans to borrowing customers and currency reserves. Then when there is a surge in the depositor demand for their money, the currency reserves will be inadequate if the surge is large enough. This ability to transition between deposits and currency is referred to as form elasticity of the money supply. Importantly, this same issue applies to what we might term *near banks*. A near bank is a financial institution that takes in money from investors and allows these investors to withdraw some or all of their investment in a specified time frame, perhaps even overnight. Because the near bank liabilities are not demand liabilities, these institutions require smaller cash reserves, but are nonetheless fractional reserve institutions.

Money market funds are an example of a common investment at a financial institution.[5] Such funds borrow short and lend short. However, the investors treat their investment as having nearly instant availability. Thus, a significant increase in the investors demand for cash, either in the form of currency or demand deposits at their bank, forces the fund to sell assets. Even though these assets are short term in nature, it may be difficult for a fund to instantly sell off a significant share of these assets.

This lack of the ability of the system to transform one form of money, bank deposits, to another form of money, currency, has led to a series of financial crises. A financial crisis occurred whenever the public decided for any reason that it desired to hold its money as currency rather than deposits. In the rush to get currency, the financial institutions had to suspend the convertibility of their deposits into currency on demand.

---

[5]The rise of money market funds as a major player in the financial markets was aided by the enforcement of Federal Reserve Regulation Q that limited the rate of interest that banks could pay on customer deposits. In the 1980s, money market funds began allowing immediate withdrawals through an instrument known as a Negotiable Order of Withdrawal (NOW). The NOW accounts paid market rates of interest and for all practical purposes were checking accounts. As the regulated banks lost deposits to the money market funds, Regulation Q had to be abandoned.

But this form of crisis does not imply that the financial institutions were insolvent, but only that their assets could not be instantly turned into currency. A central bank can deal with this, which is essentially a non-bank insolvency liquidity crisis. Here, the central bank is not supplying reserves to the money market funds but is transforming their temporarily non-liquid assets into liquidity. A central bank can either loan the financial institutions the liquidity they require or exchange liquidity for the institution's short-term assets.

A central bank can eliminate the effect of liquidity crises through its ability to augment the supply of currency by temporarily buying financial system assets through repurchase agreements. As long as the illiquid assets retain their fundamental value, the financial system will be able to honor the repurchase agreements once the crisis has ended.

However, when the crisis is the result of a fall in the value of the assets underlying the demand liabilities, and if the repurchase contracts are at face value rather than market value, then they cannot be repaid. This form of crisis is not a liquidity crisis but is the result of a real change in the value of financial assets based on real capital or output. The question is: Is there a role for a central bank when the issue is real and not nominal? Should the central bank use its ability to print money to make the investors whole, and if it does, what are the consequences of such an action?

First and foremost, a central bank cannot solve a crisis caused by a genuine fall in the value of real assets as it has no power to affect their value in real terms. However, a central bank can print money to make up the difference between the new and old values of the underlying assets. Now, the money supply is larger and with output unchanged, the price level will rise. The end result is a redistribution to the holders of financial assets whose value has fallen from currency and deposit holders.

The same rescue could have been undertaken by the Treasury through tax relief for the injured investors. Such tax relief would have been a redistribution from all non-investor taxpayers to these investors. In either solution, there is no way to restore value to real assets that are genuinely less valuable. The answer to what is best has to do with the value of a stable currency. Perhaps, we should let the Treasury do the redistribution and the central bank do what central banks do best: maintain the value of the currency.

How Central Banks Control the Money Supply

Central banks control the money supply through their role as the monopoly issuer of legal tender currency. While legal tender currency is not all of the money supply, it is the fundamental ingredient for all other forms of what can be considered money. Almost all transactions are conducted with currency or things that are convertible into currency. This includes checks, credit cards and debit cards. In fact, it is this convertibility that makes these other forms of transaction assets acceptable as a means of payment.

However, when the Federal Reserve was established, it certainly did not have a monopoly on the production of legal tender. Competing producers of legal tender included the national banks that produced national bank notes and the Treasury that produced both silver and gold certificates. The complete monopoly position of the Federal Reserve did not occur until 1971 when the United States totally abandoned tying the dollar to gold. However, for all practical purposes, the United States left the direct influence of gold on the money supply in the 1930s. After that time, while foreign countries could still buy and/or sell gold from and to the Treasury at the then-official price of $35 an ounce, the money supply was almost immune to these transactions. There were rare times after the 1930s, however, where the international transactions in gold did affect the monetary base, but in 1971, this connection was permanently broken.

To understand how a central bank controls the important components of the money supply, let's begin by assuming that the Federal Reserve is a monopoly supplier of legal tender money, as it has been since at least 1971.[6] Based on the generally accepted idea that the value of a unit of currency is related to the quantity of currency and the total value of transactions to be conducted, to control the currency issue is to control its value. For this discussion, let's further assume that the goal of the money supplier is to keep the value of its currency constant.[7]

---

[6] For a complete discussion of the influence of pre-1971 Treasury gold operations on the level of Federal Reserve production of legal tender money, see Pesek and Saving (1968).

[7] This assumption is at odds with the current published goals of all the major central banks, the Bank of England, the European Central Bank, the Bank of Japan and the Unites States Federal Reserve that the value of currency should fall between 2% and 3% per year.

Just how does the Federal Reserve, or any central bank, increase the money supply? It goes into the market and buys already outstanding financial assets, in most cases Treasury bonds. Rather than buy assets on the market, why not just buy Treasury bonds direct from the Treasury? The answer is simple. The past history of deals between treasuries and central banks have resulted in disastrous falls in the value of a nation's currency. As a result, most central banks are precluded from direct dealings with their respective treasuries.

However, a nation's central bank is essentially owned by the citizens of its country, and the Treasury is the country's financial center. Thus, one way for the citizen-owned central bank earnings to be distributed to the citizens is for such earnings to be remitted to the Treasury. In a balanced government budget world, the government would reduce citizen taxes by the amount of central bank earnings. In some sense then, the Treasury, acting for the citizens, is the owner of the central bank as it is the residual income recipient. This relationship will aid us later in understanding a central bank's balance sheet.

Given that the central bank wants to increase the money supply, how does the central bank pay for the necessary purchase of assets, either Treasury bonds or private assets? First, the central bank has the nation's only money printing press. Does it just run the money press and pay cash? Well, the answer is no. Essentially, it makes deposits to the sellers' bank accounts. The central bank buys and sells assets through the creation and destruction of bank reserves. Of course, the owners of these reserves can turn them into cash and require the currency printing press to run, but the central bank's printing press prints reserves and currency in whatever combination the public demands.

A Central Bank's Balance Sheet

Central banks are truly unique in that they are monopoly producers of a product, currency or its equivalent, bank reserves. To further their uniqueness, these products are virtually costless to produce. Finally, as icing on the cake, the sum of these products cannot be returned. That is, while currency can be turned into reserves and reserves can be turned into currency, their sum cannot be reduced or increased except by the central bank. If the public turns either currency or reserves into the central bank, all they get is currency or reserves in return.

Since the public cannot reverse the central bank's sale or purchase of assets, an open-market purchase of treasuries using the costless to produce reserves increases the asset holdings of the central bank and increases the bank's net worth. But does it? Certainly, the newly acquired bonds are assets. But is this increase in the central bank's assets offset by a liability? If so, what is the nature of the liability?

Contrast the central bank's purchase of an asset, say bonds, using costless currency or reserves, with a private citizen's purchase of bonds. When individuals purchase bonds, they do so with another asset, essentially they trade one asset for another with no change in their net worth. For an individual, a bond purchase could be financed by that individual issuing the equivalent of a bond, taking out a loan or selling another asset. In either case, an individual's bond purchase cannot increase that individual's net worth. Individuals cannot produce assets without incurring cost, but a central bank can.

Reserves and currency are not liabilities of the central bank because the decision by the holder of these assets to bring them to the central bank to be exchanged for these same reserves and currency has no effect on the central bank's income. What happens when a holder of reserves brings reserves to the central bank? They simply get currency or reserves. If it were possible for the public to bring currency to the central bank, what would they get in return? They would just receive the same amount of currency.

When the central bank uses reserves or currency to buy assets, their net worth goes up by the full purchase cost. By the same token, sales of bonds by the central bank for which they receive currency or bank reserves reduce the central bank's net wealth by the full amount of the sale.[8]

To see this as an appropriate way to distinguish assets and liabilities, think about it from the perspective of the owner of the central bank's income, the Treasury. Assets are things that contribute to the earnings of the owner, and liabilities are things that detract from the owner's income. The level of currency and reserves outstanding represent past purchases of assets by the central bank. All the earnings from these assets accrue to the

---

[8]This argument first appeared in Pesek and Saving (1966).

Treasury. The fact that the assets were purchased with costless currency or reserves does not affect the net value of the assets and has no effect on the net income to the Treasury.

The levels of outstanding currency and reserves are appropriately "off balance sheet items" because their total cannot change without actions by the central bank to increase or reduce assets. The levels of outstanding currency and reserves have no recourse back to the owners of the income from the assets obtained when the currency and reserves were issued. Importantly, the composition of the central bank-issued currency and reserves can change but their total cannot, without the central bank disposing off or acquiring assets.[9]

Conclusion

For most of its existence, our nation was without a central bank. Moreover, for most of this period, the nation experienced stable prices, i.e., a constant value of the dollar, and economic growth. In fact, our first attempt at establishing a national bank, the First Bank of the United States, was not a central bank as we know it. It did not have the power to print bank notes, currency, and as a result could not regulate the quantity of money and the value thereof.

Then, the Second Bank of the United States was established, and while it did have the authority to issue notes, its primary role in the control of the money supply was in expediting the return of state bank notes to the issuing state banks in return for specie (metallic money). It was its due diligence in expediting the return of bank notes to their issuer that led to its unpopularity, especially among the banking community.

With the demise of the Second Bank in 1836, we were without a central bank until the beginning of the Federal Reserve System in 1914. It certainly is clear that the financial world has increased, both in its complexity and in the share of the population that have regular access to it. Whether or not these changes necessitated the establishment of a central bank, we have one.

---

[9] As we shall see, the introduction of interest on reserves in 2008 made reserves real liabilities as the interest payments directly affect the transfers from the Federal Reserve to the Treasury.

Both the First and Second Banks of the United States were, for all practical purposes, privately owned banks with a federal franchise. Neither bank had a monopoly on the note issue and, as such, could not control the money supply and protect the value thereof. Ultimately, that changed with the establishment of the Federal Reserve.

The question is, has this central bank been a protector of the nation's financial well-being or has it been what the nation's founders feared, a tool of Wall Street? With this issue in mind, the remainder of this book analyzes the behavior of the Federal Reserve System. During what periods has the Federal Reserve been allowed to act as an independent central bank? The goal here is to put this behavior into the context of the current interest in reining in the Federal Reserve's freedom to act independently.[10]

---

[10] For an excellent but lengthy discussion of the theory and practice of central banking before the Federal Reserve, see Allan H. Meltzer, A History of the Federal Reserve: Volume I: 1913–1951, Chapter 2.

Chapter 2

The Early Years of the Federal Reserve: A Limited Role for Independence

Introduction

The monetary crisis of 1908 is often thought to be the harbinger of the legislation that created the Federal Reserve System. This crisis, as with those preceding it, was a product of a fractional reserve banking system that was unable to respond to large changes in how the public desired to hold their money balances. Whenever there was uncertainty about the banking system's safety, the public responded by demanding currency. This problem was apparent in the title to the Act establishing the Federal Reserve System, which explicitly refers to furnishing an elastic currency.[1]

How would a central bank ensure an elastic currency? The principal means available to a central bank that would allow the banking system to respond to runs on the banks in the system is tied to the second item in the Act's title: "...afford means of rediscounting commercial paper." This rediscounting of commercial paper would allow the Federal Reserve to supply currency to banks by temporally taking their commercial assets. Then when the crisis was over, returning these assets to the banks.

Because of the fear that a single central bank would become a tool of Wall Street and Washington, the Act established 12 Federal Reserve

---

[1] The Act is entitled "An Act To provide for the establishment of Federal reserve banks, to furnish an elastic currency, to afford means of rediscounting commercial paper, to establish a more effective supervision of banking in the United States, and for other purposes."

banks. These new regional Federal Reserve banks could convert commercial paper held by banks within their region into currency. Now, the public could be confident that banks, when faced with a run for currency, could convert their non-liquid assets into currency by temporarily sending commercial paper to their regional Federal Reserve Bank and receive currency in return. When the crisis was over, the local banks would buy back the paper.

A Federal Reserve Subject to the Gold Standard

At its outset, the new Federal Reserve System that began operation in 1914 and the Treasury were intertwined. Two members of the original seven member Federal Reserve Board were in the Administration: the Secretary of the Treasury and the Comptroller of the Currency. This close relationship was furthered by the onset of World War I soon after the Federal Reserve began operations. The independent central bank role of the Federal Reserve was mitigated by the requirement that it aid in financing the war. In the beginning, the early regional Federal Reserve banks had control over the discount rate they charged to banks in their region but little else.[2]

Also, this early Federal Reserve was subject to the vagaries of the gold standard, where inflows of gold increased the monetary base and outflows of gold decreased it. While we still have those who believe that a return to a gold standard will solve our financial problems, the experience at the beginning of the Federal Reserve highlights the problems that a system based on the market for a specific metal can have.

Just after the Federal Reserve began, the war in Europe forced European countries to leave the gold standard in an effort to finance their war effort. As a result, gold left those countries and came to the United States. The influx of gold as it fled Europe increased the United States' money supply and resulted in inflation even before the United States entered WWI. Then, our financing of the war continued this monetary expansion. Inflation began even before the United States entered the war

---

[2] The 12 regional banks had the ability to determine their own discount rates until the reforms enacted in the 1930s.

and reached 11% in 1916, the year before the United States declared war on Germany in April 1917. The inflation peaked at 18.6% in 1918, the last year of hostilities. Inflation, however, was still in double digits in 1919 at 13.8%.[3] These were inflation rates not seen again until the late 1970s.

In the 1920s, a falling price level brought an influx of gold to the United States as the real value of the fixed dollar gold exchange rate of $20.67 per troy ounce rose. To offset this increased flow of gold on the money supply, the Federal Reserve increased the interest rate at which they bought and sold assets to the banking system. These interest rate increases led to increased political pressure, especially from the agriculture sector. Once again, it was clear that the early years of the Federal Reserve System were not that of an independent central bank.

There is general agreement that Federal Reserve policy from late 1929 to 1933, or the lack thereof, contributed to the depth of the Great Depression.[4] At least part of the problem continues to this day. The obsession of equating monetary policy easing or tightening with interest rate changes has at times made central bank responses to economic conditions counterproductive.[5] For example, in the early to mid-1930s, falling interest rates were equated with an easing monetary policy. At the same time, however, the money supply was falling and the public was changing the desired form of its monetary holdings from bank deposits to currency. Just when the Federal Reserve could have made good on its directive in the original Act to make the currency elastic, it failed to do so.[6]

Not to belittle the ability or importance of Federal Reserve monetary policy while it was constrained by the gold standard, this work will concentrate on the period after the United States left the gold standard. At least leaving the gold standard was the beginning of what we might term *the modern era of Federal Reserve policy*. That is not to say that once the gold standard shackles were removed the Federal Reserve was free of outside control, but only that under the right circumstances, it could have operated as an independent central bank.

---

[3] These inflation rates are from Balke and Gordon (1986).
[4] For an excellent discussion of the role of Federal Reserve in the downturn, see Humphrey and Timberlake (2018).
[5] See Saving (1967).
[6] See Meltzer (2003).

The Post-Gold Standard Federal Reserve

With the passage of the Banking Act of 1933, the Gold Reserve Act of 1934 and the Securities Exchange Act of 1934, the Federal Reserve began a transition from a pure central bank with the sole charge of managing the macroeconomy to an agency also charged with managing certain aspects of the microeconomy.

The Banking Act of 1933 established the Federal Open Market Committee (FOMC) that is now the determiner of the Federal Reserve policy. Prior to the establishment of the FOMC, the individual bank Governors, now presidents, of the 12 banks determined the Federal Reserve policy. Importantly, during that period each bank could and did conduct independent policy. With the onset of the Banking Act of 1933, the individual banks lost most of their autonomy.

The Gold Reserve Act of 1934 broke the inflexible link between gold imports and exports and the monetary base, and ultimately the money supply.[7] However, there remained a role for gold since the issue of Federal Reserve notes required gold backing. To ensure that a lack of gold would not restrict the Federal Reserve's ability to conduct monetary policy, the official price of gold was raised from $20.67 to $35 per troy ounce, an almost 70% increase in the value of Federal Reserve gold reserves.

The fear that the Great Depression was at least partially caused by speculative investing that created a stock market bubble and ultimate crash, led to legislation to curtail such activity. The Securities and Exchange Act of 1934 authorized the first explicit role of the Federal Reserve as a regulator of financial markets. This Act established Federal Reserve Regulations T and U, which gave the Federal Reserve the power to set the margin requirement on loans to finance stock market purchases. This Act also allowed the Federal Reserve Board to establish Regulation Q, which imposed interest rate ceilings on bank deposits. Such regulation was designed to restrict bank competition in attracting deposits on the theory that such competition would lead banks to increase the riskiness of their investments in order to pay competitive rates to depositors.

---

[7] Perhaps inflexible is too strong a term when applied to the role of gold inflows and outflows and the monetary base. Prior to the two Acts, the Federal Reserve banks did discount bank paper and conducted open market operations that mitigated the effect of gold flows. On this issue, see Meltzer (2003: 166–168).

The Federal Reserve Act of 1913 explicitly highlighted the charge of the bank to ensure an elastic currency. But when the time came to make good on this charge, the precipitous downturn of 1930–1933, the Federal Reserve was found wanting. Although at that time, at least one could blame the Federal Reserve's failure on its maintenance of the gold standard even as the world's other major economies vacated it. The fact is, however, the inflows of gold from European countries vacating the gold standard could have allowed the Federal Reserve to satisfy the public's increased demand for currency. The ensuing failure of the Federal Reserve to adjust to the public's demand for currency in the early 1930s is attributed by many to have increased the depth of the early 1930s downturn.

While one would expect that a country's central bank would be the only supplier of a nation's currency; this was not the case for the Federal Reserve. In fact, it was only in the 1930s that the Federal Reserve became the nation's monopoly supplier of legal tender, at least of additional issues of legal tender. The first steps toward making the Federal Reserve the monopoly supplier of legal tender currency began in 1935 with the elimination of National Bank Notes as a currency competitor. These notes existed from 1864 when national banks were allowed to issue currency up to their holdings of special US Treasury bonds. These special bonds were retired by the Treasury, perhaps financed by the requirement that the Federal Reserve turn over its gold and gold certificate holdings to the Treasury.[8]

Also, during the latter 1930s, the issue of US notes (greenbacks) was suspended and while these notes remained legal tender, their total issue was fixed. The same thing is true of silver certificates that were also issued by the Treasury. Thus, with the issue of competitive currencies fixed, the Federal Reserve became, at least on the margin, the monopoly issuer of legal tender. After this point in time, any increase in legal tender currency that would be required as the economy grew to maintain the value of the dollar would have to come from the Federal Reserve.

---

[8] The provision for issuing National Bank Notes was terminated on August 1, 1935, when the remaining US bonds with the circulation privilege were redeemed by the Treasury. While National Bank Notes are still legal tender, although most if not all existing National Bank Notes are in the hands of numismatic collectors.

Thus, the gold standard cannot be blamed for the next 1930s Federal Reserve policy error. By 1935, system excess reserves were rising, and the Federal Reserve Board was concerned that these excess reserves could form the basis for monetary expansion and inflation. The decision was made to stop this potential inflation at the starting gate by raising reserve requirements and, thus, absorbing the excess.

The real question is why were the banks holding excess reserves that had a zero yield? If the answer was the fear of another surge in the public's desire to substitute currency for deposits and another failure of the Federal Reserve to act to ensure the form elasticity of the money supply, then these reserves were not excess from the banking system's perspective. Subsequent performance in the economy supports proposition that the "excess" reserves were not excess in the view of the banks. As a result, the series of three increases in required reserves by the Federal Reserve had a significant negative effect on economic activity as banks contracted loans to restore desired "excess" reserves. The result of this loan contraction was what many refer to as a double dip recession.

Conclusion

One might imagine that a role of the central bank would be to maintain the value of the nation's currency. But what does this mean? Simplistically, it would seem to mean that the central bank should conduct monetary policy to ensure a stable price level. Price stability of this form would allow citizens to be assured that their dollar earnings and savings would be accurate indicators of both present and future purchasing power. A second role of a central bank would be to mitigate the effect of changes in the public's desired form composition of their money holdings. On both of these grounds, the early Federal Reserve failed.

At its outset, however, the newly formed Federal Reserve System was restricted by the nation's adherence to the gold standard. While it could issue legal tender currency, an overissue, a level of currency that would depreciate the value of the dollar, would result in the dollars being turned in for gold at the then-existing rate of $20.67 per troy ounce. Moreover, as the Federal Reserve System began operations, it was not the only supplier of legal tender as National Bank Notes, greenbacks and silver certificates continued to circulate.

Even with the adherence to the gold standard, the onset of the Great Depression and the resulting falling price level left the Federal Reserve with a significant ability to handle the increase in the demand for currency. That it failed to respond to the public's increased demand for currency that resulted from the Great Depression's increased financial uncertainty, exacerbated the impact and length of the economic crisis.

The impetus for the passage of the Federal Reserve Act was to alleviate currency crises by making the money supply elastic. There was every reason for the banks to assume that a financial crisis would result in the Federal Reserve increasing its discounting of bank assets. But rather than satisfying the public's increased demand for currency by discounting bank assets, the Federal Reserve failed to do this, and the money supply fell dramatically, just when a significant increase was called for. This failure to discount bank assets ultimately led to the closing of the banks by the Roosevelt Administration.

Some of its early failures may be forgiven, as this early Federal Reserve was heavily restricted in its ability to act as an independent central bank, because the nation was on the gold standard. As a result, inflows and outflows of gold affected the money supply and limited the Federal Reserve's ability to be an independent central bank. The tie of the money supply to gold ended with the 1933 Presidential Executive Order 6102 that required all gold certificates to be presented to the Federal Reserve. That order, and the 1934 Gold Reserve Act that changed the official price of gold from $20.67 per troy ounce to $35, freed the Federal Reserve from the restrictions of the gold standard.

At its beginning, the Federal Reserve System was not a full-fledged central bank as it was not the monopoly producer of legal tender currency. All of this changed in the mid-1930s as the competitor currencies were either eliminated or their issue fixed. At that point, the Federal Reserve System became, at least on the margin, the monopoly issuer of legal tender currency. It is here that we really begin our analysis of the Federal Reserve as the principal supplier of legal tender and as the principal source of money and monetary policy.

Chapter 3

A Wartime Federal Reserve

Introduction

With the demise of the gold standard and the elimination of the national banks as competing currency suppliers, the Federal Reserve now had the power to determine the nation's money supply. Importantly, however, having the almost exclusive ability to coin money did not mean that the Federal Reserve was independent of the central government. In fact, the period from the early 1940s until the March 1951 Treasury–Federal Reserve Accord is generally considered a period of Treasury, and thus either Congressional or Administration, control of Federal Reserve policy.[1] But, as will be demonstrated below, the Treasury control of Federal Reserve policy, while seemingly strict, was not a significant factor in at least one critical area, that of financing central government deficits.

To get a perspective on what Treasury dependence would mean, consider a nation's Treasury's problem of war finance. Traditionally, when countries with central banks went to war, they suspended the ability of citizens to exchange bank notes for gold and proceeded to increase the note issued to support the war debt. This activity was tantamount to a Treasury running the central bank and the result was inflation. These inflations were exacerbated by the usual accompaniments of war: a reduction in the availability of consumer goods and the increase in the money supply as the central banks printed money to finance the war.

---

[1] In fact Allan Meltzer's classic work, "Under Treasury Control, 1942 to 1951," in *A History of the Federal Reserve*, Vol. 1, Chapter 7.

23

As we shall see, the United States World War II experience of Treasury control of the central bank was not one of buying the new debt but a Treasury imposed requirement to support the price of federal debt. Thus, while the Federal Reserve did monetize some of the World War II federal debt, the extent of this monetization was quite small.

The Treasury and the Federal Reserve

The 1930s demise of the gold standard ended the convertibility of Federal Reserve notes into gold. Consequently, even before the United States entered World War II, there was no restriction on the ability of the Federal Reserve to print money. That said, however, during World War II the Federal Reserve was not required to directly print money to purchase the debt generated by war expenditures. What it was required to do was to support the interest rate on Treasury issued debt, essentially supporting a lower bound on the price of treasuries by putting a floor on the price of both short and long-term government bonds. This Treasury debt price support was in the form of enforcing an interest rate ceiling on treasuries. Since the Federal Reserve had no direct control of market interest rates, this directive implied that the bank would buy treasuries whenever the market interest rate on treasuries approached the required ceiling.

In addition to the charge to enforce interest rate ceilings on Treasury debt, the Federal Reserve continued to enforce Regulation T (margin requirements on financial market financing of stock market purchases) and Regulation U (margin requirements on bank financing of stock market purchases). These regulations allowed the Federal Reserve to control the terms under which security dealers and banks could finance traded securities by setting a minimum margin requirement. Near the end of World War II, stock prices were 40% above their previous 1936 peak. Concern of a return of the 1920s boom and ultimate crash in 1929 led the Federal Reserve to set the maximum share of the value of a stock market purchase that could be covered with borrowing at 50%.

In addition to Regulations T and U, which were designed to control borrowing for securities purchases, Regulation W was introduced as the first non-financial market regulation assignment for the Federal Reserve. This regulation authorized the Federal Reserve to oversee the terms of loans for consumer durables. The fear was that, with the transfer of manufacturing from the production of consumer durables to military hardware, consumers would borrow and spend future income on the diminished quantity of durables, and this would result in inflation. Under this regulation, the Federal Reserve controlled both the minimum down payment and the maximum length of loan for consumer durables. However, given the extreme reduction in the production of all consumer durables as the production facilities were converted to military hardware, there is some doubt as to the relevance of Regulation W.

Throughout the World War II period, the Federal Reserve was under considerable pressure from the public, Congress and the White House, concerning policy. The primary issue involved the Federal Reserve's role in influencing market interest rates. The only interest rate that the Federal Reserve directly controlled was the discount rate, the rate the Federal Reserve used to charge banks on purchased securities (e.g., bankers acceptances or commercial paper).

Prior to World War II, the Federal Reserve was prohibited from buying treasuries directly from the Treasury. This prohibition was consistent with the fear of the founders that a central bank would simply become an agent of the federal government. This same fear still existed when the Federal Reserve was established, as evidenced by the prohibition on direct Treasury purchases. But this separation between the Treasury and the Federal Reserve ended with the passage of the second War Powers Act.[2] At this point, any semblance of an independent Federal Reserve was gone.

The Federal Reserve's role in affecting market interest rates was most effective during and immediately after World War II. This same period is one of minimum central bank independence. The Federal Reserve was really a sub-part of the Treasury and as such the Administration. It was required to maintain the yield ceiling on Treasury securities at 0.375% for T-Bills and 2.5% for long-term Treasury bonds. The only way that these interest rate ceilings were enforceable was for the Federal Reserve to stand ready to buy all treasuries presented to it at a price consistent with the ceiling rates. Of course, no purchase would be required as long as

---

[2] See P.L. 507, 77th Congress, 2nd Session (S2208), Approved March 27, 1942. An Act to further expedite the prosecution of the war.

market rates remained at or below the ceilings, i.e., prices remained above the price that yielded the ceiling rates.[3]

To put this charge in context, before the beginning of the build-up to hostilities, T-Bill rates in the third quarter of 1940 were 0.02%. The T-Bill rate gradually rose reaching the ceiling rate of 0.375% in the second quarter of 1942. It then remained there until the second quarter of 1947. Long treasuries were at 2.10% in the third quarter of 1940. They only reached the ceiling rate of 2.5% for the first two quarters of 1944, before falling below the ceiling for the duration of the war until finally rising above the ceiling in the first quarter of 1951.

The Federal Reserve Role in Financing the War

The mandate that the Federal Reserve maintain interest rate ceilings on Treasury bonds and T-Bills implied that the bank would operate in the market for treasuries in order to keep the interest rates on these securities from exceeding the Treasury imposed limits. The rates on long-term treasuries stayed between one and seven basis points below the ceiling from December 1941 through December 1944.[4]

Therefore, even though the Federal Reserve was under the Treasury's control during this period, the actual amount of Federal Reserve debt monetization due to purchases of federal debt did not approach what one would expect. In fact, the monetary base growth rate was very close to the growth rate of GDP — 14.2% for the monetary base and 12% for GDP.[5]

---

[3] For example, the yield ceiling rate of 0.375% on a one-year T-Bill meant that the Federal Reserve could not allow the price of a $1,000 T-Bill to fall below $996.25. In effect, when the price of T-Bills were in danger of falling below the Federal Reserve would enter the market as a demander of Bills.

[4] It has become a convention to express interest rate because they are small numbers in "basis points." A basis point is defined as one-one hundredth of a percent. Thus, an interest rate of 2.00% is 200 basis points. Then the World War II interest rate ceilings can be expressed as a short-term maximum of 37.5 basis points and a long-term maximum of 250 basis points.

[5] The usual explanation of inflation is too much money chases too few goods. In that context, the 14.2% rate of growth of the base versus the 12% growth of GDP would suggest little inflation. However, this was a period of price controls and rationing with serious penalties for violations. Also, the measurement of GDP in wartime is problematic in terms of goods being chased by money.

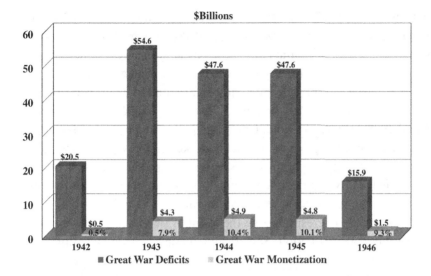

Figure 3.1. Great War Deficits and Federal Reserve Monetization

To get a feel for the magnitude of Federal Reserve involvement in financing the war effort, Figure 3.1 shows the level of fiscal deficits and monetary base growth for the 5 fiscal years of World War II; fiscal years 1942 through 1946.[6] The growth in the monetary base is almost a direct measure of Federal Reserve purchases of federal debt and is thus a measure of how much of the deficits were financed by printing money. From the beginning of the fiscal year 1942 through the fiscal year 1946, the monetary base grew 94%, an annual rate of 14.2%. In that same period, the federal debt grew 471%, an annual growth rate of just over 36%.

From the beginning of the fiscal year 1942 to the close of fiscal 1946, the Federal Reserve purchased just over $22 billion of Government securities. The federal deficit over that same period was just over $186 billion, indicating that the Federal Reserve financed just over 8.6% of the deficit.

By any measure, Federal Reserve purchases of federal debt in World War II were small relative to the period's new federal debt issued. Even though small by comparison to subsequent Federal Reserve financing of federal

---

[6] During this period, federal fiscal years began in July so that the fiscal year 1942 began in July 1941, before the onset of hostilities. Fiscal 1946 began in July 1945 just before the close of hostilities.

deficits, the level of Federal Reserve involvement was sufficient to satisfy the interest ceilings imposed by the Treasury. The question one might ask is, how such a small level of central bank involvement in financing deficits could be maintained given the Treasury imposed ceilings on interest rates?

The answer to this question can be attributed to two aspects of World War II that contributed to the public's heavy participation in financing the war deficits. This heavy voluntary participation in purchasing federal debt helped support the price of this debt and kept interest rates low. In addition, the concentration of resources on military production made materials available for private investment scarce. As a result, there was little demand by the private sector for investment funding.

Essentially, interest rates are the result of two forces that were unique to the World War II period. Specifically, on one side we have time preference by consumers, and on the other side investment opportunities for investors. Both of these forces contributed to the low level of World War II interest rates. These two players represent the supply of funds, consumers, and the demand for funds, investors. Interest rates are low when consumers have low time preference and/or when there are few investment opportunities. How do these two factors relate to the wartime experience?

First, war-time rationing, both explicit and as a result of the simple lack of availability of durable goods, gave consumers little opportunity to use their earnings on current consumption. Thus, even if consumers preferred present consumption goods to saving for future consumption goods, these goods — especially durables — were just not available. This lack of ability to consume now, lowered the observed time preference of the public. In effect, even though consumers would want to have goods now rather than wait, the fact that goods were not available resulted in *de facto* low-time preference.

Figure 3.2 contains estimates of household consumption expenditures for the 1941–1944 period.[7] The total transportation and furnishings and equipment categories fell between 20% and 40% during this period. At the same time, income rose which implies that while consumers had the funds

---

[7]The underlying data are from surveys done during World War II by the Bureau of Labor Statistics and the Department of Agriculture. An excellent summary of the results can be found in Henderson (2015). Available online at https://www.bls.gov/opub/mlr/2015/article/consumer-spending-in-world-war-ii-the-forgotten-consumer-expenditure-surveys.htm.

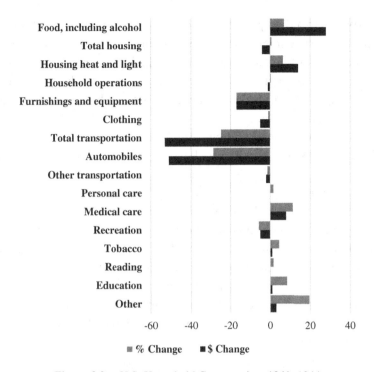

Figure 3.2. U.S. Household Consumption: 1941–1944

to purchase durables, such as automobiles and home appliances, their general unavailability resulted in significant reductions in their consumption.

Second, World War II controls on investment opportunities for non-war production made the effective return on investment lower. These two factors reduced the extent that the Federal Reserve had to support this market in order to maintain the Treasury imposed interest ceilings.

As a result, the special conditions that existed during World War II resulted in the requirement that the Federal Reserve conduct monetary policy under the direction of the Treasury having little effect on actual Federal Reserve policy.

Conclusion

Once freed from the discipline of the gold standard, the Federal Reserve was at least able to behave in an independent fashion. But this free-to-be-independent period was short-lived as the onset of World War II once again brought the Federal Reserve under the yoke of the Treasury. The directive was to maintain a ceiling on the interest rates on both short-term and long-term treasuries. As it turned out, only the short-term ceiling was in danger, which resulted in Federal Reserve holdings of treasuries being almost entirely short term.

The level of federal deficits required to finance our tremendous involvement in World War II was beyond anything in our nations' past. But, in spite of these significant deficits required to finance the war, the actual Federal Reserve involvement in war finance was small. In fact, the Federal Reserve financed just over 8.36% of the deficit. Two factors contributed to limiting the involvement of the Federal Reserve in war financing. First, war-time rationing, both explicit and as a result of simple lack of availability of durable goods, gave consumers little opportunity to use their earnings on current consumption. Second, the concentration of resources on military production made materials available for private investment scarce. As a result, there was little demand by the private sector for investment funding.

Thus, the history of other nation's central banks suspending convertibility in order to directly purchase their nations wartime debts that resulted in significant inflation, did not happen here. In fact, even the limited expansion of Federal Reserve holdings of federal debt largely disappeared by 1950. Further, as I show in the following chapter, the Treasury's role in dictating Federal Reserve policy ended with the Treasury Federal Reserve Accord of March 1951.

Chapter 4

The Federal Reserve's First Decade Free of the Treasury

Introduction

The tie between the Federal Reserve and the Treasury brought on by the special conditions of financing World War II, continued until March of 1951. At that time, members of Congress led by Senator Paul Douglass of Illinois, a former economist at the University of Chicago, put forth what has become known as the Treasury–Federal Reserve Accord. This Accord, finally allowed the Federal Reserve to pursue a monetary policy that was not based on maintaining an interest rate ceiling on the federal debt.[1]

Prior to the Accord, the requirement that the Federal Reserve conduct its open-market operations to maintain the interest rate ceilings on federal debt instruments took money supply decisions out of the hands of the central bank, whenever the ceilings were binding. The Accord allowed the Federal Reserve to base its purchases and sales of federal debt on how changes in the money supply would affect the economy. However, the lack of a formal restriction on Federal Reserve actions does not mean that monetary policy could be conducted without regard to fiscal issues. In

---

[1] For an excellent history and discussion of the events leading up to the Accord, see Hetzel and Leach (2001).

particular, this first decade after the Accord included the war in Korea, among other issues.[2]

1950s Deficits and Federal Reserve Monetization

Figure 4.1 shows the fiscal year deficit and dollar growth in the monetary base for the 10 fiscal years of the 1950s. The last nine of these fiscal years followed the March 1951 Accord. The first 9 months of fiscal 1951 preceded the Accord. During this decade, federal deficits ranged from a surplus of $6.1 billion to a deficit of $12.8 billion. A simple inspection of Figure 4.1 confirms that the monetary base growth was unrelated to the level of the federal deficit. During this period of almost a decade, federal deficits averaged just over 0.27% of GDP. Even the decade's largest deficit, fiscal year 1959, was only 2.5% of GDP. This deficit, while double the decade's second largest deficit in 1953, was small compared with the smallest World War II deficit, the 7% of GDP deficit of fiscal year 1946.

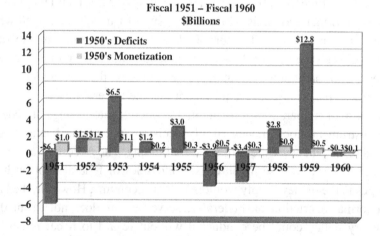

Figure 4.1.   Deficits and Federal Reserve Monetization

[2] In spite of the Accord, the Treasury and the Federal Reserve are connected in a way that cannot be undone by any legislation. As required by law, the Federal Reserve must distribute to the Treasury the residual earnings of each Federal Reserve Bank after providing for the costs of operations, payment of dividends and the amount necessary to equate surplus with capital paid-in. As the residual income owner in some sense, the Treasury is a non-voting owner of the Federal Reserve.

In spite of the 1960s being the decade of the Korean War, that began in mid-1950 and lasted until the Armistice was signed on July 27, 1953, federal deficits as a share of the nation's GDP were small relative to the World War II years. As a result, the Federal Reserve was under little pressure from the Treasury to accommodate fiscal issues. Moreover, there were federal surpluses in three of the 9 years. During this same 9-year period, the growth rate of the monetary base was less than 2%. The message is that it is easy to be an independent central bank when there is no pressure, either politically or financially.

Inspection of Figure 4.1 suggests that the level of monetization and federal deficits for the entirety of the post-Accord 1950s, are unrelated. If so, then what accounts for the monetary growth in that period? A simple goal of price level stability, one interpretation of coining money and regulating the value thereof, would require that the growth in the nation's money supply keep pace with the growth in the nation's output. Is the growth in the money supply implied by the monetization depicted in Figure 4.1 consistent with the goal of preserving the value of the dollar?

The Federal Reserve and 1950s Inflation

While the Act that established the Federal Reserve does not explicitly mention a role in maintaining the value of the dollar, clearly protecting dollar valued assets is important. Figure 4.2 shows that the path of the price level,

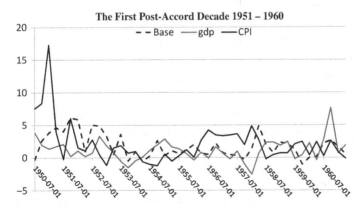

Figure 4.2. Monetary Base, CPI and Real GDP Growth

the value of the dollar, during this decade was variable, ranging from inflation of 6% in 1951 to deflation in 1954. The question is what was the role of Federal Reserve monetary policy in the path of inflation? One way to measure monetary policy is the path of the monetary base. While the money supply is heavily dependent on Federal Reserve policy, it is also affected by the public's desired composition of its money holdings.

As a way to address the role of the Federal Reserve in preserving the value of the dollar, Figure 4.2 shows the annualized growth rate by quarter of the monetary base, real GDP and the Consumer Price Index (CPI), for the post-Accord 1950s, beginning with the first post-accord quarter, the third quarter of fiscal year 1951.[3] The period between the Accord and the end of the decade was a period of rapid, but variable, real GDP growth and modest increases in both the monetary base and consumer prices. During the post-Accord 1950s, the average real GDP growth rate was 2.79%, while the monetary base grew at a very modest 1.65%, and the price level growth averaged just over 1.45% per year.

This first decade of post-Accord central bank independence was characterized by stable prices as the federal government deficits remained small. Not surprisingly, the period of the Korean War (1950–1953) saw the fastest growth of the monetary base. For the entire decade, federal deficits averaged less than 0.27% of GDP. As a result, the Federal Reserve was under little Treasury pressure to accommodate fiscal issues.

The effect of the financing of the Korean War on the Federal Reserve is indicated by the growth of the monetary base during the first third of this decade. That same monetary base growth also corresponded with the early years of higher than average inflation. In the middle of the decade, both the inflation rate and the monetary base growth rate fell. Then, both monetary base and price growth stabilized for the last 2 years of the decade. Overall, this decade was characterized by low federal deficits in comparison to the World War II years. The relatively low federal deficits was especially true for the early years of the post-accord period considering that they were the years of the Korean War.

---

[3] The GDP series is growth rate in the annualized seasonally adjusted real GDP from the United States Bureau of Economic Analysis, bea.gov. Since GDP is a flow, the annual change in GDP for any year is the result of the prior four quarters of growth. As a result, the total percentage growth in GDP will exceed any of the preceding four quarters.

The Federal Reserve and 1950s Interest Rates

Throughout its history, to both the public and the press, the Federal Reserve has been most associated with market interest rates. This association makes sense in that interest rates are directly observable and impact everyone.[4] Indeed, for the World War II period, the only financing for the war requirement of the Federal Reserve was to buy treasuries if the interest rate on short-term federal debt threatened to go above 0.375% or on long-term debt threatened to exceed 2.5%. In this first post-Accord decade, the Federal Reserve was free from supporting the yield on treasuries.

Figure 4.3 shows the yields on 10-year and 1-year treasuries for the period from the first quarter of 1953 through the first quarter of 1960 and the CPI inflation rate. The figure also contains the Federal Reserve discount rate, the rate that member banks paid to borrow from their regional Federal Reserve Bank.[5] The discount rate was the only interest rate the Federal Reserve had direct control of during this period. Further, except for financial crises, the term of discount rate borrowings is in the form of 30- to 90-day repos. While the difference between market rates of interest and the discount rate could be a major source of monetary expansion, at

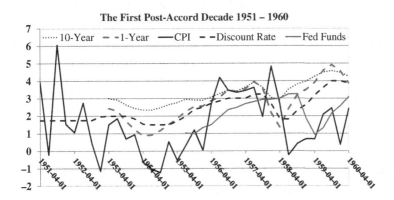

Figure 4.3. Treasury Interest Rates and CPI-Inflation

---

[4]We will argue in Chapters 13 and 15 that, for all practical purposes, the Federal Reserve is an interest rate taker not an interest setter.

[5]The discount rate is the rate paid by member banks borrowing from the Federal Reserve. Bank borrowing from the Federal Reserve was limited so that member banks could not arbitrage between the Federal Reserve and financial markets.

least during this period the discount rate was not a major tool of monetary policy. Finally, the chart contains the beginning of reporting the Fed Funds rate, the rate at which banks pay for overnight borrowing of reserves to meet the Federal Reserve's reserve requirements.

By the first quarter of 1953, the yield on 10-year treasuries exceeded the World War II 2.5% ceiling that was in place before the Accord. Given any market determined real rate of interest, the above-shown nominal rates should be that equilibrium real rate plus the rate of inflation. Not surprisingly, the yields on both the 1-year and 10-year debt followed the path of inflation. Further, the Federal Reserve discount rate tracked the market rates on 1-year treasuries. The bank overnight borrowing rate, the Fed Funds rate, which currently gets the most press attention, also tracks the 1-year treasury rate.

As noted above, this time period saw the introduction in 1955 of reporting the interest rate that the current press seems to be obsessed with, the Fed Funds rate.[6] To bring this rate into perspective, it existed well before any reporting of the rate. The Fed Funds rate is affected by market interest rates because as market interest rates rise, banks economize on reserves, and in that world of scarce reserves, the Fed Funds rate is an indication of their scarcity. Federal Reserve purchases and sales of assets directly affect bank reserves and, therefore, affect the Fed Funds rate. Not surprisingly, the Fed Funds rate tracks the alternative that banks have for reserves, market interest rates. An announced increase or decrease in a Fed Funds target rate is an indication of future Federal Reserve actions in financial markets.

Conclusion

The first decade of the Accord-free Federal Reserve in pursuing its mandated goals of protecting the value of currency, promoting full employment and modest long-term interest rates, was in the most sense successful. This period included the Korean War (1950–1953) which affected the early years of the post-Accord period. Not surprisingly, the first

---

[6]The Fed Funds rate is the interest rate at which banks lend reserve balances to other banks overnight. Banks with surplus balances in their accounts lend those balances to institutions in need of larger balances to meet reserve requirements.

post-accord decade was characterized by highly variable rates of inflation and monetary growth.

The effect of the Korean War is obvious from the path of the monetary base, as shown in Figure 4.2. The first years of this war were characterized by rapid monetary base growth averaging 3.9%. The remainder of the decade had a monetary base growth rate of only 1.1%. These facts point to a reality that will be apparent in subsequent decades, that when it counts, the Treasury and the Administration, even without a formal arrangement, have considerable sway when it comes to Federal Reserve policy.

Over the entire decade, monetary base growth was a modest 1.72%, and CPI growth was an even more modest 1.45%; the difference is explained by the relatively robust growth rate in real GDP of 2.79%. With modest growth in the price level, long-term interest rates, as measured by the yield on 10-year treasuries, were within long-term values and ranged from 2.5% to 4.5%.

Chapter 5

The Federal Reserve in the Vietnam Decade: The 1960s

Introduction

This second decade of Federal Reserve freedom began with the escalation of the Cold War, as evidenced by the construction of the Berlin Wall. Then, it was on to the Cuban Missile Crisis and finally, the escalation of the war in Vietnam. Given the level of political turmoil, it is not surprising that federal deficits rose significantly. The 9 years of the post-Accord 1950s saw average deficits of just over $2 billion. In contrast, the 1960s average deficit was triple that at just under $6 billion, and the 1968 deficit was a then-astounding $25.2 billion, a level of deficit that exceeded any prior non-war year.

To compound the fact that fiscal deficits were seemingly out of control, the participation of the Federal Reserve in funding the deficits was at an all-time high. For the entire decade of the 1960s, the Federal Reserve printed money to fund more than 40% of the decade's federal deficits. Not surprisingly, this level of Federal Reserve involvement led to rising inflation that exceeded 6% by the end of the decade.

1960s Deficits and Federal Reserve Monetization

The second decade of the post-Accord period presented even more of a challenge than the Federal Reserve's first decade of freedom from the Treasury's direct control. Figure 5.1 shows the federal deficits and the

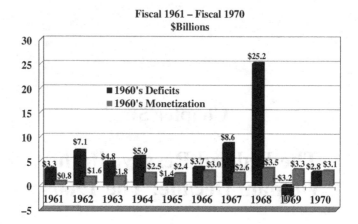

Figure 5.1.   Deficits and Federal Reserve Monetization

growth in the monetary base for this decade. Deficits averaged 0.8% of GDP, up from the 0.27% of GDP in the prior decade. Toward the close of the decade, the expansion of the war in Vietnam placed increased fiscal pressure on the monetary authority.

During this decade, the monetary base grew at an annual rate of 4.8% in comparison to an annual real GDP growth rate of only 0.9% and a total decade real GDP increase of only 9.3%. This minimal real GDP growth decade meant that protecting the value of the currency would have entailed only a 9% growth in the monetary base. Actual decade base growth was 55%, six times the rate consistent with stable prices and value of money.

A rough estimate of the share of the deficit financed by printing money can be had by a comparison of the level of monetary base growth to the total decade federal deficit. An unadjusted for GDP growth share of the deficit financed by printing money is 41.3%. However, adjusting for the level of money growth required to maintain the value of the dollar, the Federal Reserve monetized a smaller but still significant 37.5% of the decade's federal deficits.

The Federal Reserve and the 1960s Inflation

One would expect that the level of debt monetization, coupled with modest growth in real GDP would result in rising inflation. Figure 5.2 shows

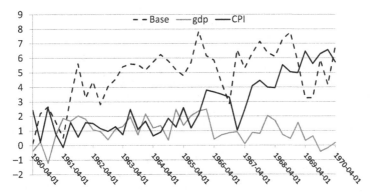

Figure 5.2.   Monetary Base, CPI and Real Growth 1960–1970

the annualized growth rate for the monetary base, real GDP and the Consumer Price Index (CPI) for the decade of the 1960s. This was a period of sporadic real GDP growth, rapid increases in the first half of the decade and then much slower growth in the second half. The monetary base grew at a 4.81% rate for the entire decade, rising from the 1.72% growth rate of the first post-Accord decade. Real GDP grew for the decade at 4.00%, just a bit faster than the previous decade. The last half of the 1960s decade saw a significant increase in the growth rate of the monetary base. At the same time, real GDP growth fell significantly to almost zero at the close of the decade. Not surprisingly, the acceleration of base growth accompanied by a deceleration of real GDP growth led to rising CPI inflation that reached 6% by the decade's end.

The combination of faster monetary base growth and slower real GDP growth depicted in Figure 5.2 suggests that the price level growth should have increased. This is exactly what did happen as CPI growth rose from the first post-Accord period of the 1950s from 1.45 to 2.64%. This second decade of central bank independence was characterized by rising prices as federal government deficits rose. The period of the expansion of the war in Vietnam shows up in the rising rate of growth in the monetary base. For the entire decade, federal deficits averaged 0.80% of GDP, as compared to the less than 0.27% of GDP for the previous decade. As a result, the Federal Reserve was under increased pressure from the Treasury to accommodate fiscal issues and it responded with growth in the monetary base that exceeded the growth in GDP by a wide margin.

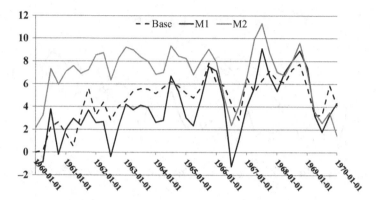

Figure 5.3.   Base, M1, M2 Growth Rates, 1960–1970

The monetary base is not itself the money supply, but forms the basis for measures of the money supply. Inflation comes from, in simple terms, too much money chasing too few goods. Figure 5.3 shows the growth rates of the monetary base as shown in Figure 5.2 and the growth rates of the two most used measures of the money supply, denoted simply as M1 and M2. The first one, M1, is most simply described as the sum of currency outstanding and checkable deposits, that is, deposits that are easily transferred on demand.[1] The second, M2, is M1 plus other less easily transferable deposits.[2]

The narrower money stock measure, M1, tracks the growth in the base very closely. For the decade, the monetary base grew at an average rate 4.69% and M1 grew at 3.83%. This close connection of M1 and the monetary base is not surprising as M1 consists primarily of components that are either directly in the base, currency and demand deposits that use bank reserves as an input.

---

[1] M1 includes funds that are readily accessible for spending. M1 consists of the following: (1) currency outside the US Treasury, Federal Reserve Banks, and the vaults of depository institutions; (2) traveler's checks of non-bank issuers; (3) demand deposits; and (4) other checkable deposits (OCDs), which consist primarily of negotiable order of withdrawal (NOW) accounts at depository institutions and credit union share draft accounts. See Federal Reserve Bank of St. Louis; https://fred.stlouisfed.org/series/M1SL.

[2] M2 consists of M1 plus: (1) savings deposits (which include money market deposit accounts, or MMDAs); (2) small-denomination time deposits (time deposits in amounts of less than $100,000); and (3) balances in retail money market mutual funds (MMMFs). See Federal Reserve Bank of St. Louis; https://fred.stlouisfed.org/series/M2SL.

On the other hand, the growth rate of the broader measure of the money stock, M2, while it moves with the monetary base, its rate of growth exceeded base growth for most of the period. For the decade, the broader based money stock grew at an average rate of 6.9%. One important factor in the rapid growth of the broader money stock is that until the 1980s Federal Reserve Regulation Q was in effect. This regulation, enacted in the 1930s, prevented banks from paying interest on demand deposits and controlled the interest that could be paid on time deposits. Thus, as interest rates rose the rate of return on less transferable deposits began to dominate the return on the components of M1.

The Federal Reserve and 1960s Interest Rates

Figure 5.4 shows the yields on 10-year and 1-year treasuries for the period from the first quarter of 1960 through the first quarter of 1970, the CPI inflation rate, the Fed Funds rate and the Federal Reserve discount rate. As a reminder, the Fed Funds rate, or at least the Fed Funds target rate, is the rate that the Federal Reserve uses to broadcast monetary policy. The discount rate applies to bank borrowings from the Federal Reserve which, except for financial crises, are in the form of 30- to 90-day repos. As such, the discount rate is not a major part of monetary policy. That said, however, this figure as well as Figure 4.3 shows that both the Fed Funds rate and the Federal Reserve discount rate simply follow rather than lead interest rates in general.

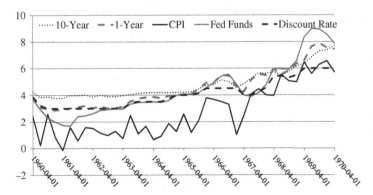

Figure 5.4.   Treasury Interest Rates, Fed Discount Rate, Fed Funds Rate and CPI-Inflation 1960–1970

The early years of the decade saw the rapid rise in the monetary base growth rate and a resulting fall in the Fed Funds rate, as reserves were increasing at a rapid rate. For most of the decade, the Fed Funds rate was below the 1-year treasury rate. As the inflation rate rose, the 1-year treasury rate rose with inflation. Not surprisingly, the 10-year treasury rate rose but more slowly as it is long-run inflation expectations that play a large role in long-term interest rates. Thus, not surprisingly, toward the close of the decade with continued inflation, the 10-year treasury rate rose rapidly. Rising inflation and interest rates put extreme pressure on bank reserves, and the Fed Funds rate toward the close of the decade exceeded the 1-year treasury rate by as many as 100 basis points. This rise in the Fed Funds rate coincided with the fall in the rate of base growth, as is clear in Figure 5.2.

Conclusion

The second decade of the Accord-free Federal Reserve in pursuing its mandated goals of protecting the value of currency, promoting full employment and modest long-term interest rates was certainly less successful than the first. The decade began with the crisis surrounding the April 1961 Bay of Pigs invasion early in the administration of President John F. Kennedy. Next we were faced with the initiation of the construction of the Berlin Wall in August 1961. And then to top that off we had the October 1962 Cuban Missile Crisis.

Crises such as these create public uncertainty, and such uncertainty leads to increases in the demand for currency as money in hand is viewed as safer than in a financial institution. The response of the Federal Reserve in its role ensuring the elasticity of the currency is to expand the monetary base to accommodate the increased currency demand.

The expansion of the early on called police action in Vietnam turned into a full-scale war by mid-decade. By the latter part of the decade, federal deficits grew and the initial early decade increase in the rate of growth of the monetary base never subsided. As a result, the monetary base grew at 4.8%, more than double the 1.72% of the previous decade. Moreover, almost all of this growth occurred in the latter half of the 1960s.

Finally, in spite of robust real GDP growth, price level growth, while modest for the first half of the decade, rose to over 6% by the decade's end. Not surprisingly, the rapid rise in the inflation rate resulted in 10-year treasury yields rising from the 4.8% that prevailed for the first half of the decade to almost 8% by the decade's end. This rise of inflation and interest proved to be a precursor of the double digit inflation and interest rates of the 1970s.

Chapter 6

The Federal Reserve and the Rise of Inflation: The 1970s

Introduction

The third post-Accord decade presented the biggest challenge in terms of political pressure on the Federal Reserve since the pre-Accord period of World War II. Deficits continued to grow as a share of GDP, especially in the latter half of the decade. At this time, these deficits were up to that time the largest since World War II. Importantly, the deficits of this decade cannot be blamed on the war in Vietnam, which was largely over by mid-1973, before the rapid acceleration of the decade's deficits.

In fact, the deficits were small immediately following the removal of US troops from South Vietnam. But by mid-decade, the deficits rapidly accelerated. This deficit acceleration was accompanied by levels of inflation and interest rates that were unheard of from a historical perspective. While the deficits at the close of the 1960s seemed large by non-war standards, they paled in comparison to the deficits of the 1970s. If we measure the role of the Federal Reserve by the extent to which it facilitated the financing of the deficits, then it might seem that the Federal Reserve was much more expansionary in the 1960s than what we shall see from the evidence presented in Figure 6.1. Although, an even less expansionary Federal Reserve in terms of the percentage of the deficit financed can be overwhelmed by a decade of previously unheard of deficits.

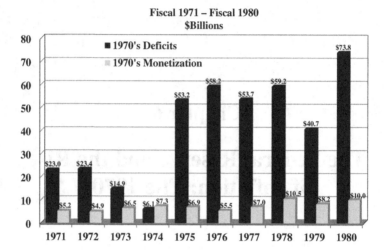

Figure 6.1.   Deficits and Federal Reserve Monetization

1970s Deficits and Federal Reserve Monetization

Figure 6.1 shows the deficits and the growth in the monetary base for the 1970s. Adjusted for the growth in the base due to GDP growth, the Federal Reserve monetized 17.7% of 1970s federal deficits. While this level of monetization may seem small in the abstract, when it is considered with the scale of the deficits, the effect on the inflation rate was indeed significant. For the entire decade, federal deficits averaged 2.15% of GDP, as compared to the 0.80% of GDP for the previous decade. The level of these deficits put the Federal Reserve under increased pressure from the Treasury to accommodate fiscal issues. In the end, however, the extent of monetization of the deficits was the largest of the post-Accord Federal Reserve era. During this decade, the Federal Reserve monetized more than 17% of the decades' deficits. In contrast, the Federal Reserve monetized less than 10% of World War II deficits.

Whatever the reason, federal deficits beginning with fiscal 1975 exceeded any prior deficit, even those of World War II. The Arab Oil Embargo that began in late 1973 and ended in March of 1974 was entirely in fiscal 1974, the lowest federal deficit of the decade. But with fiscal 1975, deficits jumped to levels that turned out to be harbingers of the next 20 years. Surprisingly, as we shall see after 20 years of as yet unheard of deficits, it all turned into the federal budget surpluses of the late 1990s.

The Federal Reserve and 1970s Inflation

To see the effect of the level of federal deficit monetization on the price level, Figure 6.2 shows the annualized growth rate for the monetary base, real GDP and the Consumer Price Index (CPI) for the 1970s. This was a period of sporadic real GDP growth, beginning with a rapid decline, as the rise of the Organization of the Petroleum Exporting Countries (OPEC) reduced the world's supply of petroleum. In effect, OPEC reduced the ability of the world to produce all output and especially energy intensive output. OPEC actions on the supply of crude oil reduced the nation's production frontier and as a result reduced our national output. In fact, the rise in the CPI during the middle of the decade could be attributed to falling GDP in response to a reduction in the effective level of world resources as the OPEC cartel reduced oil production.

The monetary base growth rate for the 1970s was consistently above the average for the previous decade. For the entire decade of the 1970s, monetary base growth averaged 7.88%, an increase from the 4.81% rate of the previous decade. Real GDP growth for this decade fell from the previous decade's 4.25–3.41%.

In fact, this decade saw two periods of negative real GDP growth. The first period of negative GDP growth, the third quarter of 1973 through the third of quarter 1975, were the 2 years following the Yom Kippur War and the effective formation of OPEC. During that time, the nation and the world experienced the equivalent of a significant inward shift in the

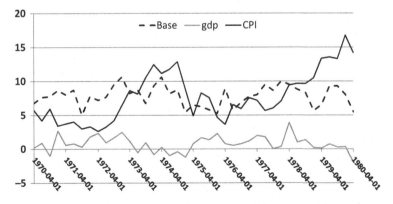

Figure 6.2. Monetary Base, CPI and Real GDP Growth 1970–1980

effective production possibility frontier.[1] The combination of continued rapid monetary base growth and declining output led to double-digit inflation. This episode is a reminder that inflation can be caused both by the printing of too much money or by producing too few goods.

The second period of declining and, at times, negative real GDP growth was in the second quarter of 1978 through the first quarter of 1980. Here, a continuation of rapid monetary base growth coupled with falling or slow-growth real GDP. That combination led to 2 years of double-digit inflation, the second such period in the 1970s.

The oil cartel inflation rate of the mid-1970s fell but still remained above the level of the beginning of the decade. By the beginning of 1977, the inflation rate accelerated and reached more than 15% at the close of the decade. A 15% inflation rate was the greatest over the entire 20th century. In summary, this third decade of central bank independence was characterized by rising prices as the federal government deficits rose further in spite of the end of the Vietnam War.

Figure 6.3 shows the effect of monetary base growth on the two most used measures of the money supply, M1 and M2. Just as in the

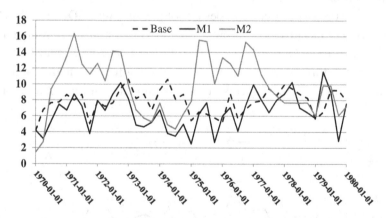

Figure 6.3.   Base, M1, M2 Growth Rates, 1970–1980

---

[1] The effect of OPEC was greatly enhanced by the US Congress enacting what I have referred to as "the OPEC relief act." In effect, Congress eliminated the most effective deterrent to the cartel's effectiveness by placing price controls on US oil production. Thus, rather than the largest non-OPEC supplier of crude oil increasing output in response to the OPEC induced increase in the price of petroleum and thereby reducing the effectiveness of the cartel, we reduced output and made the cartel a permanent feature of the world petroleum picture.

decade of the 1960s, the Federal Reserve Regulation Q limiting bank deposit interest rates remained in effect. As a result, the broader based measure of the money supply, M2, grew much faster than the narrower based measure, M1, as rising interest rates increased the incentive of investors to utilize less transferable forms of deposits. For this decade, the monetary base grew at an average rate of 7.79%, while the M1 money stock grew at 6.52% and the M2 money stock grew at a much greater rate of 9.61%.

The Federal Reserve and 1970s Interest Rates

Given the level of inflation for the 1970s, interest rates were at levels not seen, perhaps ever in the United States. Figure 6.4 shows the paths of 1-year and 10-year treasuries, CPI inflation and the Fed Funds rate.

If we take the Fed Funds rate as an indicator of monetary policy, then what does the path of the Fed Funds rate over this period indicate? The falling inflation rate and rising Fed Funds rate for the period from the beginning of the decade through mid-1973 coupled with the falling rate of growth in the monetary base is consistent with a restrictive monetary policy. Then, we have the OPEC-caused increase in world energy prices. Here, the Federal Reserve increased the monetary base, and as a result, the Fed Funds rate fell. It remained at the early 1974 rate until inflation again began to accelerate in 1977. This rise in the inflation rate was accompanied by an increase in monetary base growth.

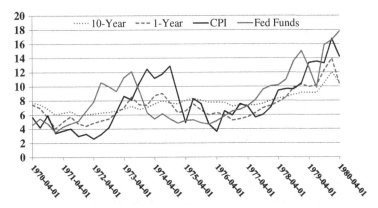

Figure 6.4. Treasury Interest Rates, Federal Funds Rate and CPI-Inflation 1970–1980

While it is true that the Fed Funds rate rose along with interest rates in general, this was not the result of restrictive monetary policy as indicated by the monetary base growth. Once the yields on both the 10-year and 1-year treasuries reached double digits, there was tremendous pressure on the bank overnight lending rate. Essentially, with alternative assets yielding double-digit returns, there was no way that overnight lending rates would not also be double digit. No Federal Reserve policy was involved in these equilibrium overnight lending rates. Rather than leading the rise in interest rates, the Fed Funds rate followed the market.[2]

An Expanded Regulatory Role for the Federal Reserve

The decade of the 1970s was more than just about a rapidly growing monetary base and virtually unprecedented inflation. It was also a decade of perhaps unprecedented non-wartime political pressure on the Federal Reserve. This pressure manifested itself in two ways. First, the Federal Reserve was charged with enforcing the Truth in Lending Act (1968), the Equal Credit Opportunity Act (1974) and the Community Reinvestment Act (1977). Second, the Federal Reserve was under significant political pressure to aid the potential bankruptcy of New York City, to buy agency securities of the Federal National Mortgage Association (Fannie Mae) to help the housing industry, and to act as the fiscal agent for the Treasury guarantees to Chrysler Corporation.

If one is to pretend that the Federal Reserve during the 1970s was really independent, why did it allow the level of growth in the monetary base that formed the basis of the continued inflation?[3] There is simply no way to imagine that the interest rate targets for the Federal Reserve consisted of the greater than 10% yields on the 1-year, 10-year, 20-year and 30-year Treasury securities.

---

[2] In Chapter 13, I present an analysis of the role, if any, of the Federal Reserve in market interest rate determination.

[3] During the middle years of the decade, the federal government introduced the Whip Inflation Now (WIN) program introduced in the Ford Administration. The basis of the program was that inflation was the fault of the public rather than excessive monetary growth. The Carter Administration continued the fallacy that inflation was somehow the result of excessive spending by citizens rather than excessive federal deficits and the resulting monetary growth.

The paths of Fed Funds rate and interest rates, in general, during this decade throws some light on the current belief that the Federal Reserve controls market interest rates. To believe that the Federal Reserve was responsible for the level of interest rates in the latter half of the 1970s, one must argue that 1-year treasuries were 14% because the Fed Funds rate was 16%. In reality, the Fed Funds rate was 16% because short-term treasuries were yielding 14%. Given the inflation of the era, one would hope that a Fed Funds rate of 16% indicated a restrictive monetary policy, i.e., a decline in the rate of growth of the monetary base. However, such a decline in monetary base growth is not apparent in the data.[4]

Conclusion

The decade of the 1970s began with falling inflation and monetary growth — not that the rate of inflation was low by historical standards, as the decade began with inflation above 5%. The rate of inflation fell to a low of 2.6% before beginning a rise that was accelerated by the OPEC effect on world oil markets. During the height of the oil crisis, inflation would reach double-digit levels. It fell just after mid-decade to between 4% and 6%, excessive by today's standards, before beginning a rapid rise back to double digits.

The federal deficits for this decade were the largest since the end of World War II, although they were to be eclipsed in later decades. The Federal Reserve participated in funding these deficits to the tune of almost 18% to the decade's total deficits. The resulting changes in the money supply and the ballooning of federal spending certainly contributed to the then-record inflation levels. The next decade saw the undoing of inflationary Federal Reserve policy and a return to what were considered normal amounts of inflationary pressure.

---

[4] Restrictive monetary policy consists of decreases in Federal Reserve holdings of assets. Such a restriction is consistent with a rising Fed Funds rate. However, if market interest rates rise faster than the target Fed Funds rate, then setting a "restrictive" Fed Funds target may actually result in an expansive monetary policy. See Saving (1967).

Chapter 7

The Federal Reserve and the Taming of Inflation: The 1980s

Introduction

As we began the 1980s, the inflation rate exceeded 15%, and the rate of interest on 1-year treasuries was 14%. The decade was also characterized by deficits that were the largest since World War II. Even with the pressure of unprecedented peacetime deficits, the Federal Reserve monetized only a small portion of this debt. This was a period where the almost unprecedented double-digit inflation of the latter 1970s, was reduced although it remained at levels well above any long-run average. It is not as if this reduction in inflation was accomplished by stringent federal budgets. Indeed, federal deficits in the 1980s exceeded the deficits of the 1970s by a factor of two.

What was unique about the 1980s was that this decade saw the first significant reform of the tax code, since the so-called Kennedy tax cuts of 1964.[1] The 1980s reform was in two parts; the so-called Reagan tax cuts of 1981 and 1986. The first of these reduced marginal income tax rates across the board and, for the first time, introduced indexation of the marginal tax rate break points. The second reform simplified the tax code and further reduced marginal tax rates. The net result was decreased inflation and increased economic growth in spite of the increased federal deficits.

---

[1] Actually proposed by President Kennedy in his 1963 state of the union address. Became the law when signed by President Johnson in 1964, subsequent to President Kennedy's assassination in 1963. See United States Revenue Act of 1964 (Pub.L. 88–272).

1980s Deficits and Federal Reserve Monetization

The fourth decade after the Accord began with double-digit inflation and a greater than 2% negative GDP growth rate. Deficits continued to grow as a share of GDP, which put increased fiscal pressure on the monetary authority. Figure 7.1 shows the deficits and the growth in the monetary base for the 1980s decade. It is clear that the scale of federal deficits in the latter half of the decade of the 1980s were the largest since World War II, averaging 3.87% of GDP. Even the first fiscal year deficit exceeded the maximum deficit of the previous decade. The entire decade had record deficits that would continue into the middle of the next decade.

Based on the increases in the monetary base as a share of the period's deficits, the Federal Reserve monetized just over 9% of the total of the periods federal deficits. However, some monetary growth is required to maintain the ratio of the money supply to the nation's output. For this decade, the rate of monetary growth adjusted for GDP growth indicates that the Federal Reserve monetized only 4.8% of the 1980s federal deficits. This level of GDP growth adjusted monetization was about one-fourth of the level of adjusted monetization of the 1970s. This lower level of adjusted monetization is consistent with the 1980s inflation rate that was much reduced from the double-digit inflation of the latter part of the 1970s.

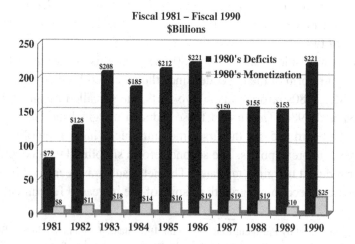

Figure 7.1.   Deficits and Federal Reserve Monetization

The Federal Reserve and 1980s Inflation

The decade of the 1980s was characterized by large deficits, increased GDP growth, a falling but still significant inflation rate and relatively rapid growth in the monetary base. Figure 7.2 shows the annualized growth rate for the monetary base, real GDP and the Consumer Price Index (CPI) for the 1980s. This was a period of sporadic real GDP growth, beginning with a rapid decline as the impact of the unprecedented inflation of the previous decade had a significant effect on the economy. For the 1980s as a whole, real GDP growth rose modestly from the previous decade's 3.1–3.3%.

This fourth decade of central bank independence was characterized by falling inflation, in spite of rising federal government deficits. For the entire decade, federal deficits averaged 3.89% of GDP as compared to the 2.15% of GDP of the previous decade. The decade's large deficits placed the Federal Reserve under increased pressure from the Treasury to accommodate fiscal issues. Indeed, this accommodation shows up in the rate of growth in the monetary base. The Federal Reserve increased its assets by $145–280 billion, but that increase paled in comparison to the decade's federal deficits of $1.565 trillion. In effect, the Federal Reserve monetized on a gross of GDP growth just over 9% of the 1980s federal deficits.

The tax code changes of the Reagan Administration resulted in a significant recovery for the economy for the period from 1983 through 1988, as real GDP grew at a 4.5% annual rate. The monetary base growth rate

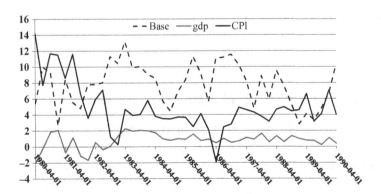

Figure 7.2. Monetary Base, CPI and Real GDP Growth 1980–1990

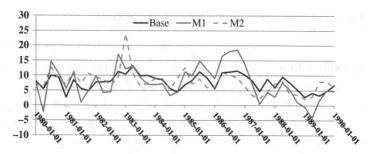

Figure 7.3.   Base, M1, M2 Growth Rates, 1980–1990

stayed virtually the same as the previous decade, falling only slightly from 4.88% to 4.75%. But the big change was in the level of CPI inflation that fell significantly from the 7.63% of the previous decade to 4.98%. Clearly, the combination of relatively stable monetary base growth rate and increased real GDP growth led to a reduced rate of inflation.

Given the level of deficits, even monetizing just over 9% of the debt increase resulted in significant growth in the popular measures of the money supply. Figure 7.3 shows the growth rates of the monetary base and the two most used measures of the total money supply, M1 and M2. Monetary base growth averaged 7.76% and was above 5% for essentially the entire decade. However, there are several anomalies in the data that are worth some discussion. In particular, the period surrounding the S&L crisis of 1985–1989 was perhaps responsible for the large increase in the M1 growth rate that averaged 7.62% for the decade and declining M2 growth rate as it fell from the 9.61% of the 1970s to 7.9% as the public clamored for cash. Overall though, monetary growth averaged over 7% for all three monetary definitions. This 7% monetary growth rate is consistent with the decade average inflation rate of 5% and real GDP growth of just less than 1%.

The Federal Reserve and 1980s Interest Rates

Given the relatively rapid decline in the inflation rate as shown in Figure 7.2, it is not surprising that nominal interest rates fell as well. Figure 7.4 shows the Fed Funds rate, the 10-year and 1-year treasury rates and CPI inflation. It is easy to see the effect of inflation on interest rates. As inflation falls and investors adjust their beliefs to a continuation of falling inflation, nominal interest rates (the sum of the real interest rate

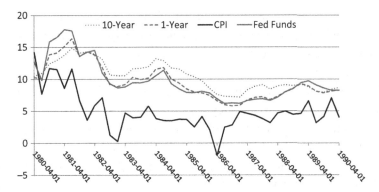

Figure 7.4. Treasury Interest Rates, Fed Funds Rate and CPI-Inflation 1980–1990

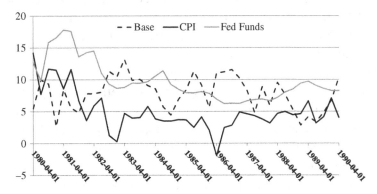

Figure 7.5. Monetary Base Growth, CPI and Fed Funds Rates 1980–1990

and the rate of inflation) fall. Indeed, that is exactly what Figure 7.4 depicts. Also, if we think of the interbank overnight lending rate, the Fed Funds rate, as short-term rates fall, the pressure to control bank reserves becomes less important so that overnight lending rates should fall as well.

It is clear from Figure 7.4 that the Fed Funds rate and Treasury interest rates are related. Changes in the Fed Funds rate will occur naturally when interest rates rise without any Federal Reserve actions. However, Federal Reserve announcements of changes in the targeted Fed Funds rate is generally taken by the market as a precursor of Federal Reserve actions. To get a feel for the connection between the Fed Funds rate and actual Federal Reserve policy, Figure 7.5 contains the rate of growth in the monetary base, the CPI and the Fed Funds rate. Actual Federal Reserve policy consists of its operations in financial markets. These operations are summarized in the change in the monetary base. The effect of these policies then show up in the Fed Funds rate. But as we have seen in Figure 7.4, inflation plays a large role in the determination of the nominal interest rate and the level of the Fed Funds rate.

To understand the underlying basis for Figure 7.5, we must review the nature of Federal Reserve policy. In normal times, the Federal Reserve conducts monetary policy by buying and selling treasuries, usually with maturities less than 1 year. These operations are referred to as open-market sales or purchases because the Federal Reserve deals in the secondary market. That is, the Federal Reserve is precluded by law from buying federal debt directly from the Treasury in these operations. A significant purchase of treasuries during a specific period will increase the demand for treasuries and reduce the quantity of treasuries available on the market. As a result, the price of treasuries will rise implying a decline on the yield on treasuries.

The direct effect of a significant purchase of treasuries will be to increase bank reserves. Assuming that the market effect of the purchase is a fall in the yield on treasuries, this decline in treasury yields coupled with the increase in bank reserves will make banks more willing to lend in the overnight reserve market and drive down the Fed Funds rate.

There is ample evidence that investors understand that inflation erodes the nominal return on financial assets. Thus, an increase in the rate of inflation will increase nominal interest rates, immediately on short-term assets and then as inflation continues, on long-term assets as well. Given this understanding what we should see in Figure 7.5 is an inverse relation between the rate of growth in the monetary base, the measure of Federal Reserve operations in the bond market, and the Fed Funds rate. Indeed, casual observation confirms just such a relation. Increases in the rate of growth of the monetary base results in falls in the Fed Funds rate and interest rates in general. However, these changes are short-run for we know that the long-run relation between inflation and nominal interest rates is positive.

Conclusion

The decade of the 1980s began with double-digit inflation and short-term interest rates that reached 15%. The rate of inflation began falling once the rate of monetary expansion fell. In fact, CPI inflation fell quickly and stabilized at around 5%. In spite of the decade being characterized by deficits that averaged $171 billion, the Federal Reserve only monetized just over 9% of these deficits.

There were three significant events in the decade of the 1980s. First, the deregulation of the petroleum pricing that led to a significant reduction in oil prices. Second, the dramatic reduction in the top income tax rate, which one could argue was responsible for the deficits early in the decade. Third, the overall tax code reform of 1986.

The federal deficits for the 1970s had been the largest since the end of World War II. However, the 1980s made those seem small as the average deficit was $171 billion. Here, the Federal Reserve showed much more restraint in funding the deficits. Some attribute this restraint to the advent of Paul Volcker as the new Chairman of the Federal Reserve Board of Governors. The fact that the Federal Reserve covered almost 18% of the 1970s deficits but only funded just over 9% of the larger 1980s deficits if attributed to Volcker, makes him the 1970s inflation killer.

Chapter 8

The 1990s: Turning Deficits into Surpluses

Introduction

Each decade since World War II has seen growing federal deficits interspersed with rare surpluses. In fact, in the 58 years since 1960, there have only been 5 years of federal surpluses. One in the 1960s and three in the 1990s with the last surplus in fiscal year 2001. Each decade since 1950 has seen that decade's deficit as a share of GDP grow relative to the previous decade.

That said, we turn to the 1990s and the unique set of circumstances that led to actual federal government surplus by the end of the decade. Some argue that a high top marginal tax rate on income has two effects, both of which lead to lower real output. First, high marginal tax rates affect the willingness of the most productive to fully employ their skills. Second, these same high marginal tax rates encourage behavior that limits tax liability at the expense of output.

The tax reforms of the 1980s are attributed by some to be the seed of the growth of national output that occurred in the 1990s. In addition, the 1990s was the decade of welfare reform legislation that, for the first time in many decades, increased the return to work relative to idleness. The gradual retraction of these reforms made this decade the last decade of increased labor force participation.

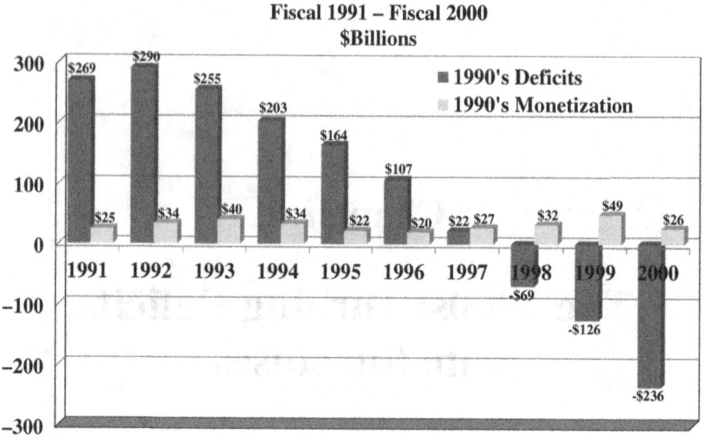

Fiscal 1991 – Fiscal 2000
$Billions

Figure 8.1.   Deficits and Federal Reserve Monetization

1990s Federal Budgets and Federal Reserve Monetization

The decade of the 1990s is only the third decade in the last 70 years with budget surpluses. Figure 8.1 shows the federal budget deficits (surpluses) and monetary base increases for each of the decade's fiscal years. The close of the decade was characterized by falling deficits that became surpluses and rising rates of increase in the monetary base. For the decade, GDP grew at a rate of 3.44%, while the monetary base grew at 7.84%. Adjusting the monetary base growth for the growth in GDP suggests that during this decade the Federal Reserve monetized 32.9% of the decade's total, but much smaller, deficit.

The federal deficits peaked in fiscal 1992 and then fell for every subsequent fiscal year in this decade. The fiscal 1997 federal deficit of $22 billion was the smallest federal deficit in more than 20 years. Then, this smallest in two decade deficit preceded an almost unheard of era of four consecutive surpluses! These surpluses reached an almost astounding $236 billion in fiscal 2000 and were still at $128 billion in fiscal 2001. It is clear from Figure 8.1 that the monetary base growth is unrelated to the budget surpluses during this decade.

The Federal Reserve and 1990s Inflation

Figure 8.2 shows the annualized growth rate for the monetary base, real GDP and the Consumer Price Index (CPI) for the decade of the 1990s.

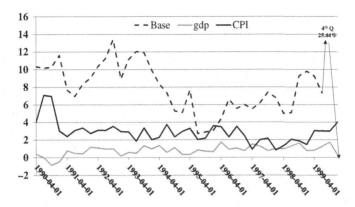

Figure 8.2.   Monetary Base, CPI and Real GDP Growth 1990–2000

This fifth decade after the Accord began with growing inflation and declining GDP growth. Both of these trends were quickly reversed. The relatively high monetary base growth continued through the first third of the decade and then declined significantly. In the latter half of the decade, deficits fell as a share of GDP and at the close of the decade became surpluses. Both the monetary base growth and the path of federal deficits indicate some accommodation by the Federal Reserve.

This decade was also unique in that publicly held federal debt as a share of GDP was lower at the close of the decade than at its start. In addition, monetary base growth slowed as deficits fell. The effect of deficits on the Federal Reserve policy can be seen by comparing the first half of this decade's growth in the base of a 9.3% annual rate to the pre-Y2K close of the period rate of base growth of 5.3%.

The question that this data raises is; would an independent central bank policies have been to monetize debt proportional to the size of the deficit? The deficit for the first half of the decade was $1.18 trillion, while the second half of the decade saw surpluses totaling $302 billion. This accommodation policy shows up in CPI growth of 3.34% for the first half of the decade compared to 2.43% in the second half of the decade. By way of comparison, GDP growth for the decade as a whole was 4.3% almost exactly the GDP growth of the latter half of the decade of 4.2%.

A last point of interest concerning this decade is the spike in the monetary base growth rate at the end of the decade. This spike in the level of the monetary base shows the Federal Reserve's response to the growing reliance of markets and industry on computer technology coupled with the fear that Y2K would result in a technological meltdown. This meltdown fear was based on the fact that when the underlying computer programs were written memory space was limited and only two digits were allowed for representing the year. If the first year of the new century was noted as 00 and if such a year was not allowed by the program, the program would have crashed.[1] It was even feared that given the increased use of computer technology in automobiles that the update from year 99 to year 00 would just shut down all aspects of the automobile's operation.

The fear of a technological meltdown given the increased reliance of financial markets on technology led to a run for currency, a pure non-technology based money. As it turned out, none of these fears materialized, and the rate of base increase of 25.44% in the fourth quarter of 1999 designed to handle any resulting liquidity crisis was quickly reversed. This is an example of central bank behavior at its best.

The growth in the two measures of the money supply follow the growth in the monetary base but in quite different ways. Figure 8.3 shows the quarterly growth rates for the monetary base and the M1 and M2 money stock measures. The average rates of growth for all three measures are very similar but the path of the growth rates is very dissimilar. For the entire decade the monetary base grew at an average rate of 7.37%, M1 grew at 7.15% and M2 at 6.97%. But the path of the two

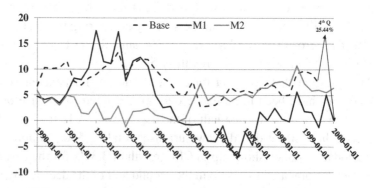

Figure 8.3.   Base, M1, M2 Growth Rates, 1990–2000

---

[1] This concern and the fact that many of the business-oriented software programs were written in Common Business Oriented Language (COBOL) led to a boom in the demand for programmers' proficient in COBOL, so that older programs could be revised.

money stock measures was very different. For the first half of the decade M1 grew faster than the monetary base while M2 grew more slowly, while just the opposite was true in the latter half of the decade. In fact, the M1 growth rate was negative for almost 3 years from the end of 1994 to late 1997.

The Federal Reserve and 1990s Interest Rates

Given the relatively rapid decline in the inflation rate in the first year of this decade, as shown in Figure 8.2, it is not surprising that nominal interest rates fell as well. Figure 8.4 shows the Fed Funds rate, the 10-year and 1-year treasury rate and CPI inflation. It is easy to see the effect of inflation on interest rates. As inflation fell and then stayed well below the rate of the previous decade, the market interest rates adjusted. Although what is surprising is that after the beginning of 1994, interest rates rose rapidly from the low of 3.5% for 1-year treasuries to well over 6% and then stabilized around the 5% level. But as investors adjust their beliefs to a continuation of falling inflation, nominal interest rates (the sum of the real interest rate and the rate of inflation) fall. Indeed, that is exactly what Figure 8.4 depicts. Also, if we think of the interbank overnight lending rate, the Fed Funds rate, as short-term treasury rates fall, overnight lending rates should fall as well.

It is clear from Figure 8.4 that the Fed Funds rate and Treasury interest rates are related. Even with no action by the Federal Reserve, Fed

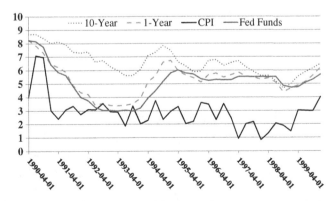

Figure 8.4. Treasury Interest Rates and CPI-Inflation 1990–2000

Funds rates will follow market interest rates. This relation is a result of the fact that as market interest rates rise it becomes more expensive for banks to hold reserves. Reserves then become scarcer and the overnight borrowing rate rises. This normal relation between the Fed Funds rate and market interest rates does not eliminate the expectation of the investment community that a change in policy is in the offing when the Federal Reserve announces a change in its target for the Fed Funds rate. If an increase in the Fed Funds target rate is to be realized, then the Federal Reserve must make reserves scarcer, which requires a reduction in the monetary base through an open-market sale of Federal Reserve assets.

To get some feel for the connection between the Fed Funds rate and actual Federal Reserve policy during the 1990s, Figure 8.5 contains the rate of growth in the monetary base, the CPI and the Fed Funds rate. The announcement of a change in the target for the Fed Funds rate is not, in itself, policy. Actual Federal Reserve policy consists of its operations in financial markets. These operations are summarized in the change in the monetary base. The effect of these policies then shows up in the Fed Funds rate. Federal Reserve purchases of securities in the market put money into the economy and increase bank reserves. The increase in reserves makes them more plentiful and the supply of funds in the Fed Funds market increases, reducing the Fed Funds rate. An asset sale by the Federal Reserve has the opposite effect and reduces reserves and raises the Fed Funds rate.

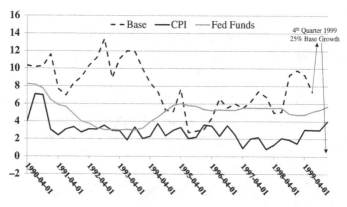

Figure 8.5.   Monetary Base Growth, CPI and Fed Funds Rate 1990–2000

While changes in the Fed Funds rate can be a signal of future Federal Reserve policy, they also happen in response to changes in market interest rates. As market interest rates rise, banks conserve on reserves and the Fed Funds rate rises. Since nominal market interest rates are composed of the equilibrium real interest rate and the rate of inflation, the movements in the CPI depicted in Figure 8.4 should be associated with interest rate changes. At least for the early part of the 1990s, the relation among the rate of inflation, the Fed Funds rate and the growth in the monetary base are consistent with this association. We see an increase in the monetary base that would be required if the Federal Reserve desired to reduce the Fed Funds rate. Almost simultaneously, the reduction in the rate of inflation would have without any Federal Reserve actions reduced the nominal interest rate.

Conclusion

The decade of the 1980s began with the largest deficits since World War II. Then, the tax reforms of the 1980s began to have their full effect on federal government finances. The lower marginal tax rates from the 1980s reforms actually increased federal revenues as tax-payers reduced inefficient income hiding activities. By 1997, federal deficits had fallen to $22 billion, a level not seen since the early 1970s. Moreover, the next year, 1998, saw the beginning of a string of federal budget surpluses, something not seen since the late 1950s. The decade was marked with declining rates of growth in the monetary base that began in 1993 and continued until the Y2K crisis at the close of the century.

This decade also saw an excellent example of a central bank doing what only central banks can do: dealing with a fear-induced increase in the demand for currency. The crisis was induced by the fear that the onset of the year 2000, referred to as Y2K, would cause a stoppage in all computer-driven hardware. It was feared that such a crash would result in an output and financial crash. Thus, the tremendous increase in the demand for cash. The Federal Reserve responded to this fear by increasing the monetary base in the fourth quarter of 1999 by 25%, a gigantic one-quarter change. As it turned out, the Y2K crash never occurred, and the Federal Reserve restored its previous asset position by undoing the increase in the base.

Chapter 9

The Federal Reserve in the Early 21St Century

Introduction

The fourth post-Accord decade ended with the special circumstance of the Y2K scare that led to a spike in monetary base growth. But that spike paled in comparison to the rate of monetary base growth that occurred after the onset of the 2008 liquidity crisis. Two periods in the early 21St century stand out in terms of monetary base growth — first, the quarters immediately following the World Trade Center terrorist attack on September 11, 2001, and second, the quarters following the liquidity crisis of September 2008.

Because of the events leading up and subsequent to the September 2008 liquidity crisis, it makes sense to separate this decade into two parts. Part 1 includes the eight fiscal years from 2001 through 2008 (a period that closed with the financial crisis of September 2008, the last month of fiscal 2008). Part 2 consists of the nine fiscal years from 2009 to 2017. This separation is especially relevant because of the October 2008 introduction by the Federal Reserve of paying interest on bank reserves. This change is especially important because it makes changes in the monetary base no longer a measure of Federal Reserve accommodation to Treasury financing issues.

Early 2000s Deficits and Federal Reserve Monetization

Here, we deal with the deficits and monetary base growth for the first eight fiscal years of the decade. Figure 9.1 shows the federal budget deficits (surplus) and the increases in the monetary base from fiscal year 2001 through the first 11 months of fiscal year 2008. The close of this period was characterized by a surge in the federal deficit and the monetary base. For this abbreviated decade, GDP grew at a rate of 2.01% while the monetary base grew at 6.40%. Adjusting the monetary base growth for the growth in GDP suggests that during this decade, the Federal Reserve monetized 11.1% of the 7-year deficits.

The first 8 years of the decade saw the rapid transition from a rare period of federal budget surpluses to budget normality, deficits. From the fiscal year 2001 surplus of $128 billion, 1.2% of GDP, the next year saw a deficit of $158 billion, 1.4% of GDP. Future deficits then rose rapidly, reaching 3.4% of GDP in 2004. Then, after a brief period of deficits falling as a share of GDP, deficits rose again and peaked in fiscal year 2008 at $459 billion, almost matching fiscal year 2004's share of GDP, at 3.3%. As history shows, this was to be the smallest deficit for many years to come. The increase in the base in fiscal year 2001, more than double the fiscal 2000 increase, was the result of the Federal Reserve's appropriate reaction to the 9/11 attack on the World Trade Center. The increases in the monetary base then fell until fiscal 2008, the beginning of the "Great Recession."

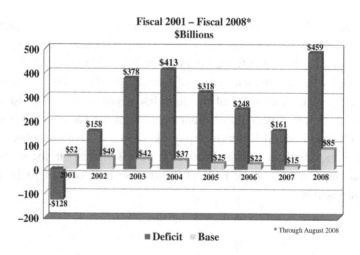

Figure 9.1.   Deficits and Federal Reserve Monetization

The Federal Reserve and Early 2000s Inflation

Figure 9.2 shows the growth rate of the monetary base, real GDP and the CPI for the period from the third quarter of 2000, the beginning of fiscal year 2001, through the close of fiscal year 2007. Just as the Y2K episode had a dramatic effect on the monetary base, the tragic 9/11 World Trade Center terrorist attack is evident in the monetary base growth rate for the third quarter of the calendar year 2001, the fourth quarter of fiscal year 2001. In addition to the 9/11 tragedy, the market was in the middle of the dot-com meltdown in which the NASDAQ composite fell 78% in the first 2 years of the 2000s. Both of these events led to a rather dramatic change in the growth rate of the monetary base that is easily discernable in Figure 9.2.

After the NASDAQ peaked in March 2000, it then fell rapidly for the next 2 years. That crash coupled with the 9/11 incident led to above-average growth in the monetary base that continued until the end of the first quarter of 2003. Then, monetary base growth rate trended downward until a dramatic rise in September 2008 that will be discussed in the following chapter. Overall, this period was characterized by real GDP growth below the level of the previous decade and slightly higher price level growth. The monetary base grew at 4.9% compared to the previous decade's growth of 5.3%. Real GDP grew in that same shortened pre-2008 decade at 2.4% versus the previous decade's growth of 3.3%. CPI growth pre-2008 was 3.0% compared to the prior decade growth of 2.8%.

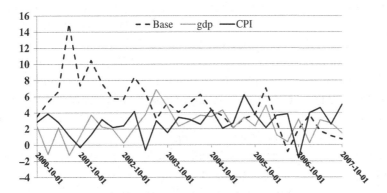

Figure 9.2. Monetary Base, CPI and Real GDP Growth 2000–2007

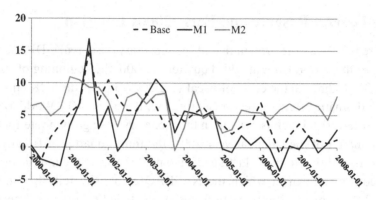

Figure 9.3.   Base, M1, M2 Growth Rates, 2000–2007

Figure 9.3 shows the growth rates of the monetary base and the two most used measures of the money supply, M1 and M2. From the figure, it is apparent that the highly variable rates of growth in the monetary base is duplicated by the growth rates in the narrower measure of the money supply, M1. The broader measure of the money supply, M2 shows much less variation in its growth rates. For the entire period, the monetary base grew at an average rate of 4.73% while M1 grew for the same period at only 3.0%. The growth of the broader measure of the money supply, M2, was much more stable and for the entire period averaged 6.21%.

The Federal Reserve and Early 2000s Interest Rates

Figure 9.4 shows the 10-year and 1-year treasury interest rates, along with the rate of CPI inflation and the Fed Funds rate. The reduction in inflation that was a characteristic of the decade of the 1990s continued in the first decade of the 21st century, or at least through 2007. From the figure, it is easy to see the effect of inflation on interest rates. Inflation stabilized and stayed below the rate of the previous decade. This history of lower inflation is consistent with the gradual falling 10-year treasury rates. From the beginning of 2003 through the beginning of 2004, short rates fell from 6% to just over 1%. Then, an upward trend in CPI inflation occurred, and these short rates rose again reaching the 5% level of the 10-year treasuries.

For this entire mini decade, the Fed Funds rate and the 1-year treasury rates marched almost in lockstep. Throughout the 7 years depicted in

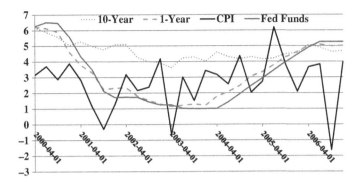

Figure 9.4. Treasury Interest Rates, Fed Funds and CPI-Inflation 2000–2007

Figures 9.2 and 9.3, the rate of growth in the monetary base declined from 10% in the first quarter of 2002 to less than 1% in the third quarter of 2007. These changes in monetary base growth seem disconnected with the changes in the 1-year treasuries and the Fed Funds rate that moved, in almost, in unison for the entire 7-year period. This observation is consistent with the hypothesis that the Fed Funds rate is driven by market interest rates rather than the reverse. This is especially relevant, since there is not a sign of changes in monetary policy in terms of base growth during the period.

Conclusion

The first 7 years of the 21ˢᵗ century saw declining monetary base growth as the initial response to the 9/11 tragedy was undone. Just as in other decades, severe financial events put the Federal Reserve in the position of having to flood the market with liquidity. The 9/11 tragedy dramatically affected money markets as the center of much of financial trading was conducted by firms occupying the World Trade Center. The Federal Reserve responded as a central bank should and indeed as only a central bank can. This period also saw a precursor of the low interest rates that would be with us for the following decade. In fact, the 1-year treasuries fell to almost 1% in 2003 and then rose back to the norm of the 1990s. But these 7 years were to be just the tip of the financial iceberg as the other nine-tenths was to begin in 2008, which is the subject of the following chapter.

Chapter 10

The Federal Reserve and the Great Recession Financial Crisis

Introduction

Until the beginning of 2007, the first decade of this century was similar to the past half-century at least in terms of Federal Reserve behavior. This similarity can be seen in the assets used by the Federal Reserve to conduct monetary policy over the entire pre-2007 period. In particular, the Federal Reserve open-market operations were exclusively conducted in Treasury securities. In fact, except for brief periods of "operation twist" transactions where policy was designed to make the interest rate yield curve flatter, Federal Reserve operations were almost exclusively done with short-term treasuries.

All changed with the onset of the 2008 financial crisis led by the collapse of the Mortgage-Backed Securities (MBSs) market. Although, prior to September 2008 financial collapse, in early 2008, the Federal Reserve had entered short-term credit markets by reducing their holdings of short-term treasuries and substituting short-term commercial assets. In fact, the Federal Reserve's holdings of treasuries only returned to their January 2007 level in mid-2009.

In this chapter, I discuss the responses to the initial financial crisis during the period from January 2007 to the close of 2009.

A Central Bank Performing as a Central Bank

Let's begin by chronicling the Federal Reserve's response to that part of the crisis that was pure liquidity in nature. Figure 10.1 shows the path of the monetary base from the beginning of 2007 to 2009. This period includes the peak of the previous expansion, December 2007, as well as the June 2009 trough of the recession. The monetary base remained virtually unchanged from the beginning of the downturn until the September 2008 financial crisis. As shown below, the fact that the monetary base remained unchanged during this period does not mean that the Federal Reserve was not playing an active role in controlling the beginning of a financial crisis. After this relatively stable period in terms of the Federal Reserve's total assets, the base almost doubled in the next 3 months from its September 10th level of $875 billion to a December 31st level of $1,691 billion.

At the beginning of the Great Recession, Federal Reserve assets were almost entirely short-term treasury securities. But as shown in Figure 10.2, the Federal Reserve began to substitute liquid financial market assets for treasury securities almost 9 months before the September 2008 liquidity crisis. The transition from Treasury securities to financial market assets began slowly in late 2007 and then accelerated at the beginning of 2008. As the recession that began in December of 2007 accelerated, financial

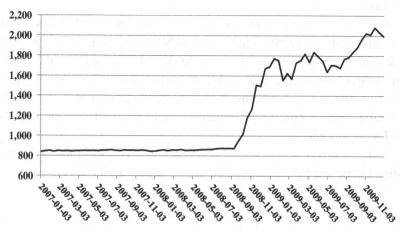

Figure 10.1. The Monetary Base Before and After September 2008 Crisis

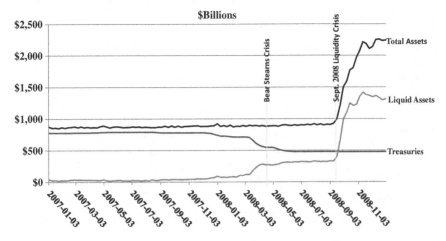

Figure 10.2. Federal Reserve Asset Responses to the Recession

institutions such as Lehman Brother and Bear Stearns were faced with potential bankruptcy. In fact, Lehman Brothers declared bankruptcy in September of 2008. The financial distress of these near banks resulted in a further replacement of treasury securities with financial market assets. During this entire period, there was essentially no change in the total asset holdings of the Federal Reserve, only a change in its portfolio away from treasuries toward commercial assets. As a result, there was almost no growth in the monetary base from the beginning of 2007 to September 2008.

Now, we get to a real liquidity crisis — September 2008. Here, the Federal Reserve responded by increasing its portfolio by purchasing commercial assets and providing the equivalent of currency to the economy. The Federal Reserve sold almost one-half of its Treasury holdings and added commercial paper assets, while doubling its assets from $1.1 trillion in September of 2008 to over $2.2 trillion by the close of the calendar year 2008. These actions were traditional central bank responses to the form of liquidity crisis that the economy was facing during this period. At least two aspects of this period are important.

First, the month of September 2008 was the month that interbank lending disappeared, for all practical purposes, and we were in a real liquidity crisis as far as the banking system was concerned.

Second, almost immediately the money market funds faced unprecedented demand by depositors for cash. These funds were faced with the

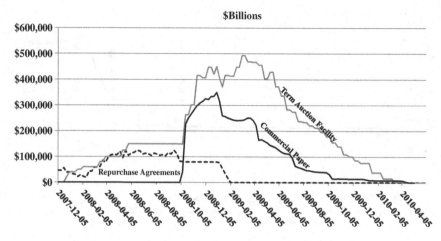

Figure 10.3.   Federal Reserve Pure Liquidity Crisis Response

prospect of not being able to honor these requests as the market for commercial paper had all but disappeared.

In response to these two events, the Federal Reserve abandoned its previous response mechanism of simply replacing treasuries with commercial financial assets and did what a central bank is supposed to do in a liquidity crisis: flood the market with liquidity. This flooding the market with liquidity took several forms, all consistent with giving the financial system access to short-term assets. Figure 10.3 shows the path of three major programs designed to flood the market with liquidity.

First, as the crisis began, the Federal Reserve increased lending to the banking system through repurchase agreements, the dashed line in Figure 10.3. In these agreements, banks give up assets to get cash now and agree to repurchase these assets at a later time. From the normal level of such repurchase agreements of about $30 billion, by the middle of 2008 bank borrowing from the Federal Reserve using the repurchase agreements more than tripled to over $100 billion. Eventually, this rise in repurchase agreements stabilized and then was replaced completely by the availability of funds via the next major program.

Second, as the severity of the crisis worsened, the Federal Reserve established the Term Auction Facility (TAF) to lend money to financial institutions at interest rates determined at auction. The establishment of the TAF in December 2007 coincided with the rise in the level of repurchase agreements, but by February 2009, this facility completely replaced repurchase agreements as the mode of bank borrowing from the Federal Reserve. The level of these borrowings was substantial and reached almost $500 billion in March 2009 before gradually tapering off, so that by April 2010 the facility was gone.

Third, the crisis affected the ability of the money market funds to instantly honor requests by depositors as the liquidity crisis resulted in a rush to cash. Even though these funds hold only short-term commercial paper assets, their liabilities, deposits by you and me, are demand in nature, although not legally so. However, once a fund does not treat its liabilities as demand liabilities, they will be out of business. To alleviate this problem, the Federal Reserve bought commercial paper directly to make an instant market for these assets.

It is during this span of time that we have a historical episode that demonstrates the real value of an independent central bank, as part of the financial crisis, was one of pure liquidity. A pure liquidity crisis occurs, when the long-term financial assets supporting the shorter-term liabilities have maintained their intrinsic value but simply cannot be converted to cash in large amounts on short notice. The response is to provide the market with large quantities of cash by acquiring these assets. In the end, when the crisis is over, these assets are simply returned to the market. As such, the assets held by the central bank would return to their before-crisis level. However, for many of the assets underlying the general financial crisis this period represented more than an issue of pure liquidity.

While the above discussion concerns the appropriate response to a pure liquidity crisis, the length of the crisis and the size of the response suggests that the episode that began in September 2008 was not a pure liquidity crisis. That this was not a pure liquidity crisis is clear from the fact that the assets underlying the deposits at financial institutions had undergone a significant depreciation. Thus, this was more than just the public suddenly wanting more currency and financial institutions with long-term assets being unable to quickly dispose of such assets. Rather, disposing of their assets would have resulted in many of these institutions being declared insolvent.

This period is also unique in terms of the scale of Federal Reserve involvement. The sum of Federal Reserve holdings of the collateral for the

TAF, plus their holdings of commercial paper peaked at the close of 2008 at more than $850 billion. This level of holdings used to aid the financial markets in the crisis almost equaled the entire Federal Reserve pre-crisis August 27, 2008, total reserve bank credit of $884 billion.

Now, we get to the second phase of Federal Reserve actions. These actions were by and large not a response to a pure liquidity crisis, but to the onset of the recession that began in December 2007. However, even before the onset of the recession, the so-called housing bubble had burst. The fallout from falling prices in the housing market, coupled with the rising share of sub-prime mortgages led to a significant rise in non-performing mortgages. Importantly, these mortgages were the asset underlying the MBSs market. Given the heavy involvement of the financial industry in this previously booming part of the financial market, the fall in value of MBSs brought many financial institutions once thought to be fail-proof to their knees, as any mark to market requirement would have resulted in insolvency.

To deal with financial market issues beyond the simple liquidity crisis response, the Federal Reserve provided funding for institutions not directly in the banking industry. Figure 10.4 indicates some of these Federal Reserve responses. Because of the general concern as markets were falling, equity investors were cashing in accounts. The issue was that both mutual funds and broker–dealers were experiencing runs on their accounts at the same time

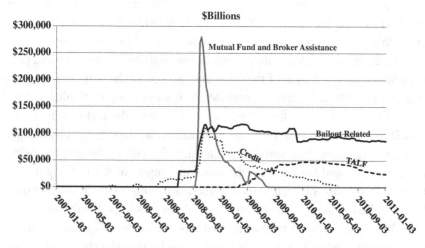

Figure 10.4. Federal Reserve Financial Market Responses

(September 2008), as well as more traditional financial institutions. This issue is similar to the pure liquidity crisis response shown in Figure 10.3 and the response lasted about a year peaking in October 2008 at just under $280 billion. In addition, the Federal Reserve expanded its credit to the financial industry. This expansion began as early as late 2007, but became significant in September 2008 peaking at just over $100 billion in November 2008 and then gradually declining until disappearing in mid-2010.

A Central Bank Doing What the Founding Fathers Feared

There were at least two Great Recession Federal Reserve actions that were outside of the normal role of central banking. They are shown in Figure 10.4 and labeled *Bailout Related* and *Term Asset-Backed Loan Facility* (TALF). The former began as Maiden Lane I, LLC in July 2008 with the bailout of Bear Sterns to aid in the disposition of their assets. It then continued when in September 2008, the American International Group (AIG) faced potential insolvency due to the effect of the massive meltdown of MBSs on AIG-issued credit default swaps. Here, the Federal Reserve established Maiden Lane II, LLC to bail out AIG's lending division and then Maiden Lane III, LLC to bail out AIG's credit default swap division.

As a continuation of the Federal Reserve's direct actions in the economy that were not liquidity crisis-related, the TALF was created to supply resources to the consumer lending industry. This industry packages loans into securitized instruments much like MBSs, except that the underlying securities may be auto loans, student loans, credit card loans, equipment loans, floorplan loans, insurance premium finance loans, small business loans fully guaranteed as to principal and interest by the US. Small Business Administration, and receivables related to residential mortgage servicing. Not surprisingly, the market for these Asset-Backed Securities (ABSs) dried up with the collapse of the MBS market. The Federal Reserve provided funds to the industry for the purpose of making the underlying loans more attractive to issuers. The expressed purpose of TALF was to make credit available to consumers and businesses on more favorable terms by facilitating the issuance of ABSs and improving the market conditions for ABSs more generally.

The actions of the Federal Reserve to provide funds to solve a pure liquidity crises that occurred when there was no fundamental decline in the value of the real assets underlying the financial system, are an excellent example of appropriate central bank responses to a liquidity crisis. These situations were handled by the Federal Reserve through the Term Auction Credit program and the outright purchase of commercial paper. The first of these efforts provided liquidity to the banks, while the second ensured that the market for commercial paper did not collapse. Since these markets did not collapse, the Federal Reserve made money on both of these endeavors.

The surge in liquid assets held by the Federal Reserve that began in January 2008 had declined from a peak of $1.5 trillion to a mere $244.9 billion by the end of 2009. Further, Federal Reserve holdings of treasuries that had declined during the peak of the crisis to $475 billion had returned to their pre-crisis level of $777 billion.

However, as early as the spring of 2008, the Federal Reserve began to pursue policies that involved individual private firms. This trend of market interference began after the Lehman Brothers difficulties that ultimately led to their declaring bankruptcy in mid-September 2008 and the political fallout that followed. It was this political fallout that moved the Federal Reserve from an independent central bank to a central bank that embodied the founding fathers' worst fears. Part of these fears were that a central bank would directly interfere in private markets. Indeed, the Federal Reserve did just that. There were three main areas of this direct interference.

First, the Federal Reserve entered the market for mortgages in the form of supporting the market for securitized mortgage packages, MBSs. Here, the problem was that the underlying value of these products had declined. The response was exactly what the founding fathers feared — that a central bank would become captive to financial interests.

In this regard, the Federal Reserve began buying MBSs guaranteed by Fannie Mae and Freddie Mac as a way of relieving the "too big to fail" private banks of their holdings of these now-questionable assets. As Figure 10.5 shows, Federal Reserve holdings during this initial MBS buying program peaked in June 2010 at just under $1.2 trillion. At that point, the Federal Reserve held over one-third of the outstanding MBSs that were guaranteed by Fannie Mae and Freddie Mac.

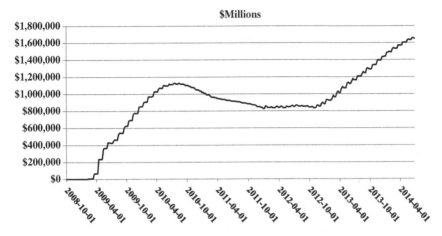

Figure 10.5. Federal Reserve MBS Holdings

After an asset acquisition hiatus, the Federal Reserve resumed purchases of MBSs as part of the second round of quantitative easing (QE2) that began in October 2012, the beginning of fiscal year 2013. At this point, Federal Reserve holdings of MBSs had declined from their June 2010 level of $1.2 trillion to $835 billion. This second round of purchases continued until finally ending in October 2014. In Figure 10.5, the two periods of Federal Reserve MBSs market participation are clearly visible.

Second, the Federal Reserve directly interfered in private financial markets in cooperation with the US Treasury by rescuing large financial institutions, such as Citi Bank, from potential bankruptcy by providing liquidity to these institutions on a favorable basis, guaranteeing a large share of the Citigroup assets whose value had fallen. This approach put the government in the position of insuring a significant slice of Citigroup's balance sheet on the basis that they were "too big to allow to fail." In exchange for the bankruptcy protection, Citigroup gave the government warrants to buy shares in the company. In addition, the Treasury Department injected $20 billion of fresh capital into Citigroup that came on top of the $25 billion infusion that Citigroup received as part of the broader US banking-industry bailout.

Third, the Federal Reserve made loans to AIG and forced, what was for all intents and purposes, a takeover of AIG at a price per share that the

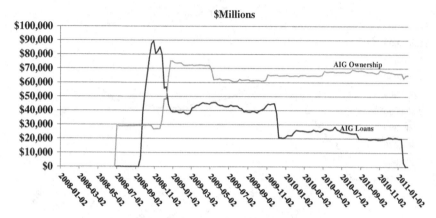

Figure 10.6.   Federal Reserve AIG Bailout

shareholders felt was below market value. Because of the dictated share price paid by the Federal Reserve for their holdings of AIG, taxpayers got all of their money back and then some, receiving a profit of more than $20 billion. Much of this profit was at the expense of the AIG shareholders.[1] Figure 10.6 shows the path of loans to AIG and the Federal Reserve ownership of AIG.

As Figure 10.6 shows, the ownership part of Federal Reserve involvement in AIG began in June 2008 on a relatively small scale. This was accomplished via the establishment of two LLCs, Maiden Lane II and III that bought shares in AIG. With the onset of the liquidity crisis of September 2008, the Federal Reserve made significant loans to AIG. These loans quickly reached almost $90 billion in late October 2008. Then, the loan part of the AIG subsidy fell at the same time that Federal Reserve ownership rose from $30 billion to almost $75 billion. Loans to AIG remained above $29 billion until the close of 2010 when they rapidly fell to zero. However, Federal Reserve ownership remained, and although it had almost disappeared by the beginning of 2015, it still remained at $1.7 billion in June 2015.

---

[1] At least one federal court has agreed with AIG shareholders that the Federal Reserve overstepped its authority in taking control of 79.9 % of the company at a price that shareholders argued convincingly was below market value, nearly wiping out many of its shareholders. At this juncture, it is not clear how this decision will affect the plaintiffs in this case.

Conclusion

The final establishment of a central bank for the United States was due to repeated monetary crises in the banking system, as it existed prior to the enactment of the Federal Reserve Act of 1913. Those monetary crises were the result of the public desiring to dramatically increase the currency share of their money balances. Since the banking system, then and now, has only limited availability of currency available, such changes can virtually shut down normal banking operations. The ability of the system to move seamlessly from deposits to cash is referred to as *the form elasticity of the money supply*. In fact, guaranteeing the form elasticity of the money supply is part of the 1913 Act establishing the Federal Reserve.

As the Great Recession monetary crisis began, the Federal Reserve responded in three ways that were traditional in that they helped give the money supply form elasticity.

First, they established the TAF in which banks could make interest rate bids for liquid funds. The TAF replaced the usual repurchase agreements between the Federal Reserve and banks. The basic difference is the scale of the program as the TAF reached $500 billion at the peak of the crisis. To put the magnitude of the TAF in perspective, the total Federal Reserve assets before the crisis were only $700 billion.

Second, they bought commercial paper directly as the ability of the money market funds to instantly honor requests by depositors disappeared, as the commercial paper market collapsed. At this program's peak, the Federal Reserve holdings of commercial paper reached almost $350 billion, almost half of the pre-crisis Federal Reserve total asset holdings.

Third, the Federal Reserve provided assistance to the mutual fund and broker industries to prevent these important financial entities from entering bankruptcy. That bankruptcy would have exacerbated the demand by the public for liquid assets. This program was brief and peaked at $275 billion.

These three programs in the first 3 months of the crisis reached over $1 trillion. To put this in perspective, the total assets of the Federal Reserve prior to October 2008 was $1.1 trillion. All three programs were over by the end of the first quarter of 2010. Even then, this length of response to a liquidity crisis was the longest in Federal Reserve history.

The Federal Reserve then moved away from traditional liquidity crisis behavior in two ways.

First, they aided in the bailout of AIG by taking an ownership position beginning in June 2008. Then, in October 2008 at the height of the liquidity crisis, they made loans to AIG. These loans were $90 billion by the end of October 2008. They fell almost as fast as they rose to about $40 billion by the close of 2008. They remained about $40 billion until falling to $20 billion at the close of 2009 and remained at $20 billion before disappearing at the close of 2010.

Second, they changed the long tradition of holding almost exclusively Treasury securities. Beginning in January 2009, the Federal Reserve began investing in private assets, namely MBSs. This program expanded rapidly and by February 2010, exceeded $1 trillion. After a brief decline to total Federal Reserve holdings, they once again increased holdings of MBSs to $1.8 trillion, about 40% of Fannie Mae and Freddie Mac MBSs.

Chapter 11

Expanding the Federal Reserve's Mission

Introduction

How has our central bank done in resisting pressure from government to help in times of deficits by creating money, and as a result creating inflation? I address this issue in part by outlining the Federal Reserve's role in mitigating at least the inflation potential of the tremendous deficits of the Great Recession. There is little doubt that the period beginning in October 2008 through the end of the third Federal Reserve Quantitative Easing in mid-2014 was unique in our financial history.

The economy experienced a collapse of financial markets, coupled with unprecedented federal budget deficits. These unprecedented deficits were accompanied by an unprecedented increase in Federal Reserve assets through the purchase of both new Treasury debt instruments and previously existing Mortgage-Backed Securities (MBSs). While the purchase of MBSs was not the first Federal Reserve excursion into the private economy, this episode represents the largest by a great margin.

Here, I delve into the details of this expansion of Federal Reserve assets beginning with the relation between the federal deficits and Federal Reserve assets purchases. Then, I proceed to an analysis of the scale of these actions relative to the economy in general. While the discussion is on the same wavelength as the discussion of the previous decades of Federal Reserve monetary policy, it differs because of the sheer scale of Federal Reserve actions.

The Federal Reserve and Government after the Onset of the Great Recession

To get a better feel for the dramatic change in Federal Reserve policy during this period, let's concentrate on the period from January 2007 to the present. Both the rate of change in the CPI and real GDP were at historic lows for any similar length period, or at least since 1950. Real GDP growth was a meager 1.35%, and CPI growth was 1.88%. Moreover, the federal deficits in terms of levels of absolute dollars and share of GDP were at post-World War II records. In keeping with the way the previous decades were discussed, Figure 11.1 shows the levels of fiscal year federal deficits and the corresponding changes in Federal Reserve assets holdings.

In the discussion of previous decades, the changes in Federal Reserve assets represented either running the money printing press, in the case of increasing assets, or destroying money in the case of Federal Reserve asset reductions. On this basis, it would appear that for the fiscal years 2009–2015, the Federal Reserve financed over 47% of the federal deficits by running the printing press. But this was not an ordinary period, so things are not as simple as they seem.

The increases in the Federal Reserve assets holdings during this period represent increases in Federal Reserve holdings of securities. But unlike almost all previous periods, the securities purchased were not all federal

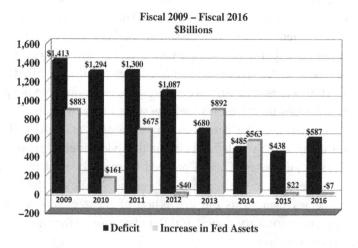

Figure 11.1.   Deficits and Federal Asset Purchases

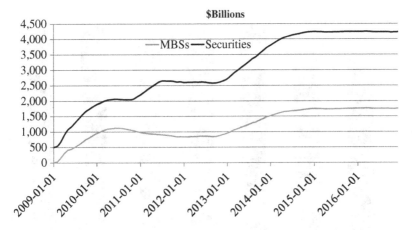

Figure 11.2. Total Securities and Mortgage Backed Securities

debt. The Federal Reserve was buying assets, principally both treasuries and MBSs, but only the treasuries were directly reducing the level of federal debt held outside the government. As we shall see below, Federal Reserve purchases of non-treasury assets affect the real cost of servicing the federal debt in the same way as the direct purchases of treasuries.

Figure 11.2 shows the aggregate level of Federal Reserve security holdings and the subset of those holdings that were MBSs. The figure includes only Federal Reserve holdings of treasuries and MBSs, since they were the subject of the three quantitative easing programs. The short-term adjustments in Federal Reserve assets to directly restore liquidity to the economy were the subject of Chapter 10. Bear in mind that prior to the liquidity crisis, Federal Reserve assets consisted almost entirely of treasuries. However, during 2007, in response to pre-Great Recession liquidity issues, the Federal Reserve sold treasuries and bought commercial assets. At the beginning of 2009, Federal Reserve holdings of treasuries were $500 billion down from the $700 billion level that existed at the beginning of 2007. However, the Federal Reserve was holding over $1 trillion in Term Auction Credit, loans, commercial paper and AIG assets. As a result, the Federal Reserve securities holdings were well less than 50% of Federal Reserve assets.

Does the Federal Reserve holdings of MBSs, and other assets for that matter, contribute in any way to the level of monetization? To solve this

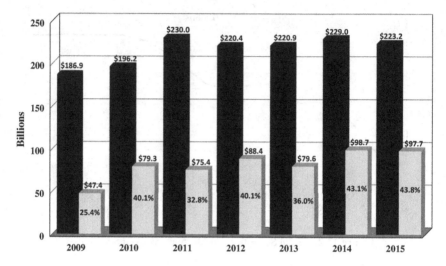

Figure 11.3.   Federal Reserve Transfer to the Treasury and Net Debt Serving Cost

puzzle requires analysis of what happens to the revenue from the MBSs and other Federal Reserve assets. By law, all profits of the Federal Reserve after costs revert to the Treasury. Thus, the Treasury is the residual income recipient of Federal Reserve asset holdings and so, in one sense at least, the Treasury owns the Federal Reserve. All Federal Reserve earnings on treasuries, MBSs and other assets accrue to the Treasury and reduce the net servicing cost of the federal debt. Figure 11.3 shows the level of the net debt servicing cost of the federal debt and the level of Federal Reserve transfers to the Treasury for the fiscal years 2009–2015.

Since Federal Reserve holdings of MBSs and other non-treasury assets all create income for the Treasury, these assets offset federal debt. Therefore, their purchase is equivalent to the Federal Reserve buying treasuries. As a result, the entire increase in Federal Reserve holdings of securities and other assets represent monetization of the federal deficits. In fact, over the fiscal years 2009–2015, the transfers from the Federal Reserve financed more than 40% of the servicing cost of the debt.

The above post-2008 deficits and monetization chart indicates the extent that the Federal Reserve's increased assets contributed to the monetization of the massive federal debts of this period. But this simple view of the federal debt world ignores the fact that the Federal Reserve increased its liabilities almost in lock-step with the increase in assets. This increase in liabilities was the result of the introduction in October 2008 of the payment of interest on bank reserves, making these reserves a short-term debt of the Federal Reserve. Further, the fact that all earnings of the Federal Reserve offset the servicing cost of the federal debt implies that bank reserves are now the equivalent of short-term federal debt. The Federal Reserve throughout the three periods of quantitative easing (QE) was buying the equivalent of long-term federal debt and selling the equivalent of short-term federal debt.

Before interest payments on bank reserves, Federal Reserve actions that increased bank reserves led to an increase in the money supply. Since bank reserves did not earn interest, banks moved these reserves into market investments, loans, Treasury securities or other investments. This activity increased the money supply and such money supply increases affected the price level. Now, these same bank reserves represent member bank income earning assets.

Figure 11.4 shows the interest rates on required and excess reserves and 1-year treasuries for the period from the beginning of reserve interest payments through the first 6 months of 2018. At the onset of reserve interest payments, the rate of return for holding reserves matched the rate on 1-year treasuries. For the period from January 2009 until September 2010, the rate of return on the 1-year treasuries exceeded the return on reserves. From September 2010, the return to holding reserves exceeded the 1-year

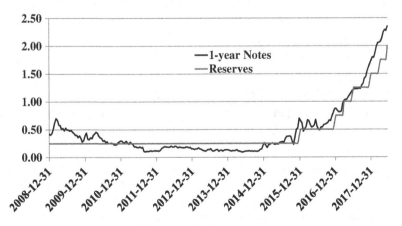

Figure 11.4. Interest Rate on Reserves and 1-Year Treasuries

treasuries rate until August 2015. In response to rising 1-year treasuries rates, the interest rate on reserves expressed in basis points was raised to 50, 75, 100, 125, 150, 175 and finally, in June of 2018 to 200 basis points.[1]

Essentially, what the Federal Reserve did was to sterilize the growth in the base by making reserves a short-term liability of the central bank. By sterilize, I mean that the normal effect of an increase in bank reserves on the money supply was eliminated by paying member banks to hold reserves, rather than increase their holdings of assets, either loans or securities. Since the interest rate on reserves exceeded the interest rate on 1-year treasuries, banks had an incentive to refrain from using the increase in reserves to make investments in loans and treasuries. As a result, any potential effect of these increased reserves on the money supply was mitigated or eliminated entirely.

The Federal Reserve during each QE was buying long securities in the form of treasuries and MBSs and creating short-term liabilities in the form of bank reserves. The excess reserve component of the monetary base could not contribute to financing the federal debt, since it is the equivalent of federal debt. Figure 11.5 is an amended version of the previous *Deficits and Federal Reserve Monetization* for fiscal years 2009–2015 shown in Figure 11.3 that accounts for the inclusion of the increase in bank reserves as an offset to Federal Reserve asset growth.

In Figure 11.5, the column labeled Adj Base is the difference between the traditional measure of monetary base growth and growth in excess reserves. This difference represents the actual level of monetization of the fiscal year deficits. For the entire seven fiscal year period, the level of deficit monetization was just over 9%. Thus, in spite of the tremendous annual growth in the traditional monetary base of 18.8%, the annual inflation rate for the entire period averaged just over 1.2%. For the period beginning fiscal years 2009–2015, the adjusted monetary base grew at 7.9%. For the same period, real GDP grew at a historically slow rate of 1.76%. These 7-year growth rates leave us with an unexplained lack of

---

[1] During our later discussion of implications for the future, this path of reserve interest rate changes match the upper bound of the Fed Funds target rate. That will continue to hold so long as bank reserves pay interest. We also show when we analyze the Federal Reserve's path to normal asset restoration that the Federal Reserve under these conditions is an interest rate follower, as is apparent in Figure 11.4.

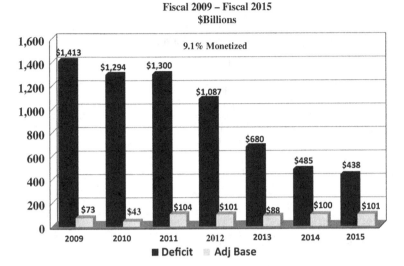

Figure 11.5. Deficits and Federal Reserve Monetization

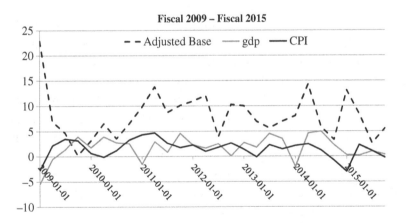

Figure 11.6. Adjusted Monetary Base, CPI and Real GDP Growth

inflation since the difference between adjusted base growth rate and the real GDP growth rate is just over 6%. To illustrate these differences, Figure 11.6 shows the rate of change in the adjusted base, real GDP and the CPI.

In contrast to the above figure's representation of the path of monetary policy during the Great Recession, consider the following chart. A glimpse

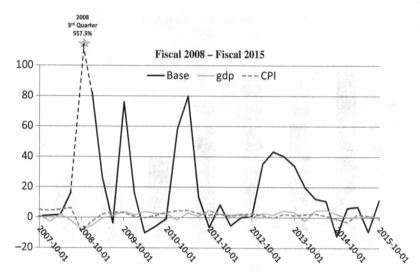

Figure 11.7.   Monetary Base, CPI and Real GDP Growth

at Figure 11.7 indicates an astounding feature of this unique period. In no period in the history of the Federal Reserve has there been growth in the traditionally measured monetary base that was so variable. During the almost 8-year period from the third quarter of 2008 to the third quarter of 2015, a period of 28 quarters, we have seen nine quarters with annual monetary base growth rates exceeding 30%. The period as a whole experienced annual growth in the monetary base of 18.8%. The contrast between Figures 11.6 and 11.7 is simply astounding!

Now, we get to what might be the worst part of this episode as the Federal Reserve facilitated the financing of the unprecedented peacetime federal deficits. Figure 11.8 shows the fiscal year deficits and the level of Federal Reserve purchases of that fiscal year's Treasury issue from 2010 to 2014. Overall, the Federal Reserve purchased more than 35% of the 5-year accumulated deficit. By way of contrast throughout the entirety of World War II, the Federal Reserve purchased just over 10% of the accumulated deficit. Indeed, this was the founding fathers' central bank fears in spades! That fear was that a central bank would be used to allow the government to expand expenditures almost without constraint.

To add insult to injury, the Treasury and the Federal Reserve are inextricably related because all revenue after the cost of operations are turned

$Billions

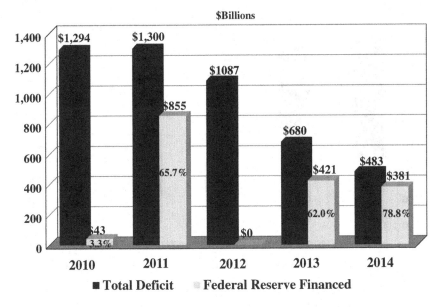

■ Total Deficit   Federal Reserve Financed

Figure 11.8.   Federal Deficits and Federal Reserve Treasury Purchases

over to the Treasury. Consequently, the Treasury is the residual income recipient of the Federal Reserve operations. This financial relationship affects Treasury debt service costs in two ways. First, the interest payments on the federal debt owned by the Federal Reserve are simply returned to the Treasury so on net reported Treasury debt service is reduced by that same amount. Second, Federal Reserve revenue from its holdings of MBSs is the same as revenue from treasuries. Thus, any addition to Federal Reserve assets are the equivalent to Federal Reserve purchases of treasuries. Figure 11.9 incorporates this idea to show the real role that the Federal Reserve played in funding the deficits of the last 6 years. In fiscal years 2013 and 2014, the Federal Reserve financed 135% and 152% of the federal debt. For the entire five fiscal years depicted, the Federal Reserve financed more than 55% of all deficits.

The Federal Reserve's behavior, since the onset of the Great Recession has led to a tremendous and unprecedented increase in the role of the Federal Reserve in the economy. To illustrate this fact, Figure 11.10 shows Federal Reserve assets as a share of the entire US economy on the weekly reporting day beginning in January 2003–January 2017. Federal Reserve assets as a share of the economy remained approximately constant at just

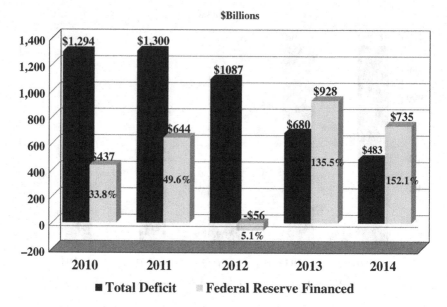

Figure 11.9.   Federal Deficits and Federal Reserve Asset Purchases

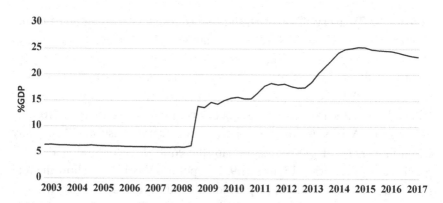

Figure 11.10.   Federal Reserve Assets Relative to GDP

over 6% of GDP from the close of 2002 until the month of extreme liquidity stress, September 2008. This observation is consistent with the idea that the money supply should grow with the needs of trade, roughly real GDP, as a way to maintain a stable price level. However, once the liquidity crisis hit in 2008, the Federal Reserve holding of assets as a share of GDP jumped significantly, and it now holds assets equal to 23% of the entire nations output. In contrast, at the close of World War II, the period of largest deficits as a share of the nation's output, total Federal Reserve holdings, as measured by the level of the monetary base, were only 14% of the economy.

Conclusion

In response to the financial distress of the 2008 liquidity crisis and the subsequent unprecedented federal deficits, the Federal Reserve moved to an entirely new way of economic intervention. For most of its existence, the changes in Federal Reserve assets represented either running the money printing press in the case of increasing assets, or destroying money in the case of Federal Reserve asset reductions.

On this basis, it would appear that for the fiscal years 2009–2015 that the Federal Reserve financed over 47% of the federal deficits by running the printing press. But this is not an ordinary period, so things are not as simple as they seem. There are two significant differences that distinguish this period.

First, unlike almost all previous periods, the securities purchased were not all federal debt. The Federal Reserve was also buying private assets, principally MBSs. Importantly, the purchases of private assets do not change the effect of asset purchases on the Treasury. By law, all profits of the Federal Reserve are transferred to the Treasury. Thus, all income from Federal Reserve private asset holdings less any cost, is transferred to the Treasury.

Second, for the first time in its history, the Federal Reserve became a major issuer of liabilities. These liabilities are the result of the institution of paying interest on bank reserves. Before interest payments on bank reserves, Federal Reserve actions that increased bank reserves led to an increase in the money supply. Now, these same bank reserves represent member bank income earning assets. As a result, the normal effect of an increase in bank reserves on the money supply was eliminated by paying member banks to hold reserves, rather than increase their holdings of assets, either loans or securities.

Because the net revenue of the Federal Reserve is transferred to the Treasury, the newly created Federal Reserve liability, in the form of bank reserves, are the equivalent of federal debt. Even so, transfers from the Federal Reserve to the Treasury over this period have financed an average of 40% of all federal debt servicing cost.

Part II

Issues From the Past and Problems for the Future

Chapter 12

The Federal Reserve: An Independent Central Bank or an Arm of Government?

Introduction

The Federal Reserve before the Great Recession was a central bank that held assets, primarily federal debt, equal to about 6% of GDP, and had no liabilities. Its response to the Great Recession converted that central bank to one that held assets that, at their peak, totaled more than 25% of GDP and issued liabilities equal to more than 17% of GDP. These changes raise a number of issues that will be the topic of this section entitled "Issues from the Past and Problems for the Future."

The historical controversy surrounding a national central bank was ultimately resolved with the establishment of the Federal Reserve System. That controversy revolved around the fear that a central bank would act as an agent of the central government and Wall Street. This fear was well founded in that the central bank most familiar to citizens of the United States was the Bank of England. Whenever the Crown needed help for war financing, the Bank of England accommodated and bought British sovereign debt through the expansion of the money stock. Since Britain was on the gold standard and bank currency was convertible into gold, the Bank of England suspended convertibility for the duration of Crown borrowing.

There is a real question as to whether beginning in 2008, the Federal Reserve became an arm of the Treasury. There is little doubt that the tremendous increase in Federal Reserve asset holdings made the unprecedented federal deficits easier to finance. In the Federal Reserve's defense, however, is the fact that every major central bank in the world engaged in similar increases in their asset holdings. The equivalent of the three Federal Reserve bouts of "quantitative easing" were also carried out by the European Central Bank, the Bank of England and the Bank of Japan.

In addition to the Federal Reserve's unprecedented actions in asset purchases, it also became a bigger player in managing the economy. Some of this economy management was in the form of entering private markets to prevent a liquidity meltdown. The Federal Reserve purchases of commercial paper is one example of appropriate action to support the economy. In fact, this action is something that only a central bank could have done. But then it also entered the market for housing, buying Mortgage-Backed Securities (MBSs). Finally in addition to its traditional role of buying and selling assets, the Federal Reserve's role in the economy was expanded as Congress assigned it more regulatory powers. Here, I review the history and the new roles for the Federal Reserve in what might be termed non-central banking.

The Expanding Role of the Federal Reserve

Over time, the Federal Reserve, which began as an agency that would solve the problem of a form inelastic-money supply, has through legislation become an enforcer of legislation designed to control the behavior of financial institutions. The first significant change was the Banking Act of 1933 that changed the name of the Open-Market Policy Conference (OMPC) consisting of all 12 regional Federal Reserve Bank presidents (then referred to as governors) to the Federal Open-Market Committee (FOMC). The OMPC recommended policy but had no real authority to require the regional Federal Reserve banks to follow its recommendations. In contrast, the FOMC established the official policy of the system, and regional Federal Reserve Banks were required to follow, thus eliminating the possibility that of independent action by the regional banks. These changes simply made the Federal Reserve a single entity, just what the original legislation was designed to prevent.

The next change to the Federal Reserve came with the Banking Act of 1935 that further centralized governance of the Federal Reserve System. Specifically, the composition of the FOMC was changed from equal representation of all 12 bank presidents to its current composition where the voting members consist of the seven members of the Board of Governors, the president of the Federal Reserve Bank of New York, and presidents of four other banks on a rotating basis. The Act also removed the ability of the regional banks to establish their own discount rates for dealing with their member banks and established system-wide reserve requirements on member banks. Ironically, for all practical purposes, the Federal Reserve System's interactions with the nation's financial markets are handled by the Federal Reserve Bank of New York, located only three blocks from the Wall Street influence that was so feared by the legislators who established the Federal Reserve System.

Up to the time of these 1930s changes, the Federal Reserve's regulatory role was restricted to ensuring that member banks had sufficient reserves and were solvent. Now, we come to the role of the Federal Reserve before and during World War II. Even before the war, the bank took on a regulatory role to control borrowing for stock market purchases and to make credit terms for consumers consistent with the war effort, specifically to make it difficult for consumers to obtain financing for the purchase of consumer durables. One might question the importance and actual effect of this regulatory role, as the output of such durables was greatly reduced as large parts of the productive capacity of the nation was devoted to military hardware. However, without specific rationing of durables, one way to limit demand was to control the terms on which purchases of durables could be made. These various regulatory roles were the beginning of making the Federal Reserve a government agency rather than an independent central bank.

Currently, the Federal Reserve is charged with enforcing some 49 regulations, only a few of which apply to what would be considered the role of a central bank.[1] While the regulatory burden began well before the 1970s, this section will concentrate on only a few of the regulations that

---

[1] A listing of all current Federal Reserve regulations with a brief explanation of each regulation's purpose is available at www.federalreserve.gov/bankinforeg/reglisting.htm.

remain relevant. Two of these are Federal Reserve Regulation BB which resulted from the 1974 passage of the Equal Credit Opportunity Act, and Regulation M, which enforces the Consumer Leasing Act of 1976.

One would expect that the regulations, if they were relevant to the Federal Reserve's role as an independent central bank, would involve ensuring the solvency of its member banks. But once politics got involved, all bets were off. Specifically, Regulation BB entails enforcement of the Community Reinvestment Act of 1977, which was to ensure that banks were making investments in lower income areas of their market. In effect, banks were required to make less than safe loans and were penalized if they did not make enough such loans.

These community reinvestment funds were often administered outside the bank, making the availability of these funds subject to the oversight, or lack thereof, of certain community groups. In response to this lack of a paper trail, we have Regulation G from the Gramm–Leach–Bliley Act of 1999. This regulation became part of the enforcement of Regulation BB which required certain reporting on the actual use of community reinvestment funds.

Of particular importance are the more recent regulations that pertain to the Dodd–Frank Wall Street Reform and Consumer Protection Act of 2010. This act imposed a significant level of authority to the Federal Reserve to determine if a company is predominantly engaged in financial activities, Regulation PP. Also, we have regulations XX and YY that involve the issue of who is "too big to fail."

In general, there are incentives for Congress to assign the scrutiny, and perhaps even enforcement, of regulatory legislation to the Federal Reserve, even if such regulation is not directly related to central banking. The primary such incentive is that no direct cost of the legislation appears on the government's books. Of course, this is illusory in that the Federal Reserve and the Treasury are inextricably tied together. All profits from Federal Reserve operations go to the Treasury. All costs associated with Federal Reserve regulation enforcement reduce Federal Reserve payments to the Treasury. As a result, taxpayers pay for all of the costs of regulations enforced by the Federal Reserve System, but without any direct accountability.

The real problem with the increasing tendency of Congress to assign regulatory chores to the Federal Reserve is that an increasing share of its resources are devoted to it being an agent of government, rather than an independent central bank. This tendency has been aided by the restructuring of the FOMC that occurred in the 1930s. As these regulatory roles for the Federal Reserve have increased, the Federal Reserve has become a New York–Washington dominated institution.

The "Liquidity Crises" Role of the Federal Reserve

Before proceeding, a brief discussion of a simple central bank might prove useful. Let's begin by considering a central bank whose only function is to maintain the value of the nation's medium of exchange. How should this entity behave? The behavior depends on factors that can influence the value of the medium of exchange. In the simplest case, it is only the quantity of the medium of exchange, money and the volume of transactions that use money. The simple equation of exchange determines everything, the only role of the central bank is getting the quantity of money right. Even here, however, over time the world evolves. Exchange technology changes and the total volume of transactions changes as output rises.

Now introduce the existence of financial institutions that are part of the transactions technology in that they facilitate the transfer of money. Such institutions, banks if you will, have in the simplest case currency deposited by individuals that are regularly transferred among like institutions by depositors, so that the total quantity of currency in each institution stays approximately the same. These banks create assets by using these deposits to make loans that have liquidity more distant than the original deposits on which these new bank assets are based. These loans become deposits as they are created. Since these deposits are easily transferable, they perform all the functions of money. These deposits are held at the will of the depositor and these financial institutions hold reserves of central bank money, currency, to cover the random variation in their deposits.

There is no doubt that these banks contribute greatly to the efficiency of commerce, but they also introduce a level of uncertainty that can, and indeed has, lead to what is called a *liquidity* crisis. Such a crisis results when individuals want to change the form of their money from demand deposits at financial institutions to currency. Such a change in the composition of money holdings can only be accommodated if the banks can dispose of their assets in an orderly market. But, if all depositors want to switch to currency at the same time, the market for bank held assets will collapse, at least temporarily. In fact, it was just this kind of crisis that led to the passage of the legislation that established the Federal Reserve System.

Because a central bank has control of the printing press, it can provide, on a temporary basis, currency to financial institutions to meet the public's increased demand for currency. How does the central bank put this currency into the financial system? The central bank puts currency into the system by temporarily taking possession of a financial institutions' assets in exchange for currency. In these "discounting" operations, central bank lends the financial institutions currency based on the collateral of their asset portfolio. This activity is often referred to as the central bank being the *lender of last resort* to the financial system.

These transactions are generally in the form of repurchase agreements, meaning that when the crisis is over, the financial institutions return currency to the central bank and take back their assets. Throughout much of the Federal Reserve's history, these collateralized loans were done at what has been referred to as the "discount window" at the "discount rate." The financial institutions borrow currency from the central bank and give the central bank assets as collateral.

In its role as the lender of last resort, the central bank uses its ability to print money to make loans to the financial system in the form of currency to satisfy the temporary demand by the public to increase the role of currency in its money holdings. This type of action by the central bank does not change the money supply, but simply changes its composition between currency and checkable deposits. The banks become smaller, as both their deposits and reserves fall by the amount of currency withdrawn by the public.

Assuming that this change in the public's desire to hold currency is temporary, when the public's desire to hold currency returns to the pre-crisis level, then the central bank undoes the transactions by returning the assets to the financial institutions. The financial sector returns to its former size as their deposits and reserves return to the original levels. Since the entirety of the operation never changed the aggregate money stock, it has no price level effect and, therefore, no effect on the fundamental value of the currency. The central bank increased the monetary base by an amount that allows the public to satisfy its demand for currency, but not so much as to increase the money supply. The transition back to the original equilibrium requires a reduction in the monetary base to its former before-crisis level.

Three Recent Federal Reserve Liquidity Crisis Episodes

The establishment of the Federal Reserve System was based on the need to aid in making the composition of the money supply elastic. But how does a central bank make the money supply composition elastic, and what is the meaning of an elastic money supply? Even though the complexity of financial markets has increased significantly since the 1913 passage of the bill establishing the Federal Reserve System, the elastic currency issue remains as important today as it was in 1913. Events that result in a significant change in the public's demand for liquid assets have the potential to cause a liquidity crisis. The crisis comes from the fact that financial institutions, banks and what might be referred to as near banks, when faced with a surge of depositors wanting to essentially cash in their deposits, have a limited ability to honor such requests using existing liquid reserves. This is where a central bank with a virtual currency printing press can come to the rescue.

In the past two decades, there have been three such episodes in which the Federal Reserve acted to avert a liquidity crisis. Two such episodes were discussed in Chapters 8 and 9, but bear repeating here to clarify the difference between Federal Reserve behavior that fits the traditional way a central bank behaves in a liquidity crisis and the expansion of Federal Reserve assets that has occurred since 2007.

The first such episode began with the fear that the coming close of the 20th century would result in a massive breakdown both in financial and real aspects of life. This meltdown fear was based on the fact that the dramatic increase in the reliance on computer technology in virtually all aspects of life in the previous decades would cause havoc with the coming of the new century. Specifically, many of the computer programs underlying the digital age were written when memory space was limited and only two digits were allowed for representing the year, so that when the new century began these programs would crash and financial markets and even automobiles would simply cease operating. During this episode, what became known as the Y2K scare, the Federal Reserve increased the monetary base to allow the public to increase its holdings of currency. Once it became clear that the computer assisted world was not going to suffer issues with dates that began 20XX, the public's demand for currency went away.

The second episode was related to the aftermath of the terrorist attack on the World Trade Center, what is now referred to as 9/11. Once again, a fear arose that the financial industry would be under siege and the safest form of money for the public to hold was currency. The Federal Reserve increased the monetary base to ensure that the public's increased demand for currency could be met without disrupting financial markets. Just as with the Y2K episode, when the crisis was over the public's increased demand for currency went away.

Figure 12.1 shows the Federal Reserve's monetary base response in each of these episodes to what proved to temporary increases in the public's demand for currency. Figure 12.1(a) labeled Y2K shows the gradual buildup of the base as the public's concern about the impact of the year

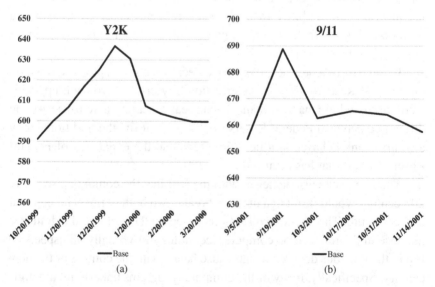

Figure 12.1. The Monetary Base in Two Traditional Liquidity Crisis Responses

2000 on the increasingly computerized financial industry increased as we neared the turn of the century. Once it became clear that the forecasts of computer doom were unfounded, the public returned to pre-crisis levels of demand for currency and the Federal Reserve returned the monetary base to the pre-crisis level. Figure 12.1(b) labeled 9/11, shows the immediate response to the public's fear that the 9/11 terrorists attack was to be part of a larger attack on the financial industry. When it became clear that this was not an all-out attack on financial markets, the monetary base returned to its previous level.

In both of these liquidity crises, the Federal Reserve quickly acted to increase the supply of currency providing the form elasticity of the money supply as emphasized in the Act establishing the central bank. The increase in the monetary base for the Y2K crisis occurred gradually over the final two months of 1999 then, over the following 3 months, the monetary base returned to its pre-crisis level. The 9/11 crisis was much more sudden since it had no warning. Here, the increase in the base took place in the first 2 weeks of the crisis and the return to normalcy in the following 2 weeks.

The third episode of Federal Reserve responses to a liquidity crisis was in the events surrounding the onset of the Great Recession. There were three programs that were prominent in the Great Recession liquidity response. These responses were increased repurchase agreements between banks and the Federal Reserve, the introduction of a Term Auction Facility (TAF) program to give banks access to reserves and finally the direct involvement of the Federal Reserve in the market for commercial paper. The path of each of these three responses are shown graphically in Figure 12.2.

The first response consisted of an expansion of repurchase agreements between the banking system and the Federal Reserve, as the level of these agreements grew from less than $50 billion to more than $100 billion. Then, the Federal Reserve began the TAF that made liquidity available to member banks on a bid basis. From its inception in January 2008, the TAF quickly surpassed repurchase agreements in volume so that by September 2008 it reached $150 billion. Then came the real liquidity crisis of September 2008. In the next few months, the TAF grew and reached a peak of almost $500 billion, replacing repurchase agreements entirely. Finally, the Federal Reserve bought commercial paper in response to the collapse

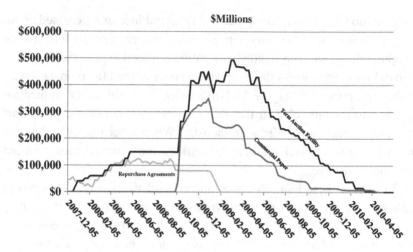

Figure 12.2.   Federal Reserve Pure Liquidity Crisis Response

of the commercial paper market as the money market funds faced almost a wholesale demand for cash by their depositors. The Federal Reserve holdings of commercial paper reached a maximum of more than $850 billion in early 2009. By April 2010, these crisis responses were gone.

The Non-Liquidity Crisis Federal Reserve Expansion

Now, we get to the Federal Reserve's two largest interferences in the economy unrelated to any standard liquidity crisis. Early in January 2009, the Federal Reserve entered the market for MBSs by buying MBSs that were guaranteed by Fannie Mae, Freddie Mac and Ginnie Mae. The stated goal of this program was to provide support to the mortgage and housing markets and to improve conditions in financial markets in general. Figure 12.3 is a reproduction of Figure 10.5 that demonstrates the extent of the Federal Reserve's involvement in this market.

Within the first year of this program, the Federal Reserve had purchased $900 billion in MBSs, an amount greater than the entire Federal Reserve pre-crisis portfolio. This first round of MBS purchases saw a peak in Federal Reserve MBS ownership of more than $1.1 trillion, almost one-third of all existing MBSs guaranteed by Fannie Mae, Freddie Mac and Ginnie Mae. After allowing their holdings to mature and fall to

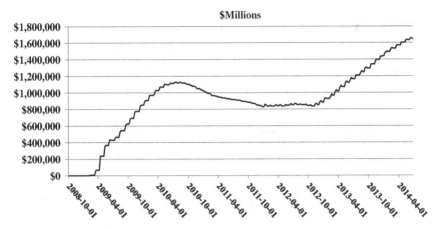

Figure 12.3. Federal Reserve MBS Holdings

just over $800 billion, the Federal Reserve, as part of a Quantitative Easing (QE) program, began monthly purchases of MBSs in October 2012. Federal Reserve holdings of MBSs in September of 2018 were just under $1.7 trillion. The Federal Reserve investment in the GSE-guaranteed MBS market has resulted in the Federal Reserve holding over 40% of total GSE-guaranteed MBSs outstanding.

The Federal Reserve compounded its interference with the economy by its efforts to stimulate activity through aiding in the funding of federal deficits. Figure 12.4 shows the path of Federal Reserve holdings of treasuries from 2007 through May 2017. This figure clearly distinguishes the initial liquidity crisis response and the subsequent quantitative easing activities of the Federal Reserve. Federal Reserve Treasury holdings began the period at their long-run share of the economy, slightly over 5% of GDP, at just under $800 billion. Federal Reserve actions during the financial crisis consisted of reducing treasuries and expanding short-term financial assets by a multiple of the reduction in its holdings of treasuries. This response occurred before the September 2008 liquidity crisis, as the Federal Reserve provided short-term economic help to the financial industry by substituting short-term financial assets for treasuries.

Examining Figure 12.4, it would appear that by the close of 2009, with the crisis behind us, the Federal Reserve had returned to normal operations. The real story, however, is that normalcy was not going to return as

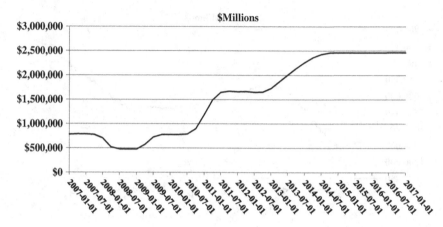

Figure 12.4.   Federal Reserve Treasury Holdings

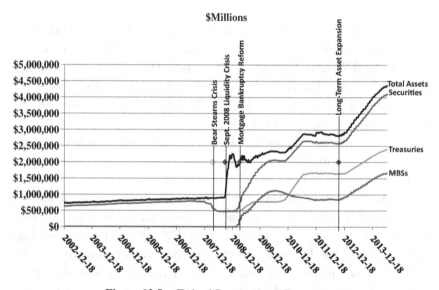

Figure 12.5.   Federal Reserve Asset Responses

the Figure 12.5 demonstrates. What began as a simple substitution of treasuries for short-term assets, the period from the close of 2007 to September 2008, was then augmented with a significant expansion of short-term assets. The Federal Reserve began by replacing the treasuries it sold with short-term financial assets and, at the same time, adding MBSs to its portfolio. Then, as the liquidity crisis response eased it that more than replaced the short-term assets by increasing its involvement in the housing industry and financing federal deficits. Figure 12.5 shows the overall extent, but not the detail, of these Federal Reserve actions.

Even with a casual inspection, the path of Federal Reserve assets in Figure 12.5 are not what one would expect if this was just a response to a liquidity crisis. A traditional response to a liquidity crisis would be an increase in the base, as currency is pumped into the economy to account for the public's desire to exchange deposits at financial institutions for currency followed by a decline as the crisis winds down.

Now, compare the two traditional liquidity crisis responses shown in Figure 12.1 to the Federal Reserve's immediate and subsequent responses to the September 2008 liquidity crisis. Figure 12.6 shows the response to the September 2008 crisis in terms of the monetary base. Two things stand out. First is the significant difference in the scale of the responses. The Y2K and 9/11 responses involved a less than 10% increase in the monetary base. In dollar terms, the Y2K response was just less than $50 billion, and the 9/11 response was just under $40 billion. The September 2008 response more than doubled the base over the 3 months following September 2008. The increase was a staggering $900 billion. Second, in the first two crises, the monetary base quickly returned to its old level. In the September 2008 response, there was no return to the prior level of the monetary base over the first year after the initial response.

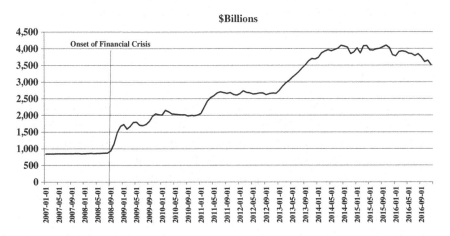

Figure 12.6. Monetary Base Before and After the September 2008 Crisis

Upon inspection of Figures 12.5 and 12.6, the September 2008 response was significant in both its length and scale. However, it was also significant in that there has been no effort to bring the monetary base back to a level consistent with the goal of an independent central bank. The fact is that the Federal Reserve was in the process of rescuing financial institutions by buying assets or lending to financial institutions. Both of these activities increased the level of reserves at member banks, essentially all banks, but not all financial institutions. Importantly, however, funds used to rescue financial institutions that were not member banks eventually became reserves at member banks.

Figure 12.5 details the involvement of the Federal Reserve in the economy. There are four distinct levels of the monetary base that are easily discernable in the figure. First, we have the initial response to the September 2008 liquidity crisis with an increase in the base from just under $800 billion in August 2008 to almost $1.8 trillion at the close of December 2008. Second, the MBS surge that began in 2009 and culminated around the close of 2010 resulted in a monetary base level of about $2.1 trillion. Third, we have the second quantitative easing, QE II, that involved the Federal Reserve doubling its holdings of treasuries from their October 2010 level of just over $800 billion to a July 2011 level of just over $1.6 trillion. Fourth, we have the QE III that involved a surge in Federal Reserve holdings of both MBSs and treasuries. This last surge in the monetary base began with a monetary base of just over $2.6 trillion and ended with a monetary base of just under $4.1 trillion.

Conclusion

What has this unprecedented increase in the monetary base during the post-financial crisis of 2008 meant? The answer requires a careful look at the two components of the monetary base, currency and member bank reserves. Financial institutions that take deposits with zero maturity have reserves either represented by actual currency in their vaults or deposits at the Federal Reserve. In one sense, these two components of reserves are one and the same. Because the Federal Reserve possesses the goose that lays the golden eggs in the form of a virtual currency printing press, deposits at the Federal Reserve are magic. They can be either deposits or currency at the command of the owners, the public.

For the moment, assume the primary role of a central bank is to preserve the value of the currency. Historically, the money supply and the value of the currency are inversely related. Further, the level of reserves determine the banking system's ability to expand their investment portfolio and this expansion increases the money supply. Before September 2008, the unprecedented expansion of the monetary base that followed the crisis would have resulted in an increase in the money supply at a rate much faster than the rate of growth in output, and price inflation would have been rampant. The following chapters will deal with this issue and others relating to the future of the Federal Reserve and central banking in general.

Chapter 13 deals with the connection between Federal Reserve, or any central bank, and market interest rates. Then, in Chapter 14, the issue of why, in spite of the great expansion of Federal Reserve assets, rapid inflation did not occur. Next, Chapter 15 considers the implications of the Federal Reserve becoming a major supplier of the equivalent of short-term debt, in the form of bank reserves that now pay interest. Most importantly, how does the payment of interest on reserves affect the ability of the Federal Reserve to conduct monetary policy. Continuing in the area of interest rates and monetary policy, Chapter 16 addresses the possibility of a continuation of the essentially zero interest rates at the beginning of the second decade of the 21st century on the ability the Federal Reserve to conduct monetary policy, a discussion that is still relevant even as the fear of a zero interest rate world has abated.

Moving away from interest rates and their determination, Chapter 17 discusses how the net worth of a central bank should be calculated using data from the Federal Reserve. Then, Chapters 18 and 19 address the problems of restoring the Federal Reserve to an asset and liability balance sheet more in line with their former share of the national economy. Now, we get to the newest entry into the money supply arena, cryptocurrency. Chapter 20 discusses the potential future for cryptocurrencies and the possible role for central banks in that future.

Finally, Chapter 21 is a summary of the issues faced in the past and the potential future for the Federal Reserve. Central Bank independence is critical if we the public are to be served well by our central bank, the Federal Reserve.

Chapter 13

The Federal Reserve's Role in Market Interest Rates

Introduction

After the beginning of the Great Recession the world's major central banks, the European Central Bank, ECB, the Bank of Japan, the Bank of England and the United States Federal Reserve, all indicated a target of maintaining low and stable inflation. Accepting that the world central banks want a modest rate of depreciation in the purchasing power of each of their currencies, what are the tools for achieving such a target?

Here, at home, the Federal Reserve affects the price level through the tools at its disposal that expand and contract the money supply. These policy levers include changing reserve requirements, buying and selling assets, changing the interest rate it pays on bank reserves and adjusting its target for the interest rate on overnight inter-bank loans, the Fed Funds rate.

This last tool often leads to the conclusion that the Federal Reserve sets market interest rates. But more importantly, the bank's primary policy goal is expressed as an interest rate target, perhaps because of the press's obsession with the interest rate role of the Federal Reserve.

Federal Reserve actions continue to be couched in terms of interest rate targets, even though the primary goal is now moderate inflation. This raised the question of what is meant by moderately stable inflation. Or in fact, why would a central bank charged with preserving the value of the currency have a goal expressed in terms of the rate at which the currency should decline in value? Is there anyone who would like the dollars they have in their wallet to be worth less than 80 cents in a decade?

The two goals of a target interest rate and rate of inflation go hand in hand because nominal interest rates are a combination of the inflation rate and the real interest rate. While the Federal Reserve can influence the money supply and the inflation rate, real interest rates are largely determined by market forces beyond the Federal Reserve's immediate control. Further, I will present evidence that markets determine interest rates and not central banks.

Monetary Policy and Fed Funds Rates

I begin this discussion by considering the tools at the disposal of the Federal Reserve to influence the economy. Before the advent of paying interest on bank reserves, a topic that will be discussed at length in Chapter 15, the Federal Reserve had only one main tool that affected the economy. That tool was operating in financial markets in ways that affected the Federal Reserve's asset portfolio. By operating in the open market for securities, the Federal Reserve either injected money into the economy by purchasing assets or removed money from the economy by selling assets. How these changes affect the economy in the short-run or the long-run has been discussed above and will be discussed further, especially in the discussion of issues for the future of monetary policy.

At least since the 1960s, Federal Reserve policy actions were expressed in terms of an interest rate target. When the Federal Reserve determined that the economy needed a boost, it would announce a target for the short-term interest that was below current market rates. Or, if it determined that the economy was over heating it would announce a target for short-term interest rates that was above current market rates.

While the announcement of a target interest rate might affect markets briefly, for any real impact the announcement must be followed with actions. An announced increase in the target for interest rates must be accompanied by an open-market sale of Federal Reserve assets. Such a sale is an exchange of currency and reserves held in the economy for assets that were being held by the Federal Reserve. Essentially, the currency and reserves are destroyed as assets are moved from the Federal

Reserve to private sector accounts. The reverse operation of the Federal Reserve buying assets, creates currency and reserves.

There are two effects of this open-market sale policy. First, the sale of assets increases the stock of such assets which has a small effect on their price and thus their yield. Second, the sale reduces bank reserves. Banks, in an effort to restore reserves must reduce investments in the economy. Both these effects work to increase interest rates, the goal of the policy action. But can this policy actually work? Can the Federal Reserve change the outstanding stock of financial assets enough to affect market interest rates? Also, how will the other suppliers of assets change their behavior in response to the short-run effect of the interest rate policy? All of these questions suggest that the Federal Reserve does not have an interest lever at its disposal.[1]

There is a rate of interest the Federal Reserve can affect through its open-market sales and purchases, the Fed Funds rate (the rate that banks pay one another for overnight use of reserves). Importantly, this is the interest rate most commonly referred to as the target of Federal Reserve policy. Figure 13.1 shows the Federal Reserve effective rate for the Fed Funds

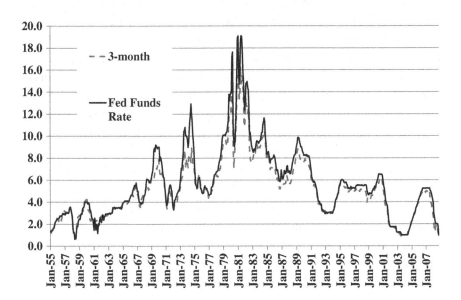

Figure 13.1. 3-Month T-Bill Rate and Federal Funds Rate

---

[1] For an excellent discussion on this point, see Fama (2013).

market and the yield on 90-day treasury bills from January 1955 to October 2008, the beginning of the payment of interest on bank reserves.[2] The two rates moved together, but there is no clear evidence that one leads the other. Did the Federal Reserve Fed Funds rate simply reflect the market for short-term interest rates, or did it determine the yield in that market? One way to ask this question is: Was the 30-day treasury rate in March of 1980 15.20% because the Fed Funds rate was 17.19% or was the Fed Funds rate 17.19% because the 30-day treasury rate was 15.20%? Essentially, is the Federal Reserve an interest rate follower or an interest rate leader?

The press equates the relation between Federal Reserve intentions and market interest rates, as if the Federal Reserve is somehow in charge of the level of all interest rates. However, historically, there has been only one interest rate directly under the control of the Federal Reserve, the discount rate, the rate charged to banks that borrow from the Federal Reserve.

The transmission mechanism of Federal Reserve actions and the Fed Funds rate is typically through the sale or purchase of treasuries. At least it was true before October 2008 and certainly was so during most of the period depicted in the Figure 13.1. A Federal Reserve sale of treasuries, or any other financial asset such as Mortgage-Backed Security (MBS), takes money out of the banking system and reduces reserves. A reduction in reserves makes reserves scarcer and increases the overnight reserves borrowing rate. A Federal Reserve purchase of treasuries or other financial assets puts money in the banking system, which increases reserves, making them less scarce and, as a result, decreases the overnight reserves borrowing rate.

These same operations also affect financial markets by making the banking system expand or contract their loan portfolio with resulting changes in market interest rates. In this sense, the Federal Reserve can influence interest rates, and it does so in two ways.

First, by changing the level of treasuries or other financial assets in the market, it affects the stock of these assets available to the public. For

---

[2] Chapter 15 is devoted to Federal Reserve policy when reserves pay interest. The introduction of interest on reserves fundamentally changed the role of the Fed Funds rate in ways that will be discussed at length in that chapter.

example, the purchase of treasuries by the Federal Reserve reduces the stock of treasuries, increases the price of treasuries and lowers yields. Second, this same purchase of treasuries increases reserves at banks and allows the system to expand loans which also reduces the rate of interest on such loans. The bottom line, however, is: does this change influence the real, after adjusting for inflation, interest rate?

Assume for the moment that the Federal Reserve wants to control a particular interest rate. How would such control be accomplished? We know how central banks across the world maintain the exchange rate between their currency and the dollar. Consider a foreign central bank with dollar reserves. When events occur that put pressure on the exchange rate, the central bank either buys or sells dollars into the foreign exchange market to keep the exchange rate within the desired range. The only hitch in these plans is that when their government finances its expenditures by printing money, continued inflation occurs. Then, the demand for dollars will rise and, ultimately, the foreign central bank will run out of dollar reserves. When that happens, the exchange rate must and will change in order to reflect the new level of prices in each country.

In a similar vein, assume that the Federal Reserve wants to raise the interest rate on 1-year securities to the average rate of 3.47% that existed prior to 2008. At this interest rate, newly issued 1-year treasuries will sell for $966.46, with a par value of $1,000. Currently (June 25, 2018), the 1-year treasury yield is 2.34% (234 basis points) so 1-year treasuries at issue are selling for $977.135. How could the Federal Reserve lower the price of 1-year treasuries from $977.135 to $966.46?

The only way this can happen is to increase the stock of 1-year notes that are as safe from default risk as 1-year treasuries. The Federal Reserve, as a central bank, owns the money printing press so it could offer special Federal Reserve 1-year notes in unlimited quantities for $966.46. In a simple supply and demand situation, this operation is equivalent to making the supply of 1-year zero default notes completely elastic, i.e., horizontal, at the $966.46 price.

A policy that reduces the market price of 1-year securities equivalently raises the yield on these securities. This action simply floods the 1-year security market and, as a result, reduces the 1-year security price and raises the 1-year security yield. In this sense, financial markets are no different than the market for any consumer good — flooding the market with goods lowers prices.

What are the consequences of such an action? Who will come up with the difference between the selling price and the 1-year redemption value on all these new bonds? There are only two candidates. First, the Federal Reserve could print money to make up the difference. Second, the Treasury could pay the difference with new tax revenues. Ultimately, tax-payers are on the hook, either in terms of the inflation that would happen in response to the increase in the money supply or in the taxes necessary to pay the interest on this new debt. This again illustrates that there is simply no way to separate the central bank from the Treasury.

Suppose the Federal Reserve has enough assets in its portfolio to provide the resources necessary to flood the market. Doesn't this mean that taxpayers are off the hook? No, since the revenue from the assets held by the Federal Reserve is transferred to the Treasury and, as such, reduces the burden on taxpayers. When these assets are sold, the revenue to the Treasury is lost and must be replaced by taxpayers. This real link between the actions of the central bank and the fiscal arm of the government indicates that the two are permanently intertwined.

The above market approach to fixing a price — and interest rates are a price — is not now, and never has been, Federal Reserve policy. The absorbing of money from the economy reduces reserves and leads the banking system to reduce the supply of loanable funds to the market. As a result, interest rates rise. We know that this is not how Federal Reserve actions affect financial markets, although reality is related to the above methodology.

What in the press is referred to as a Federal Reserve increase in short-term interest rates, is in fact an increase in the Federal Reserve target for the Fed Funds rate. However, unless the Federal Reserve takes some action that affects the availability of funds in the Fed Funds market, such an announcement can have no effect. So, what does the announcement mean? It means that the Federal Reserve is ready to sell assets and reduce the money supply. The money supply reduction reduces bank reserves and reduces the supply of overnight funds, which raises the Fed Funds rate. The reduced level of bank reserves contracts the ability of the banking system to supply loanable funds and raises interest rates.

Interest Rates and Financial Markets

In general, interest rates are related to the real return of assets in the economy and the rate of inflation. To see this relationship, it will be helpful to begin the discussion of financial markets and interest rates by examining the history of the impact of past high inflation rates on realized interest rates on longer-term notes. Figure 13.2 gives us a picture of the relation of immediate past year inflation, the current yield on 10-year treasuries and the realized real yield if a 10-year treasury after purchase had been held to maturity. It is clear from the figure that rising inflation rates result in falling realized yields, as current market rates lag the inflation trend. The period of negative realized real yields from 1963 to 1973 was characterized by just such a period of rising inflation rates, as past year inflation rose from 1.75% to 14%. Once market yields adjust to the inflation rate, positive real yields returned. In fact, at the peak of current market yields in late 1981 with rates above 15%, the real yields obtained by investors rose to unprecedented levels as inflation subsequently fell. But then as inflation rates stabilized the difference between current and realized yields fell.

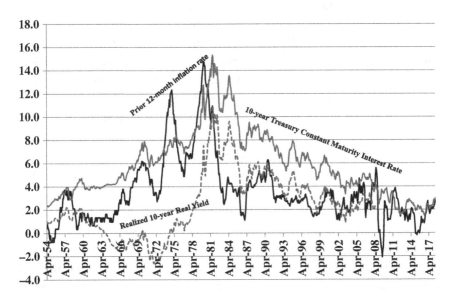

Figure 13.2. Nominal and Real Constant 10-Year Treasury Yields and 1-Year CPI Inflation

Is there a lesson in this discussion of nominal interest rates and inflation? Yes, it relates to the general belief, at least in the current popular press, that the Federal Reserve has the power to determine interest rates. Such a belief is hard to justify given the data shown in Figure 13.2. Are the movements of yields on the 10-year treasuries depicted above due to the Federal Reserve setting the interest rate? Clearly, the Federal Reserve's influence over interest rates diminishes with the length of the period to maturity with realized yields largely a result of future inflation rates. Can anyone imagine that the Federal Reserve wanted 1-year treasuries to be yielding 15.15% in late 1981, or at any time for that matter?

Accepting that interest rates are market determined, what, if anything, can the Federal Reserve do to affect interest rates? The Federal Reserve is now paying interest on reserves and has complete control over that interest rate. Given that the alternative to holding reserves for member banks is buying securities or making loans, the interest rate on reserves sets a lower bound on the yield they will accept on any alternative investment.

With the advent of interest on reserves, the Federal Reserve now has an interest rate it controls in addition to the discount rate, the interest rate on reserves. The question is whether the Federal Reserve determines that interest rate or whether it must respond to the market level of interest rates. If the Federal Reserve desires to keep the banking system holding the entire amount of reserves, essentially have a banking system with 100% reserve banking, then it must pay an interest rate on reserves equal to or greater than alternative investments available to banks. Suddenly then the Federal Reserve is an interest rate taker rather than the force that determines interest rates. We shall discuss this matter at length in Chapter 15.

Paying interest on reserves makes reserves, for all practical purposes, a new form of federal debt issued by the Federal Reserve. The fact that the earnings on the Federal Reserve's current portfolio are more than adequate to fund the interest payments on reserves does not change this fact. Federal Reserve earnings are transferred to the Treasury, and these earnings are reduced by the amount of interest payments on reserves. In effect, interest payments on reserves are equivalent to Federal Reserve sales of assets in their effect on the economy. In either case, the servicing cost of the federal debt rises and in a balanced budget world, taxpayers are on the hook.

Treasury Interest Rates and Federal Reserve Actions

Despite the lament "When is the Federal Reserve going to raise rates?" heard often in the financial press, does the Federal Reserve have any power to change the interest rate? As we have seen above, the answer is yes and no. Yes, in that the Federal Reserve can conduct policies that influence interest rates, at least nominal interest rates, and indeed can set some interest rates directly, but not market rates of interest. Most importantly, interest rates are essentially market prices, and as with any market, it is supply and demand that ultimately determine price. But what is the demand and supply that determines the interest rate?

In simple economics jargon, increasing the returns to investing makes the public, the ultimate supplier of funds to the market, willing to forego current consumption in favor of future consumption and put their money in the market. They do this by demanding bonds issued by corporations and/or governments. In a sense, the public supplies funds by increasing their deposits at investment houses or by directly demanding the bonds of corporations and governments. An increase in the demand for bonds increases their price and reduces interest rates.

Now, consider the other side of the market, demanders of funds, i.e., suppliers of bonds. Firms, governments and individuals express their demand for funds by supplying bonds to the market. These demanders run the gamut of the population. There are individuals who want to purchase cars, appliances or houses. There is the federal government who wants to finance increased expenditures or falling revenues. There are firms with market opportunities that want to fund expansion. All of these components make up the supply of bonds to the market. In the end, it is the balancing of the supply of funds to the market and the demand for these funds that determines the market interest rate.

With this picture of the demanders and suppliers of funds in mind, how can the recent level of historically low interest rates be explained? Throughout the developed world governments have financed large deficits by supplying bonds to the market. If the demand for bonds was unrelated to government finances, this dramatic increase in the supply of bonds would have lowered the price of bonds and led to an increase in the interest rate.

But the opposite occurred. Just as all governments incurred deficits and financed these deficits with bond issues, interest rates fell. For example, the yield on US Treasury 10-year notes fell from 5.1% in mid-2007 to a low of 1.53% in mid-2012. While rates have recovered, the 10-year treasuries were at 2.87% in mid-June of 2018 but still well below their mid-2007 level. Thus, the unprecedented increase in the supply of treasuries beginning in 2008 has not resulted in a falling price of these securities.

Figure 13.3 shows the path of long-term interest rates expressed as 30-, 20- and 10-year constant maturity yields from the beginning of 2006 to May 2017, the period of the Federal Reserve's biggest involvement in asset accumulation. Since the beginning of the recession, the federal government has run large deficits financed through the sale of treasuries. During the same period, the Federal Reserve was operating in the Treasury market. Figure 13.3 shows (in bold) Federal Reserve purchases of treasuries and (in italics) new Treasury issues net of Federal Reserve Treasury purchases for each fiscal year. The Federal Reserve was usually removing treasuries from the market, so the net supply increase in the treasuries market is the difference between new Treasury issues and Federal Reserve purchases.

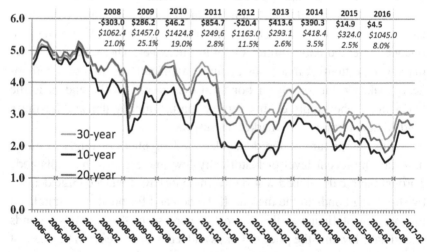

Figure 13.3.   30, 20 and 10 Year Constant Maturity Treasury Yields

Since all treasuries are marketable, there is no distinction between the securities already existing and those newly issued. The supply of any term-to-maturity issue is simply the total stock of issues; the sum of newly issued and previous issues. The change in this stock is the level of the new issues' net of Federal Reserve purchases or sales. Thus, the supply of treasuries increases by the extent to which the previously existing supply is augmented by new issues. The net increase in marketable treasuries is measured as the ratio of the new net issue and the existing publicly held debt. This percent change is reported in the italic % numbers for each fiscal year.

From the beginning of 2006 through mid-2007, 10-, 20- and 30-year Treasury yields remained at about 5%. In fiscal 2008, the first year of a string of large federal deficits, the net increase in the stock of treasuries outstanding was 21%. Part of the increase was the result of the Federal Reserve replacing $303 billion of their Treasury holdings with commercial financial assets in response to the 2008 liquidity crisis. Such a remarkable increase in the stock of marketable treasuries should have resulted in falling prices of treasuries and a resulting increase in interest rates. However, what actually happened was a decline in interest rates, implying that the demand for treasuries rose even faster than the supply.

Fiscal 2009 saw an even larger increase in the stock of treasuries in spite of the Federal Reserve restoring their position in treasuries. The outstanding stock of treasuries increases by $1.457 trillion even after subtracting the Federal Reserve's treasury purchases of $286 billion. While interest rates were very volatile during that year, at the close of the fiscal year they remained essentially unchanged from their close of fiscal 2008 levels. Thus, the demand for treasuries must have increased significantly to offset the net 25.1% increase in supply.

The stock of treasuries again increased by double digits during fiscal 2010, but without any increase in Treasury yields. In fact, interest rates at the close of fiscal 2010 were lower than the close of the previous fiscal year. In fiscal year 2011, the Federal Reserve covered just over 65% of the federal deficit so that the percent increase in the supply of treasuries to the market fell to 2.8%. However, because of the previous growth, that 2.8% still accounted for an increase in the market supply of treasuries of $250 billion.

During 2012, the Federal Reserve was totally out of the Treasury market so that the entire federal deficit resulted in an increase of over $1 trillion in the stock of treasuries and a return to a double-digit increase of almost 11.5%. Remarkably, this surge in the supply of treasuries was accompanied by a continued rise in the price of treasuries and a resulting fall in yields, just the opposite of what one might expect.

In fiscal year 2013, the Federal Reserve returned as a major player in the market for treasuries purchasing over $413 billion. Then in fiscal years the Federal Reserve purchased over $390 billion of treasuries. These purchases financed more than 57% of the federal deficit in 2013 and more than 80% in 2014.

The much smaller increase in the stock of treasuries in fiscal year 2013 of 2.6% was accompanied by a fall in the price of treasuries, and a rise in Treasury yields, again the opposite of what would have happened if demand had remained constant. In fiscal year 2014, Federal Reserve purchases of treasuries increased the addition to the outstanding stock of treasuries by 3.5%. In this case, the price of treasuries rose and yields fell, a result that is at least consistent with our usual view of how these markets work.

The problem with the preceding discussion is that it is only about the supply of treasuries. Markets are about supply and demand, not just supply. Moreover, there is no information presented on the supply of substitutes for treasuries. Specifically, the equivalent of US Treasuries from other countries in the developed world were also increasing in supply throughout the period.

Mortgage Interest Rates and Federal Reserve Actions in the Mortgage Market

The market for treasuries does not operate in a vacuum. In addition to foreign governments' bonds playing a role, long-term private securities also compete for funds in this market. Specifically, MBSs are substitutes for treasuries in any financial portfolio. Importantly, it is these securities that have been the subject of major purchases by the Federal Reserve. During fiscal year 2013, the Federal Reserve purchased just over $500 billion MBSs and in fiscal 2014 over $350 billion. When added to the

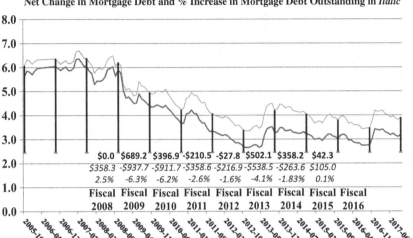

Fed MBS Purchases in Bold
Net Change in Mortgage Debt and % Increase in Mortgage Debt Outstanding in *Italic*

Figure 13.4.   30, and 15 Year Average Mortgage Rates

Federal Reserve's purchases of treasuries, these purchases more than offset the net sale of treasuries and resulted in an increased total Federal Reserve asset position.

Figure 13.4 shows the Federal Reserve's net purchases of MBSs and mortgage interest rates on 30- and 15-year fixed rate mortgages from the beginning of Federal Reserve involvement to the end of 2017. Of note is that the total stock of mortgage debt was over $13 trillion at the close of fiscal 2007 compared to publicly held federal debt of $4.4 trillion. Also, this was a period of falling interest rates and market size, even without Federal Reserve involvement. Because the size of this market was declining it is much harder to relate Federal Reserve actions to market results. However, it is clear that the stock of mortgage debt was falling both as a result of Federal Reserve policy and changes in the supply of mortgages.

There is considerably more going on in the market for securities than solely the actions of the Federal Reserve. From simple inspection of the above two figures of interest rates on longer-term securities, either Treasury or mortgages, and Federal Reserve activity in these two markets, there seems to be little relation between Federal Reserve actions and outcomes. That does not say that these policies did not have an effect, but

Figure 13.5.   30-Year Treasury Yield and Fixed Rate Mortgage Rate

simply that an analysis of these markets involves much more than just treasuries and mortgages.

To get a better idea of the relation between the market for treasuries and mortgages, Figure 13.5 shows the 30-year fixed rate mortgage interest rate and the constant maturity yield on 30-year treasuries. The movements in these two rates of interest indicates that these markets are closely related. The difference between the two rates is the risk premium attached to the mortgage instrument. Further, the rates of return on MBSs, securities consisting of sets of 30-year mortgages and the markets for treasuries and MBSs that the Federal Reserve operated in would follow the same pattern.

Taking the idea of the risk premium attached to mortgages relative to 30-year treasuries, Figure 13.6 shows that premium in two ways. The upper line in the figure shows the absolute difference in the two rates. During the period before the financial crisis, the risk premium attached to 30-year mortgages was about 150 basis points, or 1.5%. During this period, the yield on 30-year treasuries averaged about 4.8%. Subsequent to the liquidity crisis, 30-year treasuries fell to about 4% and then below

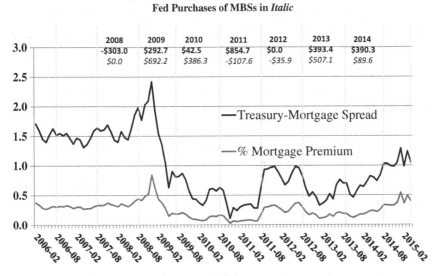

Figure 13.6. 30-Year Treasury Yield and Fixed Rate Mortgage Spread

3%. At the same time, the risk premium on 30-year mortgages fell from the pre-crisis 150 basis points to an average of about 75 basis points. To account for this change in the treasury-mortgage spread, the lower line shows the mortgage premium as a percentage of the 30-year treasuries rate. The mean risk premium percentage was 22%, but by the end of the period, the risk premium had risen to its pre-crisis level of about 35%. While this discussion only deals with two assets of similar duration, it is clear that these financial markets are all related. If and when one becomes out of sync with the others, markets adjust as arbitragers move in and quickly remove the anomaly.

All these movements in the Mortgage and Treasury markets raises serious questions concerning the Federal Reserve's ability to control interest rates. With this in mind, why were interest rates at historic lows for almost a decade? There are at least three possible explanations.

First, consumers, the ultimate suppliers of funds to the market, were so worried about the future that they were willing to give up the current consumption and set aside funds for a gloomy future, thus increasing the supply of funds to the market. Also, if this fear of the future is large enough, it could result in lower equilibrium interest rates on developed world sovereign debt. This could be a problem as the central banks of the developed world, the Federal Reserve, the European Central Bank, the Bank of England and the Bank of Japan, are all engaging in, or have engaged in, what has been referred to as quantitative easing (QE) and defined as a program to increase a central bank's asset portfolio by entering the market for sovereign debt and other market assets. For the Federal Reserve, the QEs all increased holdings of treasuries and mortgage backed securities. If the public in general had increased its level of risk aversion about the future, then we should see the risk premium on less secure assets rising. In fact, the risk premium between 30-year mortgages and 30-year treasuries shown in Figure 13.6 is consistent with that hypothesis.

Second, firms with market opportunities, the demanders of funds, have so little confidence in the future that even near-zero borrowing costs will not match the hurdle rate required to go ahead with their projects for the future, reducing the demand for funds. The evidence presented here suggests that both of these hypotheses carry weight.

Third, demographics have resulted in a decrease in the young population relative to the old population. There is a general hypothesis that individual's consumption smooth over their lifetime. Consumption smoothing results in the young borrowing, in effect supplying future income to the older parts of the population. A now-larger, older population must bid for the smaller supply of future income increasing the price of future income. Higher prices of bonds mean lower interest rates.[3]

Whatever the underlying explanation, interest rates during this period were persistently low, even in nominal terms, making them even lower in real terms. Such rates cannot exist without a lack of real capital investment opportunities. This lack of investment opportunities may have been the result of considerable uncertainty concerning the future costs of production, and not based on the usual level of uncertainty about the economy, but rather about future government policy. Intuitively, when the future is uncertain you don't build permanent structures and hire permanent labor. Instead, you put up tents that are easy and almost costless to dismantle and hire temporary workers.

---

[3] See Walker (2016) for a concise explanation of the theory underlying this hypothesis.

One cost of such historic low real rates of interest is that they lower the implicit cost of the consumption of capital. This means that as a nation we will consume capital by not maintaining it. Further, it means that the demand for capital for personal consumption, such as housing and automobiles for example, will expand, while capital for investment will decline.

Ultimately, markets determine interest rates in spite of the message to the contrary expressed in the financial press. In simplistic terms, as with all markets, it's all about supply and demand. The suppliers of funds to the market, the public, must meet the demanders of these funds, investors and the federal government.

We should not waste our time arguing that the Federal Reserve should allow interest rates to rise since they have no real way to affect the real rate of return on capital. If they could, we would want the Federal Reserve to make the return on capital higher so as to stimulate economic growth. Let's rather correct the political process and restore stability to the marketplace, at least as far as government policy is concerned. We must bring back the independent Federal Reserve and get it out of the role of being a puppet to the Treasury.

Conclusion

Interest rates present a real dilemma. Borrowers want interest rates to be low, and lenders want them to be high. Market interest rates are the culmination of the battle between these two forces. For individuals the desire to have "something now" rather than later, prompts people to enter the market as suppliers of future income, i.e., demanders of current income. That "something now" may be pure consumption, as when those in the early stage of their life-cycle earnings desire to smooth their consumption, knowing that as they age their income will rise. Or the desire to consume now may stem from the belief that investment now will yield returns greater than the cost of obtaining the funds.

Individuals saving for after retirement consumption are suppliers of current income for when their life earnings cycle turns down. In addition, individuals essentially arbitrage between what they have to pay for current income and what the capital acquired by that current income will yield in the future. These forces together determine the equilibrium real rate of interest. Then, if both sides of the market have the same expectations concerning the real value of the money they receive or pay in the future, the nominal rate of interest, what we observe in the market, will be the sum of the equilibrium real rate of interest and the rate of inflation.

Put in this context, what is the role of the Federal Reserve in the determination of the equilibrium rate of interest? We know the monetary policy statements from the Federal Reserve are couched in terms of interest rate and inflation targets. But in reality, these markets are so huge relative to any potential Federal Reserve policy that, at least in the long run, the Federal Reserve is just a real interest rate taker. While the Federal Reserve can influence the money supply and thus the inflation rate, the evidence presented in this chapter supports the argument that real interest rates are largely determined by market forces that are beyond the Federal Reserve's control.

Chapter 14

The Federal Reserve, the Great Recession and the Lost Inflation

Introduction

As the series of Federal Reserve QEs transpired, traditional monetary economists began predicting levels of inflation that would, at a minimum, rival the inflation of the late 1970s and early 1980s. Indeed, the three QEs more than quadrupled the level of Federal Reserve assets in the fiscal year 2009–2015 period. During this 7-year span, Federal Reserve assets grew at an astounding annual rate of nearly 21%.

The traditional pre-Great Recession theory of the relation among the monetary base, the money supply and prices suggested that a greater than 20% growth in Federal Reserve assets would result in at least double digit inflation. But none of these dire predictions happened. In fact, two measures of inflation, the CPI and the GDP deflator, grew at surprisingly low rates of 1.2% and 1.4%, respectively.

Beginning with the onset of the financial crisis of September 2008, did a new regime of the relation between monetary base growth and price level growth take effect? From the beginning of fiscal year 2009, October 2008, to the beginning of fiscal year 2016, the monetary base grew at an annual rate of 23.6%, real GDP grew at an annual rate of 1.8%, and the CPI grew at an annual rate of 1.2%. Applying simple monetarist arithmetic where the rate of change in the price level equals the difference between the rate of money base growth and real output growth, prices should have grown at an annual rate of 22.4% (23.6 − 1.2 = 22.4) instead of the actual price level growth rate of 1.2%. What happened?

The Great Recession and Federal Debt Monetization

In terms of Federal Reserve behavior the first decade of this century, at least prior to fiscal year 2009, was similar to other decades of the past half-century. Then came the onset of the Great Recession when everything seemingly changed. To get a better feel for this dramatic change in policy, consider the 7-year period from October 2008 to October 2015. Both the rate of change in the CPI and real GDP were at historic lows for any similar length period, at least since 1950. Real GDP growth was 1.8%, and CPI growth was 1.2%. Moreover, federal deficits for fiscal year 2009 through fiscal year 2015, were post-WWII records, expressed either in terms of absolute dollars or as a share of GDP.

Figure 14.1 shows the levels of fiscal year federal deficits and the corresponding changes in Federal Reserve assets, as reflected by changes in the monetary base. The monetary base changes presented in Figure 14.1 are the result of the changes in the level of Federal Reserve assets. In general, changes in Federal Reserve assets represent either running the money printing press — in the case of increasing assets — or destroying

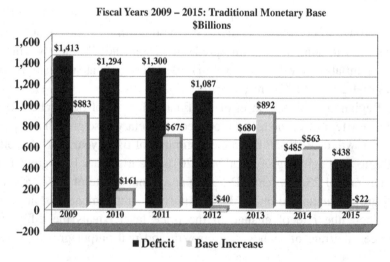

Figure 14.1.   Federal Deficits and Federal Reserve Monetization

money in the case of Federal Reserve asset reductions. Based on the data in the figure, it appears that for the fiscal year 2009 through fiscal year 2015 Federal Reserve asset acquisitions financed just under 47% of the federal deficits.

Except for Federal Reserve responses to the financial crisis in the last 4 months of 2008, the increases in the monetary base during this period were the result of the Federal Reserve increasing its holdings of securities. In fiscal 2009, the $883 billion increase in Federal Reserve assets was a more than a doubling of its asset position prior to the onset of the Great Recession. Importantly, the increase in securities held were, for the first time, not all federal debt. Here the Federal Reserve was buying private market assets, MBSs, in addition to treasuries.

Figure 14.2 shows the aggregate level of Federal Reserve security holdings and the subset of those holdings that were MBSs. From a portfolio that was traditionally 100% treasuries, the share of Federal Reserve asset holdings that were non-treasuries was almost 50% by the close of fiscal 2009. But have the Federal Reserve holdings of MBSs contributed in any way to the level of monetization? The answer to this question requires a brief discussion of how a central bank monetizes the nation's assets.

Central bank monetization is not just about buying Treasury debt. In fact, some central banks have at times been prohibited from buying government debt. This prohibition was imposed in the case of the European Central Bank. But such a prohibition never lasts. Importantly monetization occurs whenever a central bank buys assets from any entity in the

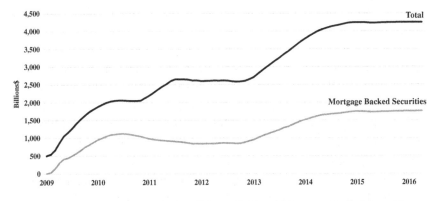

Figure 14.2.   Federal Reserve Holdings — Total and Mortgage Backed Securities

economy. Because the central bank is the monopoly issuer of legal tender, it issues the quantity of legal tender necessary to finance its asset purchases. This operation monetizes these assets as the outstanding quantity of legal tender increases by the value of the assets purchased, no matter the source of the assets.

The effect of monetization on the economy is also independent of the source of the assets purchased by the central bank. On net a central bank purchase of assets increases the public's wealth. This wealth increase is the result of a two-step process. First, the issue of new legal tender with the purchase of assets from the public leaves the public in the same wealth position as before the transaction, i.e., this transaction is a substitution of one form of wealth for another. Second, and this is the important part, the central bank is owned by the government. The revenue from the purchased assets belongs to the government and must be returned to its citizens in one form or another.

Indirectly the public is made better off when citizens give up assets for legal tender since they indirectly get the asset revenue back from the central bank. But just how does this income transfer occur? For the case of a government owned central bank, such as the U.S. Federal Reserve, the revenue belongs to the government. By law, the profits of the Federal Reserve after all costs revert to the Treasury. Since the Treasury is the residual income recipient of all Federal Reserve asset holdings the Treasury, in a sense, "owns" the Federal Reserve. In the final analysis, any transfer from the Federal Reserve to the Treasury reduces the taxes on the public required to fiancé government expenditures. Thus, the net effect of a Federal Reserve asset purchase on the public's wealth is the same as a gift of money to the public.

Since all Federal Reserve earnings accrue to the Treasury and reduce the net servicing cost of the federal debt, the issuer of the assets held by the Federal Reserve is irrelevant. In today's terms, this means that whether the Federal Reserve holds treasuries or MBSs is irrelevant to the effect of asset purchases on the public's wealth. But only Federal Reserve purchases of treasuries were directly reducing the level of federal debt held outside the government.

Figure 14.3 shows the level of net debt servicing costs and transfers from the Federal Reserve to the Treasury for fiscal years 2009–2015.

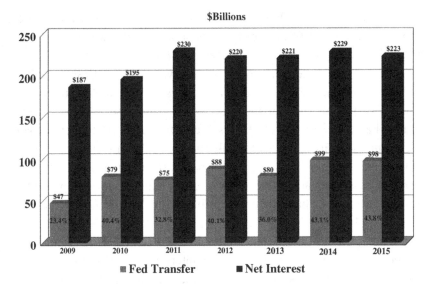

Figure 14.3. Net Debt Servicing Cost and Federal Reserve Distributions to the Treasury

Since Federal Reserve holdings of MBSs create income for the Treasury, these assets offset federal debt. In effect, their purchase is equivalent to the Federal Reserve buying treasuries. The entire increase in Federal Reserve holdings of securities represent monetization of the federal deficits. For the entire period, transfers from the Federal Reserve financed more than 37% of the servicing cost of the debt and over 43% in the 2014 and 2015 fiscal years.

Returning to the post-2008 deficits and monetization contained in Figure 14.1, it seemed that the Federal Reserve asset increases did indeed constitute monetization of a significant share of the massive federal debts of this period. But this simple view of the federal debt ignores the fact that the Federal Reserve increased its liabilities almost in lock-step with its increase in assets.

In October 2008, the Federal Reserve began paying interest on bank reserves. Essentially, the obligation to pay interest on bank reserves made these reserves a short-term debt of the Federal Reserve. Since all earnings of the Federal Reserve offset the servicing cost of the federal debt, the interest payments on reserves reduce these transfers by the full amount of the payments. In a sense, the payment of interest on bank reserves makes bank reserves the equivalent of short-term federal debt. For all practical purposes, during the QE periods, the Federal Reserve was buying long-term federal debt and selling short-term federal debt.

Before interest payments on bank reserves, Federal Reserve actions that increased bank reserves led to an increase in the money supply by a multiple of the increase in reserves. When bank reserves did not earn interest, banks moved any excess reserves into market investments, loans, or Treasury securities, and as a result, increased the money supply. These same money supply increases would have affected the price level. But now that reserves earn interest, these same bank reserves represent an increase in member bank income earning assets and do not increase the money supply.

Figure 14.4 shows the interest rates on required and excess reserves for the period from the beginning of reserve interest payments through July of 2018. At the onset of reserve interest payments, the rate of return for holding reserves matched the rate on 1-year Treasury notes. Then for the period from January 2009 until September 2010, the rate of return on the 1-year notes exceeded the return on reserves. From September 2010, the return to holding reserves exceeded the 1-year note rate until August 2015. In response to rising 1-year note rates, the interest rate on reserves was raised to 37 basis points, then 50 basis points, 75 basis points, 100 basis points, 125 basis points, 175 basis points, and finally 200 basis points.

Importantly, the Federal Reserve sterilized the unprecedented growth in the base by making reserves a Federal Reserve short-term liability. For

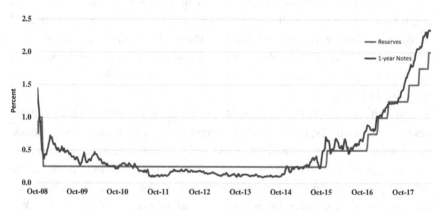

Figure 14.4. Interest Rates on Reserve and 1-year Treasuries

the entire period of QE2 and QE3, the rate of return to banks for holding reserves exceeded the rate of return on 1-year treasuries. This sterilization of reserves eliminated the normal effect of an increase in bank reserves on the money supply as member banks were paid to hold reserves rather than invest in other assets, either loans or securities. The payment of interest on reserves reduced or eliminated any potential effect of increased reserves on the money supply.

During each of the three QEs, the Federal Reserve bought long securities in the form of treasuries and MBSs and created short-term liabilities in the form of bank reserves. At a minimum, the excess reserve component of the monetary base could not contribute to financing the federal debt since it was the equivalent of federal debt. Figure 14.5 amends Figure 14.1 by netting out any increase in Federal Reserve liabilities stemming from member banks' excess reserve holdings. It accounts for the inclusion of the increase in Federal Reserve liabilities, i.e., bank reserves, as an offset to Federal Reserve asset growth.

The Adjusted Base series in Figure 14.5 is the difference between traditional monetary base growth and the growth in excess reserves for each fiscal year. The adjusted base is the appropriate measure of the ability of the banking system to expand the money supply. The Federal Reserve expanded

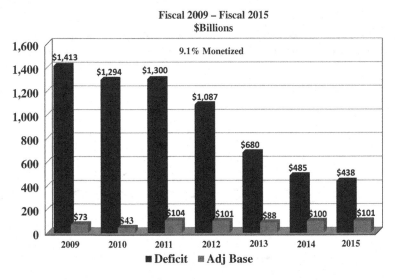

Figure 14.5. Deficits and Federal Reserve Monetization

its asset portfolio by printing money and simultaneously sequestered much of the money printed by converting it into short-term debt held by the banking system. As a result, the difference between the fiscal year federal deficit and the increase in the adjusted monetary base is an estimate of the actual level of monetization of each fiscal year's deficit. Using this measure of net Federal Reserve involvement in financing federal deficits for the entire 7-fiscal-year period, the level of deficit monetization was just over 9%.

In spite of the tremendous annual growth in the traditional monetary base of 15.7%, the annual inflation rate for the entire period only averaged between 1.2% and 1.4%, measured in terms of either CPI or GDP deflator growth. For fiscal years 2009 through 2015, the adjusted monetary base grew at 7.5%. For the same 7-year period, real GDP grew at a slow rate of 1.8%. These 7-year growth rates still leave us with an unexplained lack of inflation since the difference between adjusted base growth rate and the real GDP growth rate is just under 6%.

To illustrate these differences, Figure 14.6 presents the rate of change in the adjusted base, real GDP and the CPI. One measure of the path of monetary policy during the Great Recession is the level of monetary base growth adjusted for the transition of excess reserves to short-term equivalent debt. Even here, the disparity between the adjusted monetary base growth rate and real GDP growth still leaves the fact of low price level growth unexplained.

Without the adjustment for the policy that made excess reserves the equivalent of a market yielding asset, the disparity between monetary

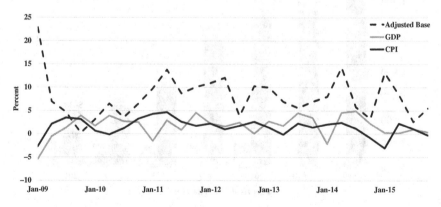

Figure 14.6.   Adjusted Monetary Base, CPI, and Real GDP Growth

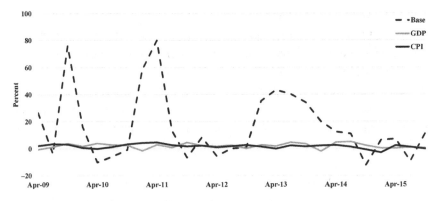

Figure 14.7. Unadjusted Monetary Base, CPI, and Real GDP Growth

base growth and inflation would be multiples of the difference shown in Figure 14.6. To show this, consider Figure 14.7, which depicts the traditional monetary base growth path without adjusting for the transition that made excess reserves a bank investment. Here, I ignore the special case of the last quarter of 2008 that included the Federal Reserve response to the financial crisis of September 2008. A simple glimpse at Figure 14.7 indicates an astounding feature of this unique period. In no period in the history of the Federal Reserve has there been growth in the monetary base that was so variable. Ignoring the fourth quarter of 2008 where the growth rate of the unadjusted monetary base was an astounding 557%, the 7-year period from the first quarter of 2009 through the third quarter of 2015, a period of 27 quarters, there were seven quarters with annual monetary base growth rates exceeding 25%. The period as a whole experienced annual growth in the monetary base of 15%.

The essential question is still why did the monetary base growth of this period, adjusted or unadjusted for the change in the role of reserves, fail to produce the inflation that would normally follow rapid monetary growth?

Is There an Inflation Mystery?

Considering the virtually unprecedented rate of monetary base growth following the onset of the Great Recession, the usual economic projection would have been inflation to match. The natural question to ask is what happened? In a simple world of a constant desire of the public to hold currency versus bank deposits and a constant desire of banks to hold reserves, the rate of change in any of the popular definitions of money would be approximately equal to the rate of change in the monetary base.

Simply put, inflation is the result of too much money chasing too few goods. To put this in perspective let the amount of money be any of the popular definitions and represent the amount of goods as the nation's GDP. Then, a measure of the amount of money relative to goods is the ration of GDP to money, the rate of money turnover in the economy or just the velocity of money.

The Federal Reserve's effect on the economy is through its effect on the money supply, however defined. In that simple world, the 15.7% rate of growth in the monetary base of the 7 years from the beginning of 2009 to 2015 should have, but did not, result in the significant inflation that many economists predicted. Why did this not happen as expected?

First, consider the traditional equation of exchange that relates the rate of change in money to the rate of change in prices adjusting for both velocity growth and real GDP growth. This equation says that the rate of inflation must equal the rate of growth of the money supply plus the rate of growth of velocity less the rate of growth of the nation's output.[1] For this 7-year period, the rate of growth in the expanded definition of the money stock, M2, was 6.3%, much less than the 15.7% rate of growth in the monetary base. For the same period, the GDP velocity of M2 fell at a rate of 2.9%, and real GDP grew at 1.8%. The result using the simple equation of exchange is an inflation rate of 1.6%, just larger than the measured rate of inflation of the GDP deflator of 1.4%.

Second, what is the reason for the disparity between the 15.7% rate of monetary base growth and the much smaller 6.3% growth in the M2 money supply? The answer lies in the change in the nature of the monetary base, in particular, the reserve component.

Traditionally, when the Federal Reserve increases its asset holdings, as they did during the three periods of quantitative easing (QE1, QE2, QE3), the proceeds of these purchases became bank reserves. Since these

---

[1] Let the rate of inflation be π, the rate of money growth be μ, the velocity of money be v and real output growth be g then we have, $\pi = \mu + v - g$. Thus, the rate of inflation, π, must equal the rate of growth in the money supply, μ, plus the rate of growth in the velocity of money v minus the rate of growth in real GDP, g.

now-excess reserves earned nothing, banks put them to use by increasing loans or security holdings. But all this changed in October 2008 when the Federal Reserve began paying member banks interest on their reserve holdings. Reserves were now investments.

In this new world, both kinds of reserves, required and excess, pay interest, but only excess reserves are truly investments of choice for banks. For the purpose of bank money creation, only required reserves matter. The traditional relation between any of the measures of the money supply and the monetary base will show a much smaller effect of a change in the base on the money supply. Now monetary base growth is a combination of required reserve growth that reflects growth in bank investments in the economy and excess reserve growth that reflects bank investments in this new form of income earning assets, bank excess reserves.

Reflecting this new reality of the money supply–monetary base relation, Figure 14.8 depicts the multiple that a popular measure of the money supply, M2, has been of the monetary base based on total reserves and for reserves adjusted for the investment component of bank reserves. The adjustment is a simple reduction in total reserves by the quantity of excess reserves. Since excess reserves before the payment of interest on reserves were for all practical purposes zero, the two multipliers were virtually identical until the onset of interest being paid on reserves. Once we get to October 2008, however, the traditional M2 base multiplier falls off the chart, while the M2 adjusted base multiplier remains almost unchanged.

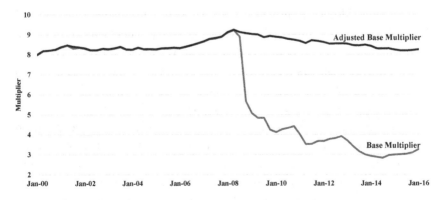

Figure 14.8. Monetary Base, M2, Multiplier

In simplistic terms, the inflation that did not happen was the result of a remarkable reduction in the velocity of money coupled with a reduction in the effect of the monetary base on the supply of money. Understanding what happened brings two perplexing issues into focus. First, at the beginning of the fourth quarter of 2008, did everything we thought we knew about how the monetary system worked become wrong? Second, if not, then why did an unprecedented expansion of Federal Reserve assets not have any real effect on the economy?

The answer to both of these questions lies in the introduction of interest payments on bank reserves. These interest payments on bank reserves created investment opportunities for banks that did not involve the economy. Simultaneously, interest payments on reserves created liabilities on the Federal Reserve balance sheet.

Prior to these interest payments, the largest Federal Reserve liability in their version of their balance sheet was currency. But in reality, as we shall discuss at length in Chapter 18 on valuing a central bank, currency should not be considered a liability in any real sense. To see this point, consider what you get when you bring currency to the Federal Reserve. You just get replacement currency. The Federal Reserve gets real resources when it issues currency, just as you would if you issued a personal bond, i.e., borrowed money from a bank. The difference is that you would be required to pay back the loan with interest, that is give up something real, while the Federal Reserve never has to pay back anything.

In this new world of interest payments on reserves, the asset purchases of the Federal Reserve have suddenly been financed, at least partially, by issuing debt. Moreover, this new debt has real consequences because all Federal Reserve earnings accrue to the Treasury. Therefore, the interest payments on reserves reduce Federal Reserve transfers to the Treasury. These reduced transfers increase the cost of servicing the federal debt and ultimately increase the federal debt burden.

Of note is that many economists, myself included, ignored the importance of paying interest on reserves as a game changer in the inflation arena. We warned about the almost certain prospect of double digit inflation as the asset portfolio of the Federal Reserve grew at a double digit rate of just over 20%. In reality, its portfolio net of increased liabilities grew at a much more modest rate of 9.9%. Over this same period, the adjusted-for-liability base grew at 7.5%, just slightly greater than the M2 growth rate of 6.3%. But, the inflation specter can come back with a vengeance should the Federal Reserve abandon paying market interest rates on bank reserves. This payment of interest on reserves has fundamentally changed our view of monetary policy.

Conclusion

In the final analysis, there is no mystery concerning the missing inflation. Further, there is nothing wrong with our more than century old understanding of the effect of monetary base changes on the money supply in a fractional reserve banking system. Those of us predicting higher inflation missed the importance of the introduction of paying banks to hold reserves at rates that were competitive with what the market had to offer. In retrospect, it is no surprise then that the combination of a falling velocity of money as the cost of holding money fell to near zero, and the payment of interest on reserves giving the banks no incentive to invest in the economy, resulted in near-zero inflation.

The unprecedented increase in Federal Reserve assets associated with QE1, QE2 and QE3 seemed to imply that the Federal Reserve financed over 40% of the period's federal deficits. Such a massive spree of running the Federal Reserve money printing press should have given us the double digit inflation we were all so certain was imminent. However, the simultaneous creation of the equivalent of federal liabilities all but negated the Federal Reserve's effect on federal debt financing. In the end, the Federal Reserve's role in financing the federal deficits was on the same order as a share of the deficits in WWII and the Reagan 1980s, about 9.1%.

This does not mean, however, that the introduction of paying interest on reserves was an insignificant change in Federal Reserve policy. Nor does it mean that this new innovation does not affect monetary policy in any significant way, beyond its effect on monetary base growth and inflation. As we shall see in the following chapter, the payment of interest on reserves is a major game changer in the Federal Reserve's ability to affect the economy.

Chapter 15

Federal Reserve Monetary Policy When Reserves Pay Interest

Introduction

The statutory objectives for monetary policy are maximum employment, stable prices and moderate long-term interest rates, as specified in the Federal Reserve Act and amended in 1977. All three of these objectives appear in releases from the Federal Reserve concerning potential policy changes. Consider the following excerpt from the FOMC (Federal Reserve Open-Market Committee) release of July 31–August 1, 2018.

Against this backdrop, the Committee decided to maintain the target "In view of realized and expected labor market conditions and inflation, the Committee decided to maintain the target range for the Fed Funds rate at 1¾ to 2 percent. The stance of monetary policy remains accommodative, _ Minutes of the Meeting of July 31–August 1, 2018 Page 11 thereby supporting strong labor market conditions and a sustained return to 2 percent inflation. In determining the timing and size of future adjustments to the target range for the Fed Funds rate, the Committee will assess realized and expected economic conditions relative to its maximum employment objective and its symmetric 2 percent inflation objective. This assessment will take into account a wide range of information, including measures of labor market conditions, indicators of inflation pressures and inflation expectations, and readings on financial and international developments.

The above excerpt mentions two of the three mandated Federal Reserve objectives of monetary policy, employment and price stability, or inflation. Further, if one interprets the Fed Funds rate (the overnight bank lending rate) as related to long-term interest rates, then the excerpt contains all three objectives. What is not mentioned in the excerpt is any actual Federal Reserve policy or policies that would result in the Fed Funds rate reaching its target and what reaching that target would mean for employment or inflation.

Except in times of extreme liquidity crises, traditional monetary policy is about actions that impact the level or rate of growth of the money supply. The inflation rate is about money growing faster or slower than real output. One way to assess the level of money relative to economic output is the availability of free bank reserves, i.e., reserves above the level required by the Federal Reserve, excess reserves. The Fed Funds rate, as the overnight borrowing rate for these bank reserves, is the connection between money and economic output through its relation to bank reserves. When output rises relative to the money supply, banks economize on reserves. As reserves become scarcer, competition among banks for reserves results in an increase in the Fed Funds rate.

With the introduction of interest on bank reserves, we have a new way to think about bank reserves — as an investment, rather than insurance against a run on the banking system. How, if at all, does paying interest on bank reserves change monetary policy? In one obvious way, the Federal Reserve now has an interest rate that it directly controls. But does paying interest on reserves change how Federal Reserve actions affect the money supply and the economy?

The Fed Funds Rate and Monetary Policy

Consider the excerpt from the FOMC in the introduction. In that statement, the Fed Funds rate is referred to as a "target." In the usual interpretation, a "target" is something a policy maker aims at on the supposition that if the target is achieved, the desired policy goal is achieved.[1]

---

[1] For a thorough discussion of the relation between a target and the subsequent direction of the ultimate policy, see Saving (1967).

The Fed Funds rate is the equilibrium cost of overnight borrowing of reserves. How does the Federal Reserve influence this equilibrium rate? It does so by taking actions that increase or decrease the availability of bank reserves. As such, the Fed Funds rate is not monetary policy in and of itself but is the result of monetary policy. As we think about policy, what policy actions could the pre-October 2008 Federal Reserve engage in to reach a specific Fed Funds rate target?

Before October 2008, when the Federal Reserve was not paying interest on bank reserve holdings, the only action available to the Federal Reserve to affect the Fed Funds rate was buying or selling assets on the open market.

As we have seen in the earlier chapters, a sale of Federal Reserve assets takes money out of the economy and reduces bank reserves. A reduction in bank reserves, everything else the same, makes federal funds scarcer and raises the Fed Funds rate.

Federal Reserve purchases of assets put money into the economy and increase bank reserves. An increase in bank reserves, everything else the same, makes federal funds more plentiful and lowers the Fed Funds rate.

Assuming the players in the market understood the above mechanism, an announcement of a change in a target Fed Funds rate to a rate above or below the current rate is an indication of intended Federal Reserve policy. Both the press and market reaction to such announcements in the immediate short-run seem to indicate that, indeed, the players did understand. What is the mechanism through which either of these monetary actions affect the economy?

A Primer on Traditional Federal Reserve Monetary Policy

Traditional monetary policy is about Federal Reserve actions that increase or decrease the money supply. These money supply changes take place when the Federal Reserve buys assets from the public or sells assets to the public.[2] What is the mechanism through which these changes in the

---

[2] In this case, "public" means not directly from the Treasury. Specifically, "public" does not mean that assets purchased or sold are not Treasury securities. In fact, for most of its existence, the Federal Reserve primarily dealt in Treasury securities purchased or sold from or to the public in the secondary market.

money supply influence the economy? Specifically, how can a change in the money supply bring employment to the maximum employment, or bring inflation to the 2% inflation rate, as specified in the July 31, 2018, FOMC policy statement?

Let's begin with a Federal Reserve purchase of securities. While such a purchase historically would have been exclusively Treasury debt, the purchase of any financial instrument, public or private, has the same effect. In such a purchase, the public gives up financial assets and gets money, e.g., currency or deposits to their bank account.

The Federal Reserve asset purchase increases the assets in its portfolio and increases its portfolio income. By the same token, the public has decreased the earning assets in its portfolio and gained currency or bank deposits, leaving its wealth unchanged. By law, the entire increase in Federal Reserve portfolio income accrues to the Treasury.[3] The Treasury must now return this increase in income to the public, either in the form of reduced taxation, increased services or lower debt issue, to cover a now-smaller deficit. Therefore, there can be no pure monetary policy. Every increase in the money supply implies a simultaneous fiscal policy action since it affects the revenue of the Treasury.[4]

As a result, after all is said and done, the public, from a budget constraint perspective, has the same income as before but has more currency or bank deposits. With the same income as before but increased currency or bank deposits, the public is wealthier. Being wealthier the public can consume and invest more. The combination of increased consumption and investment will increase the demand for goods and services on the one hand, and increase the supply of loanable funds on the other. The immediate effect of this increase in the public's wealth increases prices and reduces interest rates.

Put differently, when the Federal Reserve buys assets, it prints the money used to pay for the purchase. The purchase results in a reorganization of the public's wealth toward money and away from other assets, so no net change in wealth would occur. But the income from the assets now

---

[3] In fact, all profits of the Federal Reserve are remitted to the Treasury. These profits consist of all revenue less preferred stock dividends to the owner member banks and Federal Reserve costs.

[4] An excellent discussion of the connection between monetary and fiscal policy is in Cochrane's (2014) article.

held by the Federal Reserve goes to the US Treasury. In a balanced budget world, the increased Treasury income would be offset by lower taxation of an equal amount. This open-market purchase of assets from the public is the same as if the money dropped from the sky.

If the economy is in full employment equilibrium, nothing much can happen to "real" economic outcomes. The increase in wealth must be undone by a commensurate increase in the price level with no change in the real rate of interest. Importantly, this change in the price level is a one-time measured inflation but no in persistent ongoing inflation. Persistent ongoing inflation of, say 2% per year, would require persistent ongoing increases in Federal Reserve asset purchases and would result in an increase in nominal interest rates equal to the 2% inflation rate.

The reverse of this transaction is a Federal Reserve sale of securities, either public debt or private debt. The Federal Reserve reduces its assets and acquires currency. The public, at least directly, is no better or worse off for it has simply, and voluntarily, given up money for debt instruments. The Federal Reserve's reduced income reduces the transfers to the Treasury by an equal amount. The Treasury must now reduce services, increase taxes on the public or issue more debt. The tax increase matches the increased income that the public received in exchange for the currency they gave up. With no change in income and the loss of currency, the public is unilaterally poorer by the amount of the decrease in currency.

The now-poorer public will reduce consumption and investment. On the one hand, the combination of decreased consumption and investment will decrease the demand for goods and services, and/or on the other hand, decrease the supply of loanable funds. The immediate effect of this decrease in the public's wealth is a fall in the price level and an increase in interest rates. This open-market sale of assets to the public is the same as if the money was sucked up and burned.

Once again, if the economy is in full employment equilibrium, nothing much can happen to real parts of the economy. The decrease in wealth must be undone by a commensurate decrease in the price level with no change in the real rate of interest. Importantly, this change in the price level is a one-time measured inflation, or rather deflation.

These Federal Reserve changes in the money supply become changes in the public's budget constraint through changes in their wealth. Monetary policy has real effects on demand for the nation's output. How does the Federal Reserve meet its charge that policy be conducted to achieve maximum employment, stable prices and low long-term interest rates?

Monetary policy that changes the money supply works through what has historically been termed a "wealth" effect. This form of monetary policy in a steady state world is about a stable price level, not about an equilibrium rate of change in the price level. This distinction raises the question as to the meaning of the current Federal Reserve policy goal of 2% inflation. Does the Federal Reserve desire an equilibrium continuing 2% per year increase in the price level, or is the goal that the price level rise 2% in the next year and then stabilize?

If the goal of policy is to have steady state inflation, then policy must continually increase the money supply at a rate above the rate of growth in the economy. In this case, in addition to the seigniorage from the initial issue of currency, the government collects revenue from the public's desire to maintain its desired level of the real value of its money balances. In order to maintain the real value of its money balances, the public must continually buy the equivalent of currency from the monopoly issuer, the Federal Reserve.[5]

The current level of inflation in Venezuela of more than 180% annually is the result of the Bank of Venezuela financing the national government's deficits by running the printing press. Historically, inflation rates of this level or greater have ultimately resulted in a monetary reform that wiped out the old currency.[6]

In the United States, the money supply is not entirely generated by the Federal Reserve as evidenced by the fact that currency is just only 45% of the narrowest measure of money, M1 — defined as essentially currency plus bank checking accounts. Further currency is just over 10% of the most used broader measure of the money stock, M2, measured as M1 plus other easily transferable accounts. The fact is that the majority of what we term money is generated by the private sector. In a simple world,

---

[5] An excellent paper that traces the path of inflation is Auernheimer (1983).

[6] Maintaining the value of currency and providing currency for ordinary transactions has plagued economies for centuries. For an excellent discussion of what was a constant problem see Sargent and Velde (2001).

the greater the private component of the money supply, the smaller the maximum revenue that can be raised through inflation.[7] Whether the goal of monetary policy is a once for all change in the price level or a constant rate of change in the price level, has the introduction of interest on bank reserves changed how monetary policy works and, if so, why?

Does Paying Interest on Reserves Change Anything?

With the advent of interest payments on reserves, the Federal Reserve now has an interest rate it can set, rather than simply target. Does this fact change the monetary policy options available to the Federal Reserve? Further, does the fact that the Federal Reserve announces an increase in its target for the Fed Funds rate or raises the interest rate it pays on bank reserves mean that market interest rates are going to rise? Finally, can either the target Fed Funds rate announcement or an actual increase in the rate of interest paid on reserves be the interest rate that concerns the press so greatly?

Interest on reserves does not change the fundamental goals of monetary policy. The first goal of a central bank is to act to mitigate liquidity crises, such as the crisis experienced in September 2008.[8]

Once we move beyond the mitigation of the effect of liquidity crises, central banks have assumed the role of reducing the variation of output during business cycles. This role is exemplified in the 1977 amendment to the Federal Reserve Act that set the objectives for monetary policy as maximum employment, stable prices and moderate long-term interest rates.

Does simply setting an objective for the Federal Reserve mean that it is actually possible for it to achieve the goal? Given the cited objective of Federal Reserve monetary policy to impact the level of economic activity

---

[7] For an analysis of the effect of private money on the level of seigniorage that can be generated through inflation, see Dwyer Jr. and Saving (1986).

[8] Two other recent examples of liquidity crises were: (1) the increased demand for cash due to the fear that Y2K would have significant effects on the world economy and (2) the increased demand for cash following 9/11.

relative to the economy's full potential, what are the tools, if any, that it can use to achieve this goal? The only way the Federal Reserve affects the economy is through operations in financial markets, generally the market for treasuries. These changes then result in once-and-for-all changes in the public's nominal wealth.

With the introduction of interest on reserves, does monetary policy now take on a whole new aspect? Previously, Federal Reserve monetary policy was conducted by changes in its asset position, buying and selling assets. These operations affected the level of currency and bank reserves and had a wealth effect on the economy. Now, Federal Reserve policy consists of operations in financial markets that change its asset holdings, but simultaneously, it now issues short-term liabilities in the form of bank reserves.[9]

Now with interest on reserves changes in Federal Reserve assets holdings are only part of the picture. There is no limit to the amount of assets in the Federal Reserve portfolio, as it is the level of these assets net of liabilities that matters. As we saw in the last chapter, what matters is not the rate of growth in the gross assets held by the Federal Reserve, but its net assets. No increase in Federal Reserve assets offset by an equal increase in Federal Reserve liabilities, in the form of interest paid on bank reserves, will have any effect on the future price level.

The key here is that an increase in Federal Reserve assets fully offset by an "equal" increase in liabilities has no wealth effect because it has no effect on the public's budget constraint. No wealth effect means, no effect on output demand and hence, no effect on the price level. By the same token, an increase in Federal Reserve assets that is not offset by an increase in liabilities does have a wealth effect and, other things constant, will have a price level effect.

Simply paying market rates of interest on reserves has not changed how Federal Reserve actions that increase or decrease their net asset holding affect the economy and the price level. What this new regime does change is the appropriate measure of the effect on wealth of Federal Reserve policy.

---

[9]The other short-term liability issued by the Federal Reserve is in the form of reverse-repos. However, the scale of this aspect of Federal Reserve liability is on the order of $300 billion while the reserves liabilities total $2.4 trillion.

The appropriate measure must be based on the effect of any given Federal Reserve policy on the budget constraint of the public. A Federal Reserve purchase (sale) of assets where the public gives up (purchases) income earning assets and gets (gives up) currency results in no change in assets held by the public. These actions at first blush only change the composition of the public's asset holdings so the public is held harmless.

The issue is what happens to the income flow from the assets purchased by the Federal Reserve? To the extent that the Federal Reserve creates (destroys) liabilities equal in value to the asset purchases (sales) and uses the increased (decreased) income flow from the assets to offset the interest increase (decrease) on the liabilities, there is no effect on the public's budget constraint.[10] The increase (decrease) in currency held by the public from the purchase (sale) of assets increase (decrease) public bank deposits that yield market rates of interest equal to the interest rate on Federal Reserve assets. As a result, the public's constraint before the asset purchase (sale) remains unchanged after the asset purchase (sale).

When does a change in Federal Reserve assets affect the public's budget constraints? From the above, it is clear that a change in Federal Reserve net-of-liability assets is a necessary condition for there to be an effect on the public's budget constraint. Consider a Federal Reserve purchase (sale) of assets accompanied by a smaller increase (decrease) in liabilities. Assuming a balanced budget government, the net increase (decrease) in Federal Reserve earnings is returned to the public via tax reductions so that the public's budget constraint is increased (decreased) by the net change in Federal Reserve assets.

The effect on the public's budget constraints of net Federal Reserve asset changes can be summarized by the change in what could be called the "effective monetary base," namely, in the narrowest sense, just currency, or in a broader sense currency plus required reserves.[11] These two

---

[10] There are some issues that are ignored here. First, the assets purchased by the Federal Reserve during the interest on reserves period have been long-term relative to the liabilities created. As a result, Federal Reserve transfers to the Treasury have increased even with no change in Federal Reserve net assets. This increase in Federal Reserve transfers that is distributed to the public as a reduction in taxes increases the public's income.

[11] Lest we begin to believe that currency can be ignored because we are becoming a "cashless" society, the currency component of the money supply is $1.33 trillion while currency plus required reserves is only slightly larger at $1.47 trillion.

measures of Federal Reserve monetary policy have risen over the past 7 years at an annual rate of 7.56% and 8.28%, respectively.

So, traditional monetary policy has not disappeared with the advent of interest on reserves in the sense that we have seen an increase in non-interest bearing currency, essentially printed money. Keeping a stable value of the currency would require a growth in the money supply that equals the rate of growth in real output. However, for this period, annual real GDP growth was only 1.76%.

To bring the contrast between the growth in monetary assets and real GDP into context, let's return to the Federal Reserve goal to achieve an inflation rate of 2%. A stable 2% inflation requires that the money supply grow 2% faster than real GDP to ensure that adequate resources are available to conduct transactions. Faster money growth, absent changes in transactions technology, results in inflation above the 2% goal, while slower money growth would result in a lower inflation rate and perhaps even a falling price level, deflation.

In a very simple sense, the growth of the effective monetary base of between 7.56% and 8.28% coupled with real GDP growth of 1.76% should have resulted in about 5.5% annual inflation. But actual inflation for this period was only 1.4%, well below the above 5.5% estimate. What happened was that the economic uncertainty coupled with historically low interest rates increased the demand by the public to hold money. As a result, the income velocity of money fell at an annual rate of 3.9%. Then for this period the demand for holding money absorbed most of the increase in the adjusted monetary base.[12]

The usual relation between the usual measure of the monetary base and the supply of money seems to have broken. The various measures of the money supply grew but at a much slower rate than the monetary base that supports the money supply. Have we entered an alternate universe where the relations that existed in the previous universe no longer hold? Or is there an explanation for the past 7 years that is consistent with the universe as we have always known it?

Two distinct things have happened that have affected the normal relationship between price level growth rate (the rate of inflation) and the difference between the money growth rate and the growth rate of real GDP.

---

[12] For the effect of this velocity change on inflation, see Saving (2016).

Both of these effects are related to changes in interest rates and the difference between the money growth rate and the growth rate of real output.

First, the historically low market rates of interest reduced the cost of holding assets in the form of money balances. The GDP velocity of money has declined since the beginning of 2008; this decline is on the order of 44% for M1 and 25% for M2 and MZM. When calculating the expected inflation from a given rate of monetary growth, one must subtract the rate of growth in real GDP, for the 7 years since the onset of 2008 where the growth rate was 1.2% and add the rate of growth in money velocity, which was −8.7% for the M1 money definition, −4.2% for the M2 money definition and −4.3% for the newer MZM money definition.

Second, a new interest rate that did not exist before 2008 is the yield that the Federal Reserve is paying banks to hold reserves. In the same way that low yields on alternatives to holding cash reduce the public's desire to hold non-cash assets, a positive yield on reserves reduces the banking system's desire to find investments to use up their idle reserves.

To see the effect of the level of the interest rate on bank reserves on bank investments, Figure 15.1 shows the yields on a subset of investments for both the public and the banks and the rate of interest on bank reserves. As treasury yields fell rapidly from levels of near 2% for 1- and 2-year treasuries at the end of 2007 to 1% for 2-year treasuries and 0.5% for 1-year treasuries, holding near zero yield money balances becomes a real alternative. Further, by the middle of 2011, the yields on both the 1-year

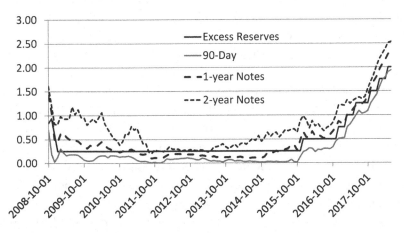

Figure 15.1.   90-Day, 1yr, 2yr Treasury Yields and Interest Rate on Reserves

and 2-year treasuries had fallen to less than 0.25%. Is it any wonder that money holdings rose and that the velocity of money reached historic lows?

Market interest rates explain why the GDP velocity of money fell and raised the idea that the road to recovery was simply to restore this money velocity to its previous level. As usual, the simple solution is no solution at all. The reduced velocity was a result of the problem and not the problem itself. But the question that still remains is why hasn't the unprecedented increase in the monetary base resulted in a close-to-equal increase in the money supply? The reason is that the fundamental relation between the monetary base and the money supply changed with the payment of interest on bank reserves.

Because the banking system is a fractional reserve system, the demand deposit component of the money supply is a multiple of the banking system's reserves. That multiple is a function of the level of reserves that the banking system holds, in effect the reserve to deposit ratio. But by paying banks to hold reserves at a rate that exceeded the rate of return on 1-year treasuries, the Federal Reserve broke the link between the monetary base and the money supply. The Federal Reserve paid banks to invest in reserves instead of in the economy. By the same token, the payment of market rates of interest on reserves broke the relation between monetary base growth and price level growth.

How did we get to this point? The Federal Reserve was clearly under extreme pressure to absorb some or perhaps all of the unprecedented federal deficits. Its response was to use its Congressional permission to institute the payment of interest on bank reserves. This change allowed the Federal Reserve to quadruple its assets but mitigate the effect on the economy by sequestering this increase through paying the banking system to hold much of their total increase in assets as excess reserves.

Thus, on balance, the net asset position of the Federal Reserve after all the QEs were done was only slightly larger as a share of GDP than it was before the financial meltdown of 2008. Does the Federal Reserve want to get back to its traditional role by shrinking its assets and liabilities with a goal of reaching its traditional net asset position of roughly 6% of GDP without liabilities? Or is this new role of influencing the economy through direct interest rate changes a superior way to conduct monetary policy?

As an aside, the creation of reserves as short-term debt would further enhance the Federal Reserve policy referred to in the past as "operation twist." In order to keep long-term interest rates low to help the housing and other durable goods markets, the Federal Reserve changed the structure of its asset portfolio that prior to 2008 consisted of mostly less than 1-year treasuries, to one that contains virtually no treasuries less than 5 years. They also added to their portfolio $1.75 trillion of long-term MBSs. At the same time, the Federal Reserve turned the excess bank reserves into short-term securities. The goal of the combination of reducing the stock of long-term securities and increasing the stock of short-term securities was higher short-term interest rates and lower long-term interest rates.

Interest on Reserves as a Monetary Policy Tool

As we have seen, the creation of a new Federal Reserve liability in the form of bank reserves does not prevent the Federal Reserve from engaging in the traditional monetary policy. Paying interest on bank reserves made these reserves a Federal Reserve liability because of the connection between the Treasury and the Federal Reserve. Before interest on reserves, Federal Reserve policy involved adding to or depleting its assets without affecting liabilities. As a result, open-market purchases or sales of assets represented changes in Federal Reserve net asset holdings. Thus, traditional policy is now about changes in the level of Federal Reserve net assets, not gross assets. In both cases policy was always about changes in the equivalent of changes in the adjusted monetary base. Without interest on reserves, Federal Reserve liabilities were zero so that changes in the monetary base were by definition changes in the adjusted monetary base.[13]

Before interest on reserves, the only way for the Federal Reserve to affect the economy was through an open-market sale or purchase of assets. In the interest on reserves world, the Federal Reserve can affect its net asset position by adding or depleting its assets or reducing or increasing its liabilities.

Let's see how this works by considering a policy to stimulate the economy. Before interest on reserves this would have taken the form of running the printing press and buying assets from the public. The public has more money and fewer assets and the Treasury has more income that

---

[13] Chapter 18 discusses the new worth of the Federal Reserve. There the issue of "what is a Federal Reserve liability," is considered at length.

it can use to reduce taxes or debt. In the interest on reserves world, there are two levers that can achieve the same effect.

As before, the Federal Reserve can run the printing press and enter the open-market and buy assets from the public. Does this policy have the same effect it did before reserves were a liability of the Federal Reserve? It does, provided that desired excess reserve holdings for the banks do not change. But desired excess reserves now depend on the return to holding reserves relative to bank alternatives. If the open-market asset purchases reduced market interest rates then reserves will become more attractive to banks. In the limit, banks might desire to hold the entire increase in their reserves as excess reserves. If so, there is no change in Federal Reserve net assets occurs and therefore, no policy effect.

Figure 15.2 shows the share of total bank assets that are invested in excess reserves, Federal Reserve liabilities and the basis point spread between 1-year treasuries and bank reserves for the period from the onset of paying interest on reserves, October 2008 to June of 2018. What the figure does not contain is the beginning of 2008, when bank holdings of excess reserves were for all practical purposes zero, 0.015%, not surprising since reserves had a zero return. Once the yield on reserves became significant, the reserve share of bank assets rose rapidly, especially during the period of negative spread that coincided with the last two QEs, the end of 2010–2014. Since the onset of a negative spread, the share of

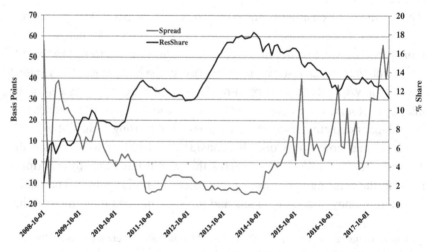

Figure 15.2. Excess Reserve Share of Total Commercial Bank Assets

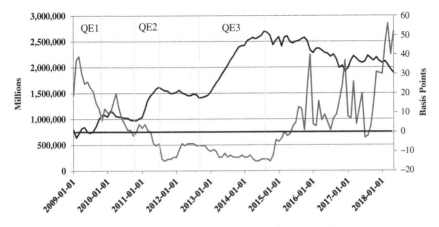

Figure 15.3. 1yr Treasury-Reserves Internet Rate Spread and Excess Reserves

excess reserves has been falling as reserves become a relatively less attractive investment.

It is clear from Figure 15.2 that banks respond to the difference between market rates of interest and the interest paid on their holdings of excess reserves. Figure 15.3 shows this relation directly. In this figure the effect of the negative spread on excess reserve accumulation is clear, as is the fact that most of the QE asset accumulation by the Federal Reserve was absorbed by the banking system as excess reserves. Thus, that period of unprecedented Federal Reserve asset growth contributed very little to the net asset position of the Federal Reserve.

Since monetary policy is really all about changes in the Federal Reserve's net asset position, changes in assets in one direction are equivalent to equal changes in reserves (liabilities) in the other direction. Either of these has the same effect on the wealth of the public and the same effect on the economy.

A contractionary interest on reserves policy

Assume that the FOMC desires to slow an overheated economy by reducing the Federal Reserve's net asset position. Assume further that they do so by increasing the rate of interest rate on reserves.[14]

---

[14] In Chapter 16, will consider the role of the Federal Reserve Fed Funds targets on the interest rate on reserves and the resulting monetary policy.

In response to an increase in the return to holding reserves, banks reduce investments in the economy and increase reserves, thereby reducing the Federal Reserve's net assets. Total bank assets remain the same as they have simply substituted investment in reserves for investment, say in short-term treasuries. The public now has more treasuries and has given up currency and/or deposits. The currency and/or deposits are now bank reserves at the Federal Reserve.

Importantly, from the banking system's perspective, total income earning assets have not changed. More importantly from the non-banking public's perspective their wealth has not changed. The public has given up currency and deposits and acquired treasuries, and they did so voluntarily. Thus, from the perspective of the total public, bank owners and non-bank owners, wealth has remained the same.

What has changed is the level of Federal Reserve transfers to the Treasury. These transfers have fallen by the amount of the increase in interest payments on reserves. In a simple world of a balanced budget government, the fall in Federal Reserve transfers to the Treasury must result in increased taxation. Therefore, the public is worse off by amount of the increase in taxation. Then if we measure wealth by the present value of this permanent increase in taxation, the public is poorer by that amount.

Consider the alternative to increasing the interest on reserves method for decreasing net assets, by the more direct approach of an open-market sale of assets. The asset sale affects net assets initially by the amount of the sale. Then the total effect on net assets must account for the effect of the asset sale on bank reserves. Initially, the sale reduces reserves by the amount of the sale. Then, with no change in the return on reserves, banks will restore reserve holdings by selling assets. Finally, from the public's point of view, they have simply exchanged currency and deposits for income earning assets. However, since the net assets of the Federal Reserve are smaller, transfers to the Treasury are smaller, and the balanced budget government must raise taxes. Once again, a reduction in the Federal Reserve's net assets reduces the public's wealth.[15]

As a result of the reduction in Federal Reserve net assets transfers to the Treasury are reduced and the government must either raise taxes,

---

[15]This analysis is a partial equilibrium one as it ignores any interest rate effect.

reduce expenditures or issue more debt. This is the negative wealth effect that is the equivalent of an open-market sale of Federal Reserve assets prior to the interest on reserve world. In both cases, the policy leaves the public budget constraint unchanged absent consideration of the reduction in transfers to the Treasury.

An expansionary interest on reserves policy

Now, assume that the FOMC desires to expand an underperforming economy by increasing the Federal Reserve's net asset position. Assume further that they do so by decreasing the rate of interest rate on reserves. In response to a decrease in the return to holding reserves, banks increase investments in the economy and decrease reserves, thereby increasing the Federal Reserve's net assets. Total bank assets remain the same as they have simply substituted investment in, for example, short-term treasuries for reserves. The public now has fewer treasuries and more currency and/or deposits. The gain in currency and/or deposits represent a reduction in bank reserves held at the Federal Reserve.

Importantly, total income earning assets have not changed from the banking system's perspective. More importantly, from the non-banking public's perspective, their wealth has not changed. The non-bank public has given treasuries in return for currency and deposits. As in the case of interest on reserve increase, these changes are all done voluntarily. From the perspective of the total of the public, bank owners and non-bank owners, wealth has remained the same.

As in the case of the above contractionary interest on reserves policy, what has changed is the level of Federal Reserve transfers to the Treasury. Now, rather than falling as they did in the contractionary policy, they rise by the amount of the decrease in interest payments on reserves. Then, in a simple world of a balanced budget government, the rise in Federal Reserve transfers to the Treasury must result in reduced taxation. The public is better off by amount of the decrease in taxation. If we measure wealth by the present value of the permanent decrease in taxation then the public is richer by that amount.

The alternative to decreasing the interest on reserves approach to increasing Federal Reserve net assets is the more direct approach of an open-market purchase of assets. The purchase of assets affects the net assets initially by the amount of the purchase. But the total effect on net assets must account for any effect of the asset purchase has on bank reserves. Initially, the purchase increases reserves by the amount of the purchase. With no change in the return on reserves banks will restore reserve holdings by reducing investment in the economy. Finally from the public's point of view they have simply exchanged income earning assets for currency and deposits. However, since the net assets of the Federal Reserve are larger, transfers to the Treasury are larger, and the balanced budget government must reduce taxes. Once again an increase in the Federal Reserve's net assets increases the public's wealth.

The increase in Federal Reserve net assets increases transfers to the Treasury. Then the government must either lower taxes, increase expenditures or recall debt. This is the positive wealth effect that is the equivalent of a Federal Reserve open-market purchase assets prior to the interest on reserve world. In both cases the policy leaves the public budget constraint unchanged absent consideration of the increase in transfers to the Treasury.

The Net Effect of Paying Interest on Reserves

Paying interest on reserves gives the Federal Reserve an interest rate it can control. Or, can it? There is a fundamental economics axiom in a free market world: a firm can set any price it wants and accept the amount the public will buy at that price. Or it can set the quantity it wants to sell, and accept the price the public will require to purchase the set quantity.

This axiom, in the interest on reserves world, means that the Federal Reserve can set the interest rate on reserves, and accept the level of reserves the banking system chooses to hold. Or it can set the level of reserves it wants the banking system to hold, and accept the interest rate on reserves that will result in that level of bank reserves. Importantly, the fact that the Federal Reserve can set the interest rate on reserves and accept the quantity that results, or set the level of reserves it desires and accept the interest rate required to achieve that level does not mean the ability of the Federal Reserve to pay interest on reserves cannot be an effective tool for controlling the money supply.

With interest on reserves when the Federal Reserve wants to conduct a restrictive monetary policy, that is, reduce the M1, M2, and MZM money stocks, all it has to do is increase the rate of interest on bank reserves. At this new higher rate of return, banks will want to substitute reserves for other investments, and the public will substitute deposits for currency. How does the banking system accomplish this transition? Banks will not renew loans, essentially contracting their loan portfolio, or sell other assets and raise the interest rate on deposits. Both of these changes reduce all three money stocks.

Or if the Federal Reserve wants to conduct an expansive monetary policy, that is, increase the M1, M2, and MZM money stocks, all it has to do is decrease the rate of interest on bank reserves. At this new lower rate of return, banks will want to substitute outside investments for bank reserves. How does the banking system accomplish this transition? Banks will expand loans or buy other assets. Because of the new lower interest rate on reserves, the interest rate of bank deposits falls, and the demand for currency rises. The substitution of bank outside investments for reserves and the increase in the demand for currency increase all three money stocks.[16] The end result is that while total bank reserves don't fall, the proportion of total reserves that are required reserves rises.

It is now clear that the ability for a central bank to pay interest on bank reserves can be an effective tool of monetary policy. The interest rate on reserves can be used as the only policy tool or as a supplement to the usual open-market purchase and sales of private financial assets to control the money supply. In effect, by controlling the banking system's desire to hold reserves, the Federal Reserve has reduced the effect of monetary base changes on the money supply. Thus, rather than being an indicator of policy, as the target Fed Funds rate was, the interest rate on reserves is monetary policy.

An alternative way of thinking about this is that the relevant monetary base is currency plus reserves not invested in Federal Reserve issued debt. Either way, the effect of an increase in Federal Reserve assets is to increase the money held by the public, either as bank deposits or currency.

---

[16] For an excellent discussion of monetary policy based on interest payments on reserves, see Cochrane (2014).

In the traditional methodology, an increase in the monetary base gives banks excess reserves to lend or invest in financial assets. Now, however, something new is added as the banks have the option of keeping the reserves and collecting the reserve interest rate, making these newly held reserves Federal Reserve debt. This choice wipes out the usual multiple effect on the money supply of an injection of reserves by the Federal Reserve. Essentially, the newly created reserves become "sterilized" and had effect on the money supply.

It is no coincidence that the ability to pay interest on reserves came about just when it was needed to prevent a possible unprecedented monetary expansion. As excess reserves ballooned at the close of 2008 and were not eliminated as the crisis ebbed, the Federal Reserve had to prevent the normal monetary expansion that would have followed a surge in excess reserves. The approach to solving this problem was the introduction of paying interest on bank reserves, making it more profitable for banks to hold reserves rather than investing the reserves in other market assets, such as loans, public securities or treasuries.

But as the economy continues to expand, the interest payment cost of keeping reserves at a level consistent with the money supply target of the Federal Reserve will continue to rise. What is the source of the funding for these interest payments? The Federal Reserve has income earning assets totaling close to $4.25 trillion. The duration of this portfolio is roughly 13 years, 8.25 years for the Treasury component and 20 years for the MBS component. Combining the current yield curve for treasuries and at current mortgage rates, approximately 2.19% for the treasuries and 4.09% for the MBSs, results in a weighted yield of 2.98% on the entire Federal Reserve portfolio. The Federal Reserve is earning roughly $119 billion annually on its portfolio. These earnings are used to pay the costs of operating the Federal Reserve, and the remainder are transferred to the Treasury. These transfers totaled $80 billion in 2017, down from a peak of $99 billion in 2014 as the yield curve has flattened.[17]

---

[17] It might seem that the Federal Reserve could pay the interest on reserves using its ultimate weapon for funding, the money printing press, and create the annual cost of the 100 basis point interest on $2.611 trillion of bank reserves, approximately $261 billion. However, there is no legal precedent for what is essentially a helicopter drop of currency.

To put the Treasury transfer decline perspective, let's change the discussion from bank reserves to Federal Reserve debt in general. Before bank reserves paid interest, they did not represent a debt of the Federal Reserve System, as they represented no flow liability.[18] We will get back to this issue, but for now, consider a banking system in equilibrium and a central bank that has a zero balance. Further, continue to assume that this central bank is owned by the Treasury so that all earnings (positive or negative) go to the Treasury and then directly to taxpayers.

Now, let this central bank issue its own debt. The public buys this new debt and gives up money of equal value, so that from their perspective, this transaction is a wash. This is similar to what is called an "open-market operation," but in that case, the central bank is selling outside debt it has created, rather than assets it held. In every way this is a sale of a financial asset for base money and has the same effect. It destroys base money but the public is held harmless as it gives up monetary base and gets an equal in value Federal Reserve bond.

This new level of publicly held debt implies that the Treasury, as owner of the central bank, must turn over to the central bank all servicing costs of this new debt. The public gave up money and got debt of equal value, but now has new tax obligations of equal value. Thus, on net this issue of central bank debt makes the public worse off by the amount of the debt issue. Further evidence that this new debt issue is the same as an open-market sale of Federal Reserve assets.

In contrast, let the central bank buy debt from the public and issue currency to do so. The public sells the debt and gets equal value in currency, so from their perspective, the deal is a net wash. But now the central bank has revenue that belongs to the Treasury and, thus, to taxpayers. As a result, the net effect of this central bank purchase of publicly held assets makes the public wealthier by the amount of the central bank purchase.

Current Federal Reserve policy is essentially a combination of the two actions discussed immediately above: the almost simultaneous purchase

---

[18] In one sense, this addresses the issue of what is a debt? To be a debt must imply some restraint on the issuer of the debt. Reserves are like currency, and a holder of currency can take that currency to the Federal Reserve, but all they can get is new version of the same currency. Neither reserves nor currency are debts of the Federal Reserve. This issue will discussed at length in Chapter 19.

of publicly held debt and the issue of Federal Reserve bonds. After all the bailouts and other issues, it all boils down to the Federal Reserve adding about $3.41 trillion in assets to its portfolio, $1.67 trillion in treasuries and $1.74 trillion in MBSs. These additions to its assets were then partially offset by what was, for all intents and purposes, the issue of about $2.61 trillion in new Federal Reserve liabilities, bank reserves.

The Federal Reserve's net increase of its reserve liability assets from the beginning of 2008 to mid-2015 was about $800 billion, a level just about double its asset level at the outset of the crisis. Since traditional measures of the monetary base take no account of reserves as an income yielding asset of banks, these traditional measures are of little value for forecasting future inflation. For example, from the beginning of 2008 to mid-2015, the monetary base grew by 464%, but the three measures of the money stock grew by less than half the growth in the base. For this period, the M1 money stock grew by 218%, the M2 money stock grew by 160% and the MZM money stock grew by 164%.

A Corrected Measure of the Monetary Base

Clearly, in the world of paying interest on reserves, we need a new way to measure the monetary base for it to have the same meaning as what we used to term *high-powered money*. Bank investments in reserves, as income yielding assets, are different than investments using reserves to invest in the economy or in treasuries. Banks in converting reserves to market investments or converting market investment to reserves affects the money supply.

By paying interest on reserves the Federal Reserve sterilized much of their increase in assets by turning part of the monetary base, reserves, into a Federal Reserve liability. Given that the Federal Reserve fixed the rate of return on this liability, the banks determined the amount of their reserves they chose to be Federal Reserve liabilities. We averted the inflation that would have occurred if the money supply had expanded at the almost 25% annual rate of the monetary base. Instead, the various measures of the money supply increased at rates significantly below the rate of growth of the traditional base, as much of the base increase was neutralized by interest on reserves regime established by the Federal Reserve in late 2008.

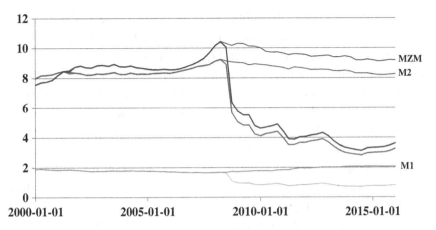

Figure 15.4. Traditional Versus Adjusted Monetary Base Money Multipliers

One way to measure the effective monetary base, defined as that part of the base that is actually available to support increases in the money stock, is to take the excess reserves out of the equation. As shown above and presented in Figure 15.4, the relation between the money supply measures, M1, M2, MZM, and the effective monetary base has remained very stable throughout the 21st century. Thus, the normal relation between the monetary base and the various measures of the money supply, appropriately adjusted for interest on reserves, remains unchanged.

Conclusion

The emphasis throughout the history of monetary policy analysis has always been on actions by central banks that increase or decrease the money supply. These money supply changes were intended to have short-run effects on the economy. In particular, in a period of economic downturn, in theory at least, an increase in the money supply would through its effect on the wealth of the public, lead to increased economic activity. Or, the monetary response to an overheated economy, a decrease in the money supply would reduce the wealth of the public, and cool the economy.

The traditional money supply actions of a central bank were accomplished through the central bank buying or selling its assets. For example, consider the response to an over-heated economy of an open-market sale of central bank assets to the public. Here the public exchanges some of its holdings of currency and deposits for central bank assets. The currency and deposits received by the central bank are essentially incinerated. The asset reduction then reduces the central bank's transfers to the Treasury, so the government must raise taxes, reduce expenditures or increase debt. On net then, the public is poorer and economic activity slows.

When the banking system is brought into the equation, the effect of the exchange of the public's currency and deposits for central bank assets raises a complication. The deposits part of the payment for central bank assets reduces the reserves of the banking system that now has to restore its reserves to their required level by exchanging investments for reserves. These exchanges reduce bank investments, which is exactly what the open-market sale of central bank's assets was intended to accomplish.

All of the above analysis assumes that the banking system holds essentially no reserves in excess of the level required by the Federal Reserve. Historically, at least for the entire post-World War II period, this was true as excess reserves earn no income for the banks. Today, we have the new world where excess reserves represent an investment for the banking system. Moreover, because these reserves pay interest that must be paid by the Federal Reserve, they represent a liability of the Federal Reserve.

The present is a new world where the Federal Reserve holds financial instruments from the economy as assets and issues financial instruments in the form of bank reserves as liabilities. However, if we concentrate only on net assets, nothing really has changed. Changes in net assets play the same policy role as changes in assets did before interest on reserves. However, because excess reserves are now an investment, reserves matter in a way they never did before. Now a reduction in reserves, assets constant, plays the same role as an increase in assets played in the before interest on reserves world.

Also, the paying of interest on reserves has given the target Fed Funds rate a whole new role in the monetary policy world. This role is the topic of Chapter 16.

Chapter 16

The Fed Funds Market in an Interest on Reserves World

Introduction

From all the press about when will the Federal Reserve raise interest rates, one would believe that the Federal Reserve has a market interest rate dial that gives it complete control of all security and loan markets. The interest rate in question for the press is the Federal Reserve's target Fed Funds rate, the rate of interest paid by banks for overnight borrowing.[1] Indeed, with the onset of paying interest on bank reserve balances, the Fed Funds rate pronouncements now have an immediate effect on the interest rate on reserves.

Prior to the introduction of interest on bank reserve balances that began in October of 2008, changes in the Fed Funds target rate were taken by the market to indicate the direction of Federal Reserve policy. An announced change in the Fed Funds target rate, for example an increase, indicated that the Federal Reserve intended to contract its holdings of

---

[1]The Federal Open-Market Committee (FOMC) sets a target level for the overnight Fed Funds rate. Historically the Fed Funds market has historically facilitated the transfer of the most liquid funds among depository institutions. The New York Federal Reserve Bank then uses open-market operations to change the supply of reserves in the system which, in conjunction with IOER, influence overnight Fed Funds to trade around this policy target rate or within the target rate range. See https://www.newyorkfed.org/aboutthefed/fedpoint/fed15.html for a more complete discussion of the Fed Funds market and its relation to interest on reserves.

assets. This contraction took the form of open-market sales of Federal Reserve assets. Such a sale would reduce bank reserves and with reserves more scarce, the overnight borrowing rate, the Fed Funds rate, would rise.

In the world of interest on bank reserves, the Fed Funds rate plays a very different role. On the one hand it is now expressed in band form rather than a single target. Second the member banks of the Federal Reserve System that before interest on reserves were on both sides of this market are now only suppliers of Fed Funds. The buyers of Fed Funds are largely foreign banks and the big suppliers of Fed Funds are financial institutions that are not members of the Federal Reserve System and as a result do not receive interest on their reserve balances.

Finally, as we shall see when reserves pay interest even no change in a Fed Funds target rate may represent monetary policy.

The Market for Fed Funds

With the onset of interest on reserves, Federal Reserve member banks were no longer on the demand side of the Fed Funds market. They had plenty of reserves and, moreover, both required and excess reserves earn the same rate of return. As a result, the market size fell significantly. Figure 16.1 shows the Fed Funds market volume for the period from October 2006 to February 2016. Prior to the introduction of interest on reserves, Fed Funds market volume averaged about $120 billion. Once the

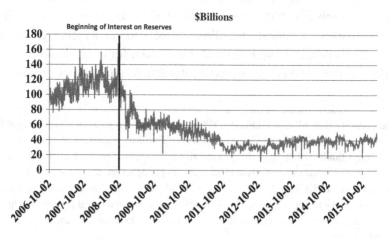

Figure 16.1.   Fed Funds Market Volume

Federal Reserve began paying interest on member bank reserves, market volume fell rapidly and by the close of 2015 was averaging $40 billion.

Also, prior to the interest rate on reserves Federal Reserve target for Fed Funds was in terms of single rate target. Changes in this target rate indicated the path of future Federal Reserve policy. A target rate increase raises market expectations that the Federal Reserve was going to engage in an open-market sale of assets. Such a sale would reduce bank reserves, making them scarcer and, as a result, increase the Fed Funds rate. The same transaction would reduce the money supply.

The introduction of interest on reserves changed how the target Fed Funds rate was announced and its implications. First, the Fed Funds rate target is now expressed as a range and the upper bound of that range is the interest rate on reserves. This is not surprising, since the level of excess reserves implies that the supply of Fed Funds is completely elastic at the reserve interest rate. Member banks will be demanders of Fed Funds only if it was possible for them to acquire Fed Funds at rates of interest below the interest rate on reserves.

Currently, the largest supplier of federal funds is federal home loan banks, but they are also supplied by GSEs, such as Fannie Mae and Freddie Mac. Not surprisingly, federal home loan banks are not members of the Federal Reserve, do not receive interest on excess reserves and supply about 75% of all federal funds. Moreover, the demanders of federal funds are largely foreign banks or bank holding companies that are, by and large, also foreign owned.[2]

The Federal Reserve participates in the Fed Funds market, it buys reserves from non-member institutions by offering overnight reverse repos. The reverse part is that Federal Reserve offers to buy overnight reserves from non-member entities at the lower bound of their Fed Funds target range. Essentially, the Federal Reserve pays these non-member entities at the lower Fed Funds target rate for overnight for a limited amount of reserves. The upper bound of the Fed Funds target range determines the interest rate on the reserves of member banks.

Figure 16.2 shows the path of Federal Reserve Fed Funds high and low target rates, the interest rate on reserves and rate at which reverse repos are offered. The figure also shows the effective Fed Funds rate defined as the

---

[2] Two sources for who buys and sells Fed Funds are Gara *et al.* (2013a, 2013b).

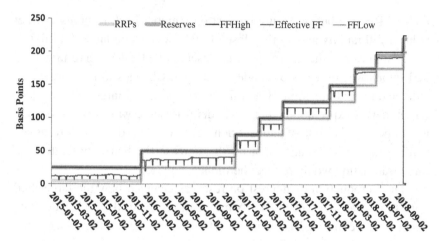

Figure 16.2.   Reserve Interest Rates, Reverse Repo Rates and Upper and Lower Fed Funds

weighted average of all transactions. As the figure shows, the rate offered by the Federal Reserve on reverse repos is the lower bound of the Fed Funds target range. Until June of 2018, the upper bound of the Fed Funds target range equaled the rate of interest offered on bank reserves. Subsequent to June, the interest rate on reserves was set five basis points below the upper bound of the Fed Funds target range. The effective Fed Funds rate is defined as the weighted average of all transactions.

Since the beginning of interest on reserves, the level of excess reserves has dwarfed the activity in the Fed Funds market. Figure 16.3 shows the levels of the potential supply of funds, excess reserves, and the level of activity in the Fed Funds market. Clearly, this is very different from the pre-interest-on-reserves Fed Funds market. Now, the potential supply of Fed Funds from excess reserves dominates the scale of Fed Funds activity. Since the interest rate paid on reserves is the upper bound of the Fed Funds target range, no member bank would supply Fed Funds at any rate below this upper bound. In general, we would not expect member banks to be a major player in the Fed Funds market.

Except at the margin member banks are not suppliers of Fed Funds. Further, the reverse repo operations conducted by the Federal Reserve are always at the lower bound of the Fed Funds target range as shown in Figure 16.2. Figure 16.4 shows a summary of the Fed Funds market for

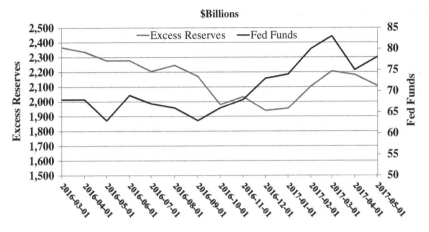

Figure 16.3. Excess Reserve and Federal Funds Market Size

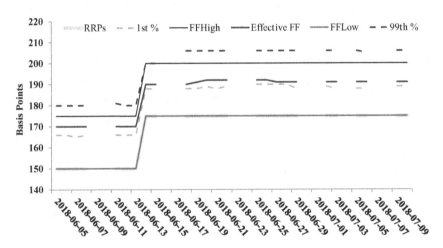

Figure 16.4. Feds Funds Transaction Distribution and Upper and Lower Fed Funds Targets

the period from June 5, 2018, shortly before the June 14, 2018 increase in the Fed Funds target range from 1.50–1.75 to 1.75–2.00. The breaks in the figure are a result of the absence of a market on holidays, July 4, and weekends.

The figure shows the target range, the 1st and 99th percentiles of the Fed Funds transactions distribution the effective Fed Funds rate and the reverse repo rate. Since eligible institutions can participate in the reverse repo offering at the lower bound of the target range even at the 1st percentile Fed Funds are traded at well above the lower bound.[3] Before the June 14, 2018 increase in the Fed Funds target from 175 to 200 basis points, the interest rate on reserves was set equal to the upper bound. Since then the interest rate on reserves has been set at five basis points below the upper bound. The fact that the 99th percentile transactions are above the upper bound indicates the minimal participation of member banks in the Fed Funds market.

Monetary Policy, Market Interest Rates and the Fed Funds Rate

In spite of the decline of the scale of the Fed Funds market, the press still seems to place great weight on the FOMC statements about future changes in their target range for the Fed Funds rate. In one sense, this press concentration on changes in the Fed Fund target range is justified; but not because it is an indication of future policy. The announced changes have to be taken in the context of movements in market interest rates. The fact that the upper bound of the Fed Funds target range is the interest rate on reserves is the key to understanding the importance of this rate.

Prior to the interest on reserves regime, announcements of changes in the then single Fed Funds rate target indicated the direction of future monetary policy. Increases in the Fed Funds target, indicated monetary actions that were designed to reduce the money supply, or at least reduce its rate of growth. What is important here is that it was Federal Reserve actions in money markets that mattered, rather than target Fed Funds rate announcements. Even more important it was the coming actual changes in the money supply that mattered. Furthermore, while changes in the economy

---

[3] Overnight reverse repos, ON RRP, operations support interest rate control by setting a floor on wholesale short-term interest rates, beneath which financial institutions with access to these facilities should be unwilling to lend funds. ON RRP operations are conducted at a pre-announced offering rate, against Treasury securities collateral, and are open to a wide range of financial firms, including some that are not eligible to earn interest on balances at the Federal Reserve. See https://www.newyorkfed.org/markets/domestic-market-operations/monetary-policy-implementation/repo-reverse-repo-agreements.

could affect the money supply, these changes were dwarfed by the effect of Federal Reserve policy on the money supply.

In the interest on reserves regime, market forces play a much bigger role in determining the money supply. The previous chapter discussed the use of the interest on reserves rate as a tool of monetary policy. Increases in reserve interest rates, market interest rates constant, result in reductions in the money supply as banks substitute market investments for reserves. Decreases in reserves interest rates, again market interest rates constant, result in increases in the money supply as banks reduce reserves and increase investments in the economy.

The caveat in the above discussion of interest on reserves as monetary policy, is especially important because it touches on a matter that is of upmost importance. Namely, in the interest on reserves world, the money supply is as much a market phenomenon as it is a Federal Reserve one. In the no interest on reserves world, money supply changes required Federal Reserve action. Now, market interest rate changes with no Federal Reserve action, affect the money supply. Suddenly a "no action" by the Federal Reserve, is a monetary policy action!

Today, we are in a world where Federal Reserve inaction is a monetary policy action! In contrast, in the old non-interest on reserves world, Federal Reserve inaction had no effect on the money supply, no matter how market interest rates changed. Now to ensure that market interest rate changes do not affect the money supply beyond the Federal Reserve target for money growth, requires careful changes in the target range for Fed Funds rate. The reality is that Fed Funds market has little to do with the money supply. Rather, it is the upper bound of the Fed Funds target range that matters since that target is the interest rate on reserves.

In this new world of interest on reserves, it is clear that the reserve interest rate is an important part of monetary policy. But it is only a part of policy. The real policy is in the relation between the reserves interest rate and the banking system's alternative to reserves in their investment portfolio. This determines the growth in the money supply. The combination of the Federal Reserve paying interest on reserves and being active in the RRP market has produced a natural limit to both the upper and lower Fed Funds rate target. First, the interest rate on reserves and the approximate $2 trillion level of excess reserves means that reserves will be completely elastically supplied at the interest rate on reserves, the upper bound of the Fed Funds target range. Second, given the level of activity in the RRP market, no supplier of reserves would take less than the interest rate on RRPs.[4] The overnight RRPs are offered at the lower bound of the Fed Funds target range.

In spite of the decline of the importance of the Fed Funds market, the press still seems to place great weight on the FOMC statements about future changes in their target for the Fed Funds rate. While the Fed Funds rate does not directly affect any other interest rate in the economy, changes in the Federal Reserve's target for the Fed Funds rate is a Federal Reserve policy rather than an indicator of a future policy.

In the world of interest on reserves, the real measure of monetary policy as it relates to interest rates is what is happening to the spread between bank market alternatives and the interest rate on reserves. Now the Fed Funds rate upper bound is tied to the interest rate on reserves and both are under direct control of the Federal Reserve.

In the interest on reserves world, changes in the target Fed Funds rate, not really a target at all since the Fed Funds upper bound is set five basis points above the interest rate on reserves. The policy is the target and requires no action in addition to the announcement itself. A Fed Funds upper target increase is a reserve interest rate increase. With no change in market interest rates then the spread between market rates and reserve rates is reduced and the banking system responds by increasing reserves at the expense of investments in the economy. The end result is a reduction in the supply of investment funds for the economy and an increase in interest rates. Both are indicative of a "tighter" monetary policy with one caveat. That caveat is that market interest rates remain unchanged except for the impact of the policy action.

In a very important sense, the market for Fed Funds is irrelevant to monetary policy. It is only the upper bound of the Fed Funds target range

---

[4]These transactions are handled by the Money Desk at the New York Federal Reserve Bank. Overnight Reverse Repos (ON RRP) operations support interest rate control by setting a floor on wholesale short-term interest rates, beneath which financial institutions with access to these facilities should be unwilling to lend funds. In a reverse repo transaction, the Desk sells securities to a counterparty subject to an agreement to repurchase the securities at a later date at a higher repurchase price. Reverse repo transactions temporarily reduce the quantity of reserve balances in the banking system.

that has any effect on the money supply. But the upper bound is not a target, but a reality, that is totally determined by the Federal Reserve. The participants in the Fed Funds market play no role in the achievement of the upper bound. Thus, the effective Fed Funds rate plays no role in determining the money supply in the current interest on reserves world.

Changes in the Fed Funds Federal Reserve determined upper bound represents real monetary policy. An increase in the upper bound, i.e., the rate of interest on bank reserves, given no change in market interest rates, will result in banks adding to their reserve holdings by contracting non-reserve investments. As banks contract non-reserve investment in order to increase reserves, the money supply necessarily falls. A decrease in the upper bound, i.e., the rate of interest on bank reserves, given no change in market interest rates, will result in banks reducing their reserve holdings and increasing non-reserve investments. As banks increase non-reserve investments in order to decrease reserves, the money supply necessarily increases.

Conclusion

By the close of 2008, the worst of the short-term liquidity crisis was over but not Federal Reserve actions that affected the economy. Many of the possible negative effects of the unprecedented expansion of Federal Reserve assets was offset by their simultaneously issuing liabilities in the form of bank reserves. The introduction of paying interest on bank reserves mitigated the effect of the huge expansion in Federal Reserve assets by offsetting much of that increase with Federal Reserve liabilities.

The change in the Federal Reserve from a central bank that did policy via changes in its asset holdings to a central bank that conducted policy through changes in what would become net assets is important. At the same time, the role of the Fed Funds market and the Federal Reserve target for that market changed in a dramatic way. In the pre-interest on reserves world, changes in the Federal Reserve Fed Funds rate target indicated the path of soon to be undertaken policy in the form of open-market treasury transactions. Now, the dual Fed Funds target sets a lower bound on the rate at which Fed Funds are traded and the upper bound is in the form of the interest rate on reserves.

The bottom line in all this is that while the Fed Funds market is important to the participants in that it gives them access to overnight reserves it is totally irrelevant to Federal Reserve policy. That said, however, the upper bound of the Fed Funds target range that prior to June 2018 was exactly equal to the interest rate of reserves, and is now just five basis points above the interest rate on reserves, is the principle element in Federal Reserve policy. Since the difference between the rate of return in the market and the rate of interest on reserves, determines bank actions, that difference affects the money supply and the economy.

These changes have put us is in a unique bind. Prior to interest on reserves, when the Federal Reserve did nothing, nothing happened to the money supply. That was true even if market interest rates changed. Now, Federal Reserve inaction when market interest rates change, has a money supply effect that must be countered if policy is to be money supply neutral. This fact explains the path of changes in the upper bound of the Federal Reserve's Fed Funds target rate as it tracks market interest rates.

Chapter 17

Can Monetary Policy Exist in a Zero or Very Low Interest Rate World?

Introduction

Despite the recent upward trend in interest rates, the unavoidable fact is that interest rates have been, on average, declining for more than 30 years. Does this trend say anything about the future of monetary policy? If monetary policy is about influencing interest rates, then are we approaching a period where monetary policy is less effective? In older economics literature equilibrium interest rates this low would have placed the economy in what was referred to as a "liquidity trap." In this so-called trap, monetary policy would be ineffective in that economic stimulation required reducing interest rates and interest rates were at their minimum. The idea was expressed in the statement that "you can pull on a string but you can't push it."[1]

Historically, central banks have produced income for their owners, the central government. Given this history, will historically low interest rates affect the ability of central banks to provide government with essentially free income? Given the unique ability of a central bank as the monopoly issuer of legal tender, it can and does run the money printing press to acquire assets. But, an unanswered question is: does this create value if the assets acquired only represent the ability to sell the asset back with no revenue generated during the period the asset was held? Essentially, the

---

[1] I encourage the reader to review any current principles of economics textbook. For a concise review of this idea and its current relevance see Arias and Wen (2014).

question is: Does monetary policy generate its effect on the economy by creating wealth or by lowering interest rates? These are the questions that are addressed in the following section.

30 Plus Years of Declining Interest Rates: Does it Matter?

The decline in interest rates has been going on for several decades as is apparent in Figure 17.1, which shows constant maturity of 10-year, 1-year and 3-month treasuries. Moreover, this decline cannot be attributed to falling inflation although inflation was slightly higher, 2.86% for the first decade as compared to 1.94% for the following two decades. As one would expect, the 3-month and 1-year treasuries are much more volatile than the 10-year treasuries. What is abundantly clear is the downward trend in all three interest rates. At the beginning of the period, in 1985, the 10-year treasuries were trading between 8.47% and 7.40% and after reaching a low of 1.37% on July 8, 2016, were still trading at below 3% on July 9, 2018.

As shown in Figure 17.1, inflation, as measured by the four quarter rate of change in the GDP deflator, fell very little over the 30-year period. Thus, the falling nominal interest rates shown in the figure are indicative of falling real interest rates as well. Figure 17.2 shows the path of real interest rates, the difference between contemporaneous nominal interest

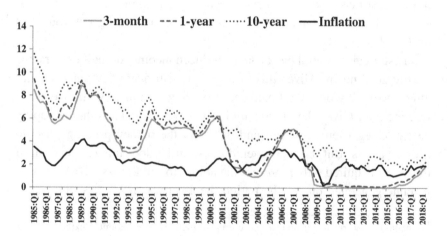

Figure 17.1.　Treasury Rates and Inflation

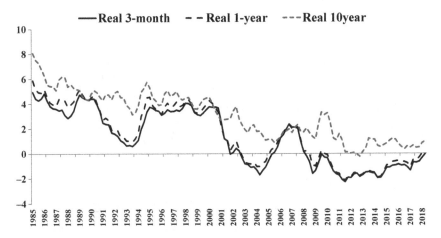

Figure 17.2.   Real Treasury Rates

rates and the GDP deflator. The downward trend in real interest rates is at least as apparent in this figure as it was in Figure 17.1. What is also apparent in both Figures 17.1 and 17.2 is that, as expected, the two short-term rates are much more closely connected with the business cycle than the long-term rates. Moreover, for the entire period, the real 3-month rates have been negative for just more than one-third of the quarters. Since 2000, more than two-thirds of the quarters have negative 3-month real rates.

In spite of the general decline in Treasury yields over this 30-year period, on average, the term structure has not changed. As Figure 17.3 shows, while the spread between the 10-year and 1-year treasuries has fluctuated considerably, these fluctuations have been around the mean spread of 1.52%. The fact that the spread between the 10-year and 1-year treasuries has remained constant over this entire period is indicative of a general decline in the entire term structure of interest rates. The real question, however, is while short-term real interest rates have been negative for most of the last decade, can this be an equilibrium? Further, if so, what is the implication, if any, for central banks and their ability to generate wealth (generate seigniorage) via money creation? Finally, can monetary policy have any effect on the economy in a zero interest rate world?

As further evidence that negative interest rates can not only exist but can also persist, Figure 17.4 shows the interest rates on Treasury Inflation Protected Securities (TIPS) for the period of January 2008–March 2018.

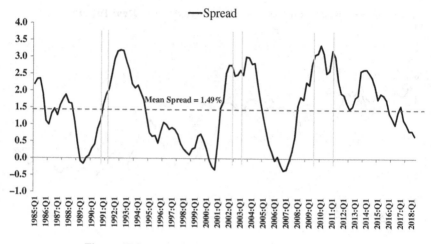

Figure 17.3.   Treasury Nominal 10-Year 1-Year Spread

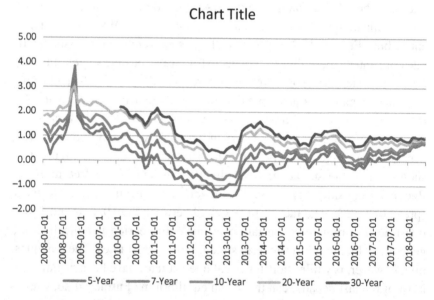

Figure 17.4.   Treasury Inflation Protected Interest Rates

In fact, all of the TIPS maturities with the exception of the 30-Year TIPS had brushes with negative yields. For the shorter-term TIPS, these brushes with negative yields were not brushes but real sweeps. The 5-year TIPS had negative yields that began as early as the beginning of

2010 and persisted until September 2014, returned briefly in 2015 and then again in 2016. The 7-year TIPS had negative yields from August 2011 until July 2013 with another shorter period in 2016. Then, the 10-year TIPS had a long period of negative yields that began in December 2011 and lasted until June 2013 and returned briefly in 2016. Even the 20-year TIPS had a very brief flirtation with negative yields in 2012. Only the 30-year TIPS escaped the projections of the market that real yields for the future looked dire.

The Possibility of a World with Zero or Negative Interest Rates

Interest rates are measures of our ability to trade present income for future income. For example, the 1-year interest rate tells us the price of a dollar of income 1 year from the present. Thus, a 1-year interest rate of 1% indicates that we can buy a 1-year-from-now dollar for a current payment of 99.0099 cents. Or a −1% interest rate indicates that the cost of that same 1-year-from-now dollar will require a current payment of $1.010101.

So much for the mechanics of interest rates. The question that must be answered is, if this is a market for future income, then how is the interest rate, the equilibrium price in this market, determined? Further, who are the suppliers and who are the demanders?

Both sides of this market stem from the fact that life is finite and that the ability to turn time into income is age dependent. For given effort and time, the lifetime age-earnings cycle can be described as parabolic. It starts low, gradually rises to its peak, and then falls for the remainder of one's working years.

Assuming that lifetime utility functions exhibit diminishing returns to consumption, individuals will maximize their utility by smoothing consumption. This consumption smoothing, coupled with a parabolic age-earnings profile, implies that individuals will borrow, i.e., supply future income, in their younger years and then save, i.e., demand future income in their middle years to be consumed when their income falls below their desired smoothed consumption.

At any point in time, it is the young that are supplying future income. That is, the young borrow to consume some of the income they will earn in the future. When they repay in the future, they supply income to those who were the lenders. As the younger generation ages, their consumption is above their earnings, but will fall below their earnings later in life. During the years of excess earnings relative to consumption, individuals become demanders of future income to be consumed as their earnings fall below their smoothed consumption.

If this is all there is, then the equilibrium interest rate will be determined by the relative amounts of suppliers and demanders of future income. Further, the relative number of young versus middle-aged will be critical. The greater this ratio, the more future income that will be supplied and the lower the price of future income, i.e., the higher the interest rate, which is the inverse of the price of future income.

Now, couple this simple, but incomplete, discussion of the equilibrium interest rate with declining fertility rates. We have an ever smaller young generation supplying future income relative to the demanders of future income. Declining supply of future income means that the price of future income is rising, i.e., interest rates are falling. Thus, demographics are one factor contributing to the declining real interest rates presented in Figure 17.2.[2]

In addition to the young as suppliers and the middle-aged as demanders, there is another factor to the supply of future income. The output of the nation is produced by a combination of capital and labor. The demanders of future income can buy capital as a substitute for promises of the young to deliver income in the future.

Demanders of future income do not care about the source of their future income, so capital and the supplying portion of the working population must compete. The rate of return on capital, the equivalent of an interest rate, and the interest rate on future income sold by the young must be equal.

The real question then is: can the rate of return on capital be negative in any long-run equilibrium? If not, then there cannot be a long run with a negative interest rate equilibrium, no matter how small the young cohort of future income suppliers gets. The recent 7-year span of negative yields on short-term treasuries suggests that a negative interest rate world can persist in the short run.

---

[2]For an interesting paper that presents this argument as a predictor of the future, see Walker (2016). https://www.fraserinstitute.org/sites/default/files/why-are-interest-rates-so-low.pdf.

In this short-run equilibrium with negative real interest rates, the question is whether the normal working of monetary policy is possible. Specifically, can central banks still deliver seigniorage to their government owners when real interest rates are negative? Finally, can traditional monetary policy still be effective when real interest is negative? Below, these two questions are addressed at length.

Measuring Seigniorage

Seigniorage was originally the price that a mint charged to turn raw precious metals into money in the form of coinage. As we have moved away from coinage, seigniorage has taken on some additional, but closely related, meanings. When paper replaced coinage as the basic form of money, this same term has been applied to the revenue received by the producers of this new form of money. In general, central banks in almost every all nation, have a monopoly in the production of essentially zero cost legal tender.[3] When central banks issue this legal money, they acquire assets from the public, generally financial assets. The value of these financial assets can be viewed as seigniorage in the same sense as the charges for minting coinage.

In the current central banking world there are two forms of seigniorage. First, as a result of the close financial connection between a nation's central bank and that nation's Treasury, central bank profits belong to the Treasury. Since these profits stem from the earnings on the assets purchased when creating money, they are flows that can be called seigniorage. Second, the flows from central bank assets can be increased by printing money faster than economic growth, i.e., through inflation. This latter form of seigniorage is usually referred to as inflationary finance of government expenditures.

How does this form of seigniorage work? It begins with the central bank buying government debt, or any asset for that matter, at a rate faster than the rate of growth in the economy. The result of this activity is a reduction in the value of the money stock. As the public desires to

---

[3] Central banks can be privately owned or what is almost universally true be part of the government. In the latter case, there is usually some form of separate control for the bank.

maintain a given level of real value of their money holdings, albeit lower than they would without a falling value of the currency, they must continually add to their nominal money holdings.[4] In responding to this demand, induced by the central bank printing money too fast, the central bank can continue to buy assets from the public. This continual increase in nominal money required to maintain a fixed real money stock can be viewed as revenue and fits the general idea behind seigniorage.

This second form of seigniorage allows government to finance expenditures by issuing debt that is purchased by the central bank. As such, it is not dependent on transfers of flows from the central bank to the government, so this from of seigniorage is unaffected by interest rates. What about the first form that appears to depend on the central bank transferring earnings on its assets to the government? It would seem that purchases of zero-yield assets by the central bank financed by printing money would not generate seigniorage. But such purchases can be used to cover government deficits.

Seigniorage with Zero-Yield Assets

Imagine a world with interest rates of zero. Certainly, short-term Treasury real rates of return were negative for at least a 5-year period. Can a central bank generate seigniorage if the assets purchased by the central bank with printing press money do not have a positive yield? The answer as we shall see is positive.

Assume a central bank increases its assets through the purchase of zero-yield newly issued 1-year government debt, either directly from the Treasury or from the public. In the case of a direct-from-the-Treasury purchase, the entire purchase is seigniorage, in the traditional use of that term, since the newly issued money goes directly to the government while the debt remains permanently with the central bank.

In the case of a private market purchase of newly issued 1-year government debt, the newly issued money goes to the public and replaces the money the public gave the government to buy the debt. However, even here the total purchase is seigniorage since the new debt now does not have to be repaid because when it matures, it is simply replaced with new

---

[4]The limits to such seigniorage are discussed in Auernheimer (1974).

debt. Therefore, buying debt from the public is equivalent to simply buying debt direct from the Treasury.

Further, assuming that the government keeps expenditures constant, the taxes that would have been necessary to repay the debt are now unnecessary. As a result, the public is better off by the amount of the purchase independent of whether the purchase was direct from the Treasury or in the open market.

Now, assume a permanent increase in central bank assets consisting of privately issued debt such as Mortgage-Backed Securities (MBSs). How does such a purchase affect the economy?

If the central bank was privately owned, then the bank owners are better off by the amount of the asset purchase, and the constraint for the rest of the public is unchanged. Therefore, the total increase in assets is still seigniorage since they are the receipts from coining money production. Importantly, this result is not dependent on the assets having a positive yield. In fact, the result is valid even if the assets have a negative yield.

If the central bank is owned by the government, which is the case for almost all central banks, then the government can use the new assets for expenditures. These new assets allow for a one-period reduction in the taxes necessary to fund that period's expenditures. Therefore, the total increase in assets is still seigniorage since they are the receipts from coining money.

From a monetary policy standpoint, the question is how is the public's budget constraint affected? If the central bank must transfer all assets to the government, then the assets rather than tax revenues can be used for expenditures. The public has the same total assets, cash plus MBSs, but their total tax bill for this period is smaller by the central bank's purchases of MBSs. In the final analysis, this case is identical to buying 1-year government debt.

Monetary Policy in the Developed World

Monetary policy that changes the money supply works through what has historically been termed a "wealth" or "real balance" effect.[5] This form of

---

[5]The effect works whether the money in question is privately or central bank issued as long as the private money is convertible into central bank money. See Saving (1970).

monetary policy in a steady state world is about changing the public's demand for aggregate output by altering the public's budget constraint. If it is a permanent change in the public's budget constraint, it must result in a once-and-for-all change in the public's aggregate demand for goods and services and must have a once-and-for-all effect on either total output or the price level.

The current goal of the developed world's central banks is in the form of an inflation target. In fact, European Central Bank (ECB), the Bank of Japan, the Bank of England and the Federal Reserve have publicly announced inflation targets of 2%. Considering that the Federal Reserve, the ECB, the Bank of Japan and the Bank of England have as one of their mandates "price stability," how is a positive inflation target consistent with this goal? Put simply, what does price stability mean? In at least one sense, it would mean maintaining the purchasing power of the Euro, the Yen, the Pound or the Dollar. But what does price stability mean in practice?

On this matter, the ECB's Governing Council has announced a quantitative definition of price stability: *Price stability is defined as a year-on-year increase in the Harmonised Index of Consumer Prices (HICP) for the euro area of below 2%.*

The Federal Reserve's FOMC judges that: ... *inflation at the rate of 2 percent (as measured by the annual change in the price index for personal consumption expenditures, or PCE) is most consistent over the longer run with the Federal Reserve's mandate for price stability and maximum employment.*

The Bank of Japan Act states that the bank's monetary policy should be aimed at achieving price stability, thereby contributing to the sound development of the national economy. Price stability from their perspective meets the following criterion:

Price stability is important because it provides the foundation for the nation's economic activity. In a market economy, individuals and firms make decisions on whether to consume or invest, based on the prices of goods and services. When prices fluctuate, individuals and firms find it hard to make appropriate consumption and investment decisions, and this can hinder the efficient allocation of resources in the economy. Unstable prices can also distort income distribution. On this basis, the Bank set the "price stability target" at 2 percent in terms of the year-on-year rate of change in the consumer price index (CPI) in January 2013, and has made a commitment to achieving this target at the earliest possible time.

The Bank of England states that *The Bank's monetary policy objective is to deliver price stability — low inflation — and, subject to that, to support the Government's economic objectives including those for growth and employment. Price stability is defined by the Government's inflation target of 2%.*

Reaching these uniform, across-the-world inflation targets requires that the money supply grow faster than real GDP, assuming that other factors that influence the public's demand for currency are unchanged. One of these factors that is of particular importance is market interest rates. As the rate of return on financial assets falls, as it has over the past 30 years, the public's willingness to hold cash even with very low, perhaps even zero return, increases simply because there is little or no cost to doing so.

For the 7-year period since the 2008 financial crisis, the rate of growth in the expanded definition of the United States money stock, M2, was 6.3%. For this same period, the GDP velocity of M2, a measure of the effect of falling interest rates on the public's willingness to hold money, fell at a rate of 2.9%. Real GDP grew at 1.8% for this same period. The result using the simple equation of exchange is a US inflation rate of 1.6%, just larger than the measured rate of inflation of the GDP deflator of 1.4%.

As a result of interest rate and money demand uncertainty, the actions required to increase the money supply or interest rate target by the appropriate amount to obtain the targeted inflation are subject to uncertainty. Part of this uncertainty is that at the time of policy implementation, the actual underlying rate of inflation and/or the equilibrium market rate of interest is unknown.[6]

If the goal of policy is to have steady state inflation, then policy must continually increase the money supply at a rate above the rate of growth

---

[6] This problem is related to the question of targets versus indicators of monetary policy and is discussed extensively in Saving (1967).

in the economy. In this case, in addition to the seigniorage from the initial issue of currency, the government collects revenue from the public's desire to maintain its real money balances.[7]

In the United States, the money supply is not entirely generated by the Federal Reserve as evidenced by the fact that currency is less than half of the narrowest definition of the money supply, M1, and just over 10% of the broader measures. Thus, the majority of what we term money is generated by the private sector. In a simple world, the greater the private component of the money supply, the smaller the maximum revenue that can be raised through inflation.[8]

Can Monetary Policy Still Work in a Zero or Negative Interest Rate World?

The primary charge of every central bank is related to price stability, defined by the world's principal central banks as a steady 2% decline in the real value of the relevant currency. If we accept the premise that the price level is related to the demand for money and its supply, then in order for the central bank to reach its inflation goal, it must have the ability to change the money supply. How do these changes happen? Principally, central bank money supply changes happen in two ways.

First, at least historically, monetary policy principally involved setting what has been referred to as the "bank rate." Here, I use the term "bank rate" to mean the rate that the central bank charges for loans to the financial markets, principally banks. A reduction in the bank rate will lead to banks borrowing more from the central bank as they arbitrage between borrowing from the central bank and investing in the market.

As a policy tool, the bank rate determined the amount of bank borrowing from the central bank. Such borrowings are assets to the central bank and of course liabilities to the banking system. In some sense, these operations could be termed "closed market" operations in that only specific financial institutions could participate. Setting this bank rate was a

---

[7]An excellent paper that traces the path of inflation is Auernheimer (1983).

[8]For an analysis of the effect of private money on the level of seigniorage that can be generated through inflation, see Dwyer Jr. and Saving (1986).

principal component of monetary policy in the early days of the Federal Reserve System.[9]

Second, at least before the payment of interest on bank reserves, the principal source of policies that affect the money supply are what are referred to as "open-market" operations. Open market refers to the fact that the central bank, actually the Trading Desk at New York Federal Reserve bank, buys and sells bonds, or other assets which recently have consisted of MBSs in addition to treasuries, in amounts determined by the FOMC of the Federal Reserve Board of Governors. Open-market purchases increase the money supply by introducing new money into the economy.

Now, for an extreme case, assume that market interest rates for treasuries with maturities less than 10-years are negative. A negative interest rate means is that the price of all $1,000 denominated less than 10-year treasuries must exceed $1,000. Assume that the 5-year treasury interest rate is -1% so that a $1,000 5-year treasury sells for $1,052.54.

Assume that the Federal Reserve engages in an open-market purchase of $1 billion 5-year treasuries, that if held to maturity, will be worth $950.986 million. The issue is whether this open-market operation is in any way different than a $1 billion purchase of 5-year treasuries when interest rates are positive. Does such a purchase increase the money supply and, if so, how does it affect the public's budget constraint?

From the perspective of the money supply, the treasuries are purchased with newly printed money so that the monetary base increases by the amount of the purchase just as it would if the yield on the treasuries was positive. No matter the yield on treasuries, a $1 billion open-market operation increases the monetary base by $1 billion.

How about the public's budget constraint? The transaction itself removes $1 billion in 5-year treasuries from the public and replaces them with $1 billion of the equivalent of cash. From this perspective, the public is whole in that it willingly gave up the treasuries for the cash. Now, the Federal Reserve, rather than the public holds the $1 billion in 5-year treasuries.

---

[9]The idea that monetary policy is about setting an interest rate rather than operating on wealth has led many to question the efficacy of monetary policy in a world with a lower bound on interest rates. See, for example, Gust *et al.* (2017).

By law, when the treasuries come due, they create income for the Federal Reserve and all profits of the Federal Reserve revert to the Treasury. Thus, the taxes that would have been necessary to redeem the 5-year treasuries will now be unnecessary. So, in 5 years, the public will get a tax reduction relative to the pre-open-market operation expected taxes. This tax reduction has a value equal to the $1 billion Federal Reserve purchase of treasuries. Therefore, the public budget constraint increases by the full $1 billion.[10]

Essentially, the public is wealthier by the full $1 billion of the open-market purchase. Is the classic Keynesian liquidity trap relevant here? The answer is no, even if such a corner solution was reached since the liquidity trap is about liquidity and not about wealth. Monetary policy that creates money by buying assets, not offset by increased Federal Reserve liabilities, from the public increases wealth. For this policy to have no effect when interest rates are zero or negative, the wealth elasticity of consumption would have to be zero!

Conclusion

There is no question that interest rates were at or near historic lows for much of the last decade. However, they began to rise in 2015 and as of July 16, 2018, 5-year treasuries were yielding 2.75% and 5-year inflation protected treasuries (TIPS) had a positive yield of 0.70%. For all the concern that we have lost control of monetary policy because interest rates are at historic lows, the effect of monetary policy is independent of the equilibrium interest rate. This is an accurate statement as long as the monetary policy in question is the simple purchase and sale of publicly held assets, normally treasuries, but recently also MBSs.[11]

The effect of traditional monetary policy works through making the public as a whole wealthier or poorer. Once we accept the premise that for the public, an increase in their wealth has an effect on their level of consumption and/or saving, monetary policy will affect the economy.

---

[10] Perhaps, the first recognition of the relation between an independent Federal Reserve System and the Treasury and then taxpayers was in Pesek and Saving (1963).

[11] For an analysis of Federal Reserve holdings of assets on the public's wealth and government debt, see Saving (2016).

The classic idea that once interest rates get low enough, the public will make all assets liquid does not affect this conclusion. The monetary policy that affects the public's wealth will have an effect on consumption and saving even if the public desires to hold all of its financial assets in liquidity. Most importantly, this result is not dependent on why interest rates are at historically low levels.

Chapter 18

The Federal Reserve and the Federal Debt

Introduction

Since the beginning of the Federal Reserve's series of Quantitative Easing (QE), its assets have increased fivefold. During this same period, federal deficits have increased the level of publicly held debt by 260%. Traditionally, the connection between increases in government debt and central bank asset growth would indicate that the central bank was providing financing for the increased federal debt. But, because the Federal Reserve increased its liabilities by paying interest on bank reserves, the actual increase in its net assets were much smaller with the result that less than 10% of the increased federal debt was financed by the Federal Reserve.

There is another important relation between Federal Reserve and the federal debt. The Federal Reserve balance sheet has a direct impact on the cost of servicing the federal debt. This direct connection between the Treasury and the Federal Reserve suggests that measures of publicly held federal debt should account for the Federal Reserve in some form or another.

The publicly held federal debt as reported by the Congressional Budget Office (CBO) is the gross of Federal Reserve holdings of Treasury debt. This treatment is based on the Financial Report of the United States Government. Specifically, the report states:

> *A number of entities and organizations are excluded due to the nature of their operations, including The Federal Reserve System (considered to be an independent central bank under the general oversight of Congress) ...*[1]

Effectively, the report's treatment of the Federal Reserve is based on the interpretation that the Federal Reserve is an independent central bank. But does this mean that there is no financial connection between the Treasury and the Federal Reserve?

The absence of a financial connection between the Federal Reserve and the Treasury would be appropriate if the Federal Reserve was a privately owned central bank. In this case, the earnings of the Federal Reserve would belong to its shareholders. These shareholders would then be the indirect holders of any federal debt held by the Federal Reserve, and it would be appropriate to ignore Federal Reserve holdings of federal debt in reporting publicly held federal debt.

But the Federal Reserve is not privately held central bank. From a financial perspective, the Federal Reserve and Treasury are connected in a very real way. Indeed, current law requires that all Federal Reserve earnings after costs and payments to preferred stock held by district banks must be transferred to the Treasury. This financial connection makes the Treasury the residual income recipient of Federal Reserve earnings.

Thus, the connection between the Federal Reserve and the Treasury is direct in that all earnings from Federal Reserve assets, Treasury securities, agency securities and Mortgage-Backed Securities (MBSs) affect the taxpayer cost of the federal debt. Any measure of the burden of the federal debt must account for this Federal Reserve–Treasury connection. The next section suggests measures of the net effect of the Federal Reserve on the taxpayer burden associated with the federal debt.

---

[1] See Financial Report of the United States Government, Fiscal Year 2015, Department of Treasury, Washington, District of Columbia.

The Publicly Held Federal Debt

The CBO estimated that the publicly held federal debt as a share of GDP was 76.5% at the end of 2017 and would rise to 96.2% in just a decade. As indicated above, these estimates ignore that the Federal Reserve must transfer all after-cost earnings to the Treasury. These earnings are equivalent to the seigniorage a nation's mint charged to mint coinage because the central bank supplies currency by taking assets from the private sector or, in effect, by negating Treasury debt.

It is clear that Federal Reserve holdings of Treasury debt reduce the cost of servicing total Treasury debt, since the interest payments on Federal Reserve held debt is returned to the Treasury. What is not obvious, but is just as true, the Federal Reserve holdings of private market assets, such as MBSs, are a source of income transfers to the Treasury as well. Thus, no matter the source of Federal Reserve transfers to the Treasury, the total directly affects the cost of servicing Treasury debt. Therefore, Federal Reserve holdings of private sector assets provide revenue to the Treasury that offsets the cost of servicing the debt. In a hard-to-imagine world of no federal debt, the revenue generated by Federal Reserve asset holdings would provide revenue to the Treasury that could reduce the taxation necessary to support government.[2]

To the extent that the Treasury receives revenue from the Federal Reserve, the burden to the taxpayers is reduced. The Treasury has debts that require interest payments and has the equivalent of assets that yield interest. The burden of Treasury debt should be considered in the same way we think about our own debt. Consider the cost of servicing our debt, and by cost, I mean the servicing cost net of any interest income on earning assets. That is certainly the way we would view our own burden of debt.

One simple way to calculate the level of debt net of asset holdings is based on the difference between the flow of interest payments on the debt and the interest receipts on the assets, essentially an income statement approach. For example, if the interest payments on all our debt, (credit card, auto loans, etc.,) totaled $1,000, and our interest earnings on our

---

[2] Importantly, the currency used to purchase assets is not convertible into anything other than currency. As such, it does not represent a liability of the issuer. For an extended discussion of this idea, search the topic of "inside versus outside" money.

assets totaled $500, what is a correct measure of our net debt? The net of these two flows is a servicing cost of $500 not $1,000, so by this way of thinking, our net debt is half our gross debt.

For an individual that has consumer debt and a Certificate of Deposit (CD), this income statement approach would calculate the net debt as the ratio of the interest received on the CD, and interest paid consumer debt, multiplied by the total of the gross debt. In the numerical example above, an individual's net debt is one-half the level of consumer debt. This calculation works even if the CD was in the form of a trust that could not be accessed by the individual.

Alternatively, we can look at our balance sheet. Here, our net debt is the difference between the liabilities that require interest payments and the assets that generate interest. With this approach, our net debt is the difference between the market value of income earning assets and market value of liabilities that require interest payments.

The debt burden approach that compares the difference between interest paid and interest received is income statement based. The alternative approach that compares market value of interest paying liabilities and interest receiving assets is balance sheet based.

Does any of this discussion have anything to do with the CBO estimates of publicly held federal debt? The answer to this question is yes on both net debt measures.

The Financial Connection between the Federal Reserve and the Treasury

On the pure asset measure, the CBO considers the Federal Reserve as part of the public and not as a government agency. Is this treatment of Federal Reserve treasury holdings appropriate when measuring the burden of publicly held debt? An extension of that question involves all income earning assets of the Federal Reserve. The answer to the determination of the relevant measure of the federal debt burden depends on who owns the interest earnings of Federal Reserve assets, including Treasury securities.

The two measures of debt discussed above apply both to private debt and federal debt. The first approach is based on the Treasury's servicing cost of the debt. Consider the publicly held debt as measured by the CBO, and compare the Treasury's net debt servicing costs to its interest income. Given the requirement that the Federal Reserve remit all profits from operations to the Treasury, these remittances are the equivalent of Treasury interest income.

In the simplest sense, because the Federal Reserve is an independent central bank, it has the authority to add to or dispose of its assets at any time. On the other hand, consider a case where you are entitled to the flow from an asset, but cannot sell the asset. Do you still own the asset? You can't get your money now, but you do get the flows from it as long as the asset is held by the entity that is required to transfer earnings to you.

By law, the profits of the Federal Reserve must be sent to the Treasury. What is the source of these profits? They come from the Federal Reserve earnings on its asset portfolio and other income.[3] The net amount that gets transferred to the Treasury is the total of Federal Reserve income less dividends to bank owners and all costs of Federal Reserve operations.

The fact that the Treasury has title to all Federal Reserve net income makes the Treasury the residual income recipient of Federal Reserve income. This residual ownership of Federal Reserve income gives the Treasury an ownership position in the Federal Reserve. However, this ownership position is attenuated in that the Treasury cannot sell the underlying assets that generate the income nor can it prevent the Federal Reserve from divesting itself of these assets. As long as the Federal Reserve is independent of the Treasury, its asset decisions are made to control the money supply and not to fund the federal government.[4]

Federal Reserve Transfers to the Treasury

As a result of the three Federal Reserve QEs, transfers from the Federal Reserve to the Treasury have grown significantly. Figure 18.1 shows the level of Federal Reserve assets and transfers to the Treasury for the period

---

[3] Federal Reserve check clearing income has all but disappeared as a significant component of Federal Reserve income.

[4] In contrast to the Bank of Venezuela where the central bank prints money at a hyperinflation rate to finance government expenditures.

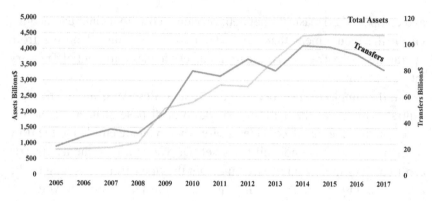

Figure 18.1.   Federal Reserve Total Assets and Transfers to Treasury

from 2005 to 2017. Both Federal Reserve assets and Treasury transfers quadrupled between 2005 and 2015, with transfers reaching nearly $98.7 billion in 2014 and $97.7 billion in 2015.[5] The transfers then began falling as total assets stabilized after 2014 and the interest rate on Federal Reserve liabilities, i.e., bank reserves, began its rise.

It is clear that the increase in Federal Reserve Treasury transfers coincided with the rise of federal deficits and Federal Reserve assets purchases. The purchased assets, whether or not they were treasuries, increased the earnings of the Federal Reserve. All of the increased earnings, less any increased bank costs, due to paying interest on bank reserves, accrued to the Treasury. The transfers as a share of Federal Reserve assets averaged 2.87% and ranged from 2.27% to 3.96% over the period depicted in Figure 18.1.

Figure 18.1 shows the total assets of the Federal Reserve and the level of transfers to the Treasury. However, beginning in fiscal year 2009, the Federal Reserve has been paying interest on member bank reserves, essentially making these reserves short-term liabilities of the Federal Reserve.

---

[5]A significant portion of these transfers are generated by Federal Reserve holdings of MBSs. The MBSs while issued by GSEs are not liabilities of the GSE's since all revenues come from the underlying mortgages. The Federal Reserve also holds some agency securities, issued by privately owned GSEs. These securities are not guaranteed by the Treasury and should be considered in the same way as MBSs. Thus, it is appropriate to treat Federal Reserve holdings of MBSs and agency debt as assets not offset by a liability of another government entity. As such, the flows transferred to the Treasury represent net income.

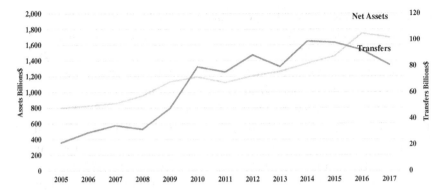

Figure 18.2. Federal Reserve Net Assets and Transfers to Treasury

Because of the financial relationship between the Federal Reserve and the Treasury, the interest payments on member bank reserves reduce the transfer from the Federal Reserve to the Treasury dollar for dollar, effectively making bank reserves a short-term federal liability.

Figure 18.2 is an adjusted version of Figure 18.1 and shows Federal Reserve net assets and transfers to the Treasury. A comparison of Figures 18.1 and 18.2 shows that net assets rose much more slowly than Federal Reserve gross assets. The rate of return to the Treasury based on Federal Reserve net assets rose from the pre-MBS Federal Reserve of between 2.69% and 4.03% to the post-MBS Federal Reserve of between 4.12% and 6.67%.

Implications for Measuring the Taxpayer Burden of Federal Debt

The usual way of reporting the scale of the federal debt is based on the amount of this debt that is held by the public. To put this measure of debt into perspective, it is often expressed as a share of the nation's GDP. In such a ratio, the debt is a stock that is being compared to a flow, GDP. For example, at the close of 2017, the CBO estimates that the publicly held federal debt was 76.5% of GDP.

Presumably, the ratio of debt to GDP is an indication of a nation's ability to at least pay the cost of servicing that debt. Any analysis of this ratio must consider that while the debt is federal, the GDP is not. The free world is not North Korea, where the government owns the GDP and lets citizens have some of that GDP. In the United States, the federal government does not own the nation's GDP, the public does. Further, the tax system suggests that the public owners of the GDP are allowing the government to use just some of this GDP — approximately 18.2% of it in 2017.

Since taxpayers are on the hook for servicing the federal debt, this federal debt is on the same footing as personal debt. The same logic used to value the net debt of any private citizen is also relevant for valuing federal debt. Figure 18.3 shows the net federal debt servicing cost as reported by the CBO along with the transfers from the Federal Reserve to the Treasury for fiscal years 2009–2017. These transfers financed 25.4% of fiscal year 2009 federal debt servicing cost. In fiscal year 2015 transfers financed 43.8% of the net federal debt servicing cost. During this 9-fiscal-year period, the outstanding federal debt rose more than 46%, while the net cost of servicing that debt rose by only 31%.

As shown in Figure 18.3, the CBO reported that the net servicing cost of the federal debt in 2017 was $262.6 billion. Given the CBO-reported level of publicly held debt at the close of 2017 of $14.67 trillion, the $223.2 billion of net interest implies a rate of interest on the total debt of 1.79%, which is just slightly above the average yield of 1.65% on 7-year Treasury notes prior to June 2016. By way of comparison, with market interest rates, the 1.79% is consistent with the duration of outstanding Treasury debt of 6.48 years. Adjusted for Federal Reserve transfers, the net debt servicing cost of the federal debt for 2017 was $182.8 billion.

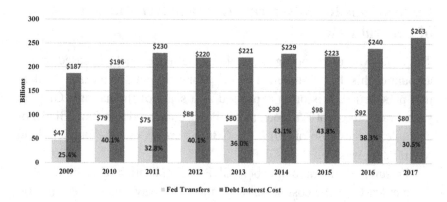

Figure 18.3.   Federal Reserve Contributions to Federal Debt Servicing Cost

The Adjusted Value of the Federal Debt

Because of the financial relation between the Federal Reserve and the Treasury and, indirectly to taxpayers, some adjustment to measures of the burden of that debt must be made. One approach is on a purely flow basis that compares the flows from the Treasury to the holders of the debt and to the Treasury from the Federal Reserve. A second approach reduces the level of outstanding federal debt by the assets held by the Federal Reserve on the theory that all the flows from these assets accrue to the Treasury and, therefore, indirectly to taxpayers. Below, we refer to these two approaches as income statement based and balance sheet based.

Income statement approach

An income statement approach takes the costs and income related to assets and liabilities and uses the result as an estimate of the level of debt underlying the income and cost figures. This approach measures the burden of a debt as the level of interest payments net of earnings on related assets required to satisfy debt holders.

In 2017, the CBO reported the servicing cost of the federal debt as $262.6 billion, and the federal debt outside government (publicly held) was $14.67 trillion. At the same time, the Treasury had revenue from its ownership interest in the Federal Reserve of $80.2 billion. Adjusted for interest revenue from the Federal Reserve, the net interest payments on the federal debt in 2017 were $182.4 billion.

This $182.4 billion net servicing cost of the federal debt was only 69.5% of the CBO reported servicing cost. In one sense, then, the effective federal debt in 2017 was only 69.5% of the reported gross-of-Federal-Reserve-transfers federal debt of $14.67 trillion. The result of this calculation is an effective federal debt at the close of 2017, from a servicing cost perspective, of $9.67 trillion, rather the CBO reported $14.67 trillion.

Further, the income statement measure of the effective federal debt adjusted for what is essentially interest income from the Federal Reserve was only 50.4% of 2017 GDP rather than the CBO reported, 76.5%. Considering that the close of 2007 pre-recession federal debt was just 35% of GDP, the adjusted-for-Federal-Reserve-transfers debt as a share of GDP rose by only 44.0%, rather than the 118% implied by ignoring the servicing cost supplied by the Federal Reserve transfers to the Treasury.

Balance sheet approach

The reported measure of publicly held federal debt, including Treasury debt held by the Federal Reserve, as of the end of 2017, was $14.67 trillion. When Treasury debt and Federal Reserve holdings are consolidated, the publicly held federal debt is reduced by Federal Reserve holdings of $2.45 trillion, to $12.22 trillion.

There is a further adjustment to the level of publicly held debt that is required due to the income of the Federal Reserve being the property of the Treasury. The other principal asset held by the Federal Reserve at the close of 2017 was $1.773 trillion in MBSs, the income of which also belongs to the Treasury. Thus, Federal Reserve holdings of MBSs are Treasury assets and as a result, they are an offset to Treasury liabilities. When all Federal Reserve assets (Treasuries and MBSs) are subtracted from reported publicly held debt, the adjusted publicly held federal debt is $10.4 trillion.

A final adjustment is required since the introduction of paying interest on bank reserves has made these reserves short-term liabilities of the Federal Reserve. In addition to paying interest on reserves the Federal Reserve has issued reverse repos to the tune of $353 billion so that at the close of 2017, Federal Reserve interest bearing liabilities totaled $2.66 trillion. Given the financial connection of the Federal Reserve and the Treasury Federal Reserve liabilities are essentially Treasury liabilities. Therefore, in the balance sheet approach it is appropriate to add the $2.66 trillion of these liabilities, because of their effect on the level of Federal Reserve transfers to the Treasury, to the $10.4 trillion above. The fully adjusted Federal Reserve balance sheet level of federal debt is then $13.06 trillion, about 89% of the current measured $14.67 trillion and 72.2% of GDP.

Some Caveats

Any evaluation of the burden of the federal debt must account for the fact that, for all practical purposes, the Treasury has an ownership position in the Federal Reserve. In any forecast of the future, the revenue from this ownership must be taken into account. But there is a caveat, and a major one at that. The level of interest transfers to the Treasury are at the discretion of the Federal Reserve. Why, you ask? The answer is that while the Treasury owns Federal Reserve profits it neither owns nor controls Federal Reserve assets and liabilities.

The Federal Reserve creates money when it adds to its portfolio and destroys money when it reduces its portfolio. As a result, the Federal Reserve's portfolio is solely at the discretion of the Federal Reserve. The Treasury owns the profits of the Federal Reserve but it does not own the assets underlying those profits. When the Federal Reserve increases its earning assets or reduces its liabilities, it adds to its transfer to the Treasury. Further, these increases in the Federal Reserve's net asset position are achieved by running the printing press. On the reverse side, when the Federal Reserve reduces net assets by reducing earning assets or increasing its liabilities, it destroys the money it created when it purchased assets or reduced liabilities.

In dealing with the unprecedented federal deficits surrounding the Great Recession, the Federal Reserve virtually sterilized its increase in assets by creating a short-term liability, bank reserves. At the same time, it dramatically lengthened the duration of its portfolio by buying long-term federal debt and private market MBSs. In effect, it was borrowing short through paying banks to hold the reserves, and lending long.

It is the difference between the rate of return on the Federal Reserve's long-term investments and the interest rate on its short-term liabilities that generates much of the transfers to the Treasury. This strategy works as long as the yield curve has enough slope. Beginning in 2014, however, the difference between long interest rates and short interest rates began to fall. Figure 18.4 shows the level of Federal Reserve transfers to the Treasury and the path of the difference between the rate of interest on 10-year treasuries and 30-day T-bills. Not surprisingly, as the Federal Reserve's cost of borrowing rises and its earnings on existing assets remains constant, transfers to the Treasury fall.

What the Federal Reserve has been doing is borrowing short, as evidenced by paying interest on bank reserves and issuing reverse repos, and investing long in treasuries and MBSs. This strategy works so long as

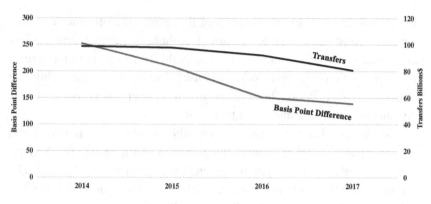

Figure 18.4.   Federal Reserve Transfers and the Yield Curve

the yield curve has enough positive slope. But transfers to the Treasury are dramatically affected by the flattening of the yield curve. This flattening has continued and by July of 2018 the basis point difference between 30-day T-bills and 10-year treasuries has fallen to 100 basis points. As a result, the 2018 Federal Reserve transfers to the Treasury will fall further.

Conclusion

The debate continues concerning how independent the Federal Reserve should be from the Treasury and what it means to be independent. From the perspective of monetary policy, that independence means that the policies conducted by the Federal Reserve are decided upon independently of the Treasury's need for deficit financing. Such policy independence does not, however, require that there be no financial connection between the two entities.

In fact, the two entities are intimately connected, at least financially. All Federal Reserve revenues after costs and payment to bank owners must be transferred to the Treasury. In the usual meaning of the word "own", the Treasury owns the Federal Reserve as it is the residual income recipient of Federal Reserve revenues. Importantly, however, the Treasury ownership status does not give Treasury the right to vote on Federal Reserve policy.

Whether or not the Treasury and Federal Reserve are connected in a political way, the Treasury is the residual income recipient of Federal Reserve revenues. Therefore, both Federal Reserve assets and income affect the taxpayer burden of federal debt. The federal debt can be adjusted for Federal Reserve's connection to the Treasury using a balance sheet or an income statement approach.

Using the income statement approach, the level of debt is determined by the net of Federal Reserve transfers debt service cost. In 2017, the transfers from the Federal Reserve were $80.2 billion and accounted for 30.5% of the net debt service cost. By this method, the reported publicly held debt burden is reduced to 69.5% of the reported $14.67 trillion, or $10.23 trillion.

An alternate approach to this calculation would be to offset the federal debt by the assets held at the Federal Reserve, even though the revenue from the sales of these assets would not accrue to the Treasury. This approach has merit since it is a balance sheet approach and given that flows from Federal Reserve net assets accrue to the Treasury. The net assets of the Federal Reserve were $2.45 trillion at the close of 2017 — the difference between outright asset holdings less the liability of bank reserves on which the Federal Reserve must pay interest. This measure of an adjusted federal debt is roughly $11.14 trillion, about 94% of the current measured $14.67 trillion and 72.2% of GDP.

Chapter 19

Measuring the Federal Reserve's Net Worth

Introduction

The power of a central bank to be the monopoly producer of legal tender money comes from the central government and, thus, ultimately from the people. For this monopoly grant to be effective, two things must happen. First, competitors must be removed. Legislation could deny legal tender status to any competing currency from other producers of currency, but that would still allow already existing competing currencies to circulate. Further, money is not only about currency. Anything that is used, or can be used, to facilitate transactions, can be a substitute for legal tender.

Once the production of competing currencies has been stopped, the central bank can begin to accumulate wealth, the flow from which has traditionally been called "seigniorage." In a simple context, the net worth of a central bank is simply the capitalized value of the flow it receives from the assets acquired as its currency replaces competing currencies. How this works will be discussed at length below. Because the nature of a central bank is so important to an evaluation of its net worth, the next section, which summarizes material presented in Chapters 1 and 2, is worth revisiting.

The Transition to a Central Bank

Most nations, including the United States, had monetary systems before they had central banks. In the early days of the United States, currency was issued by the various states and by private banks. This monetary system was essentially competitive banking. The notes, or deposits for that matter, had such a low cost of production relative to value, that assuming that the production costs were zero loses no generality.

Before getting to the transition necessary for the central bank to become the sole producer of currency, it is useful to consider a world of competitive money production. This was essentially what existed in the United States before the Civil War issue of "greenbacks" and the institution of "national bank notes." This antebellum era was a time when the country was on a metallic standard, generally the gold standard but at times on a dual metallic standard with both gold and silver being bought and sold by the Treasury.[1]

In spite of the proliferation of state-chartered banks issuing currency, the price level remained relatively stable. The question that arises is: how could a myriad of banks producing almost costless currency result in a stable price level? The answer is that in order for each currency to circulate, to be acceptable in transactions, both the holder of the currency and the other party to the transaction had to believe the currency could be used in subsequent transactions.

How, with a myriad of independent banks issuing notes, did a limit on the note issue persist? The answer is simple: for a bank's currency to be acceptable, it had to be convertible into what would then have been called "specie," gold or silver. In effect, each bank note was convertible at the issuing bank into gold or silver coin. Any excess issue of currency would literally return to the issuing bank in gold or silver coin. Because the notes were subject to convertibility this seemingly out-of-control system resulted in a stable price level. Convertibility controlled the currency issue from system of independent money issuers with the result that protected the value of the currency issued.[2]

---

[1] The bimetallic standard suffered from issues that evolved as the official relative price of the two metals would rarely be equal to the world relative exchange rate of gold or silver bullion. Then, when the market forces of supply and demand for either metal caused its bullion value to exceed its official currency value, the more valuable metal would disappear from circulation.

[2] See Saving (1976, 1977).

Our first foray into a national currency was the issue of greenbacks and then national bank notes. Interestingly, neither of these notes was convertible into gold. National bank notes were backed by Treasury bonds, and greenbacks by nothing at all. Importantly, both were legal tender and could be used to pay government taxes. As a harbinger of the future, the method used to rid the country of currency competition was a tax imposed on notes issued by competitors, in this case state-chartered banks. The result of this tax on competitors, state bank notes quickly disappeared. The fact that neither national bank notes nor greenbacks were convertible into gold, gold coins still circulated, made for interesting pricing in contracts and merchandise purchases. In particular, stores would have two prices; one for gold coin and one for paper currency.

After the conclusion of the Civil War, the country began a gradual reduction in the money supply with the goal of returning to the gold standard. This goal was achieved in 1879 when, once again, the Treasury bought and sold gold at $20.67 per troy ounce.[3] From that time until the establishment of the Federal Reserve in 1914, the nation's money supply consisted of gold and gold certificates, silver and silver certificates, United States notes (originally greenbacks) produced by the Treasury, national bank notes, and checking accounts at banks that had a varying ability to be transferred in simple transactions.

While the period after the Civil War was one of rapid economic expansion in the nation's output, it was beset with periodic financial crises, not unlike the more recent September 2008 financial crisis. These crises brought out the flaw in the monetary system of the time — its lack of flexibility. That lack of flexibility was, to a significant extent, the result of the rules regulating the production of national bank notes. As a result, whenever there was a significant increase in the public's desire to convert their bank deposits into currency, the system was often unable to respond.

The 1907 financial crisis is often credited for the passage of the Federal Reserve Act of 1913. During that crisis, in many cities, banks maintained clearing houses to settle daily transactions. These clearing houses issued extralegal clearing house certificates in denominations from

---

[3] Contracts often had gold clauses in them so that the lender had the option of demanding gold rather than currency at the contract's conclusion. Such a provision protected the lender from a suspension of convertibility such as occurred with the issue of greenbacks.

25 cents to $500. These certificates amounted to $256 million, an amount that was almost 10% of notes outstanding.[4] This crisis led to the passage of the Aldrich–Vreeland Act that ordered a major study of the US monetary system and allowed for the issue of emergency currency with a limit of $500 million. In addition, the Secretary of the Treasury was permitted to suspend the $500 million limit.

The Federal Reserve as a Monopoly Central Bank

Ultimately, the Aldrich–Vreeland Act study led to the passage of the Federal Reserve Act of 1913, and the beginning of the Federal Reserve as a Central Bank in 1914. While the institution of the national banking system coincided with the elimination of the ability of state-chartered banks to produce currency, the beginning of the Federal Reserve did not spell the end of national bank notes as circulating currency. At the beginning, Federal Reserve notes competed with national bank notes and Treasury notes. In all three cases, the ability to issue notes allowed the note issuer the rights to obtain income earning assets and collect seigniorage.

By the mid-1930s, national bank notes completely disappeared as the special government bonds that were required for their issue were eliminated. At the same time, the Treasury note issue became small enough that the Federal Reserve became the monopoly issuer of currency. As such, it became the only producer of legal tender that could be used to taxes to the federal government and to dispose of all debts, public and private.

Despite the above, it is important to recognize that the determination of what is money is not controlled by any government. Money is what money does. That is, anything that is readily acceptable in exchanges by the general population is in fact money. Clearly, a central bank producing currency that is easily recognizable as being genuine makes it easier for this currency to be used in general commerce. For something to be money, it must be generally accepted in transactions. With this criterion, Bitcoin is not money, even though it is acceptable at a subset of institutions. Bitcoin is, of course, convertible into money at what has historically been a very volatile exchange rate.[5]

---

[4] See Friedman and Schwartz (1964).
[5] Chapter 22 deals with the economics of crypto-currencies at length.

In the current environment, the Federal Reserve is the sole producer of legal tender in the United States. Moreover, except for the costs involved in replacing worn out currency, this legal tender is produced at virtually no cost. The Federal Reserve can and does acquire market valued assets by creating its own assets at no cost. Prior to the payment of interest on reserves, the level of zero cost assets created consisted of the sum of currency and bank reserves. As such, the net worth of the Federal Reserve was approximately the total of currency outstanding and bank reserves, both of which the Federal Reserve produces at virtual zero cost.

The Federal Reserve's Net Worth

One estimate of Federal Reserve net worth can be obtained from the balance sheet from the Federal Reserve. Table 19.1 shows this balance sheet from January 3, 2007, as reported by the Federal Reserve Board of

Table 19.1. Traditional Federal Reserve System Balance Sheet January 3, 2007

Assets		Liabilities	
Gold Certificates	11,037	Federal Reserve Notes	781,347
Special Drawing Rights	2,200	Reverse Repurchase Agreements	29,742
Coin	797	System Bank Reserves	20,044
T-Bills	277,019	US Treasury, general account	6,156
Notes and Bonds	501,891	Foreign Deposits	90
Repurchase Agreements	39,750	Other Deposits	239
Loans	1,262	Deferred Available Cash Items	4,840
Items in Process of Collection	5,472	Other Liabilities	5,461
Bank Premises	1,945		
Other Assets	37,152	Total Liabilities	847,920
Total Assets	878,524	Paid in Capital	15,328
		Other Capital	248
		Surplus	15,029
		Owner's Equity	30,604

Governors.[6] According to the Federal Reserve, the total owner's equity on January 3, 2007, was $30,605 million. But whose owner's equity is this number?

As originally constituted, the regional Federal Reserve banks were "owned" by banks in their respective regions. The word "owned" is in quotes because these local banks have preferred stock, not common stock, and receive dividends.[7] But who owns the residual income of the banks, the equivalent of common stock? The residual income of the Federal Reserve belongs to the grantors of the Federal Reserve's monopoly on the production of legal tender, namely the public. And what is this ownership worth? That is, what is the value of the Federal Reserve owner's equity?

The output of the Federal Reserve is legal tender currency, and it has used this output to purchase income earning assets. Basically, the Federal Reserve exchanges one asset, legal tender currency, for another of equal value, income earning assets. The yield from the asset the Federal Reserve uses to purchase income earning assets must make the two assets equivalent, or the transactions could not happen. What is the yield on the legal tender currency? It is the fact that the Federal Reserve issued currency is generally accepted by all in transactions of any form, i.e., whether these transactions involve consumables or assets.

What are the Federal Reserve's responsibilities that preserve the value of its output? Before answering this question, let's consider a firm that issues an asset, e.g., a bond, and sells it to the public. The firm's responsibility is to pay the interest specified on the bond, then when the bond comes due, pay the bond holder the face value of the bond. The firm creates an asset for the public by creating a liability for itself.

---

[6] From Factors Affecting Reserve Balances, Statement of Condition of Each Federal Reserve Bank on January 3, 2007. https://www.federalreserve.gov/releases/h41/20070104/.

[7] Member banks are stockholders in their respective regional Federal Reserve Bank. They receive dividends after all necessary expenses of a federal reserve bank have been paid or provided for. The stockholders of the bank shall be entitled to receive an annual dividend on paid-in capital stock depending on the size of the bank. In the case of a stockholder with total consolidated assets of more than $10 billion, the smaller of the rate equal to the high yield of the 10-year treasury note auctioned at the last auction held prior to the payment of such dividend; and 6%; and in the case of a stockholder with total consolidated assets of $10 billion or less, 6%.

Table 19.2. Amended Federal Reserve System Balance Sheet January 3, 2007

Assets		Liabilities	
Gold Certificates	11,037	Reverse Repurchase Agreements	29,742
Special Drawing Rights	2,200	US Treasury, general account	6,156
Coin	797	Foreign Deposits	90
T-Bills	277,019	Other Deposits	239
Notes and Bonds	501,891	Deferred Available Cash Items	4,840
Repurchase Agreements	39,750	Other Liabilities	5,461
Loans	1,262		
Items in Process of Collection	6,733	Total Liabilities	46,529
Bank Premises	1,945		
Other Assets	37,152		
Total Assets	879,784	Paid in Capital	15,328
		Other Capital	248
		Owner's Equity	831,995

In contrast, consider the monopoly issuer of currency. Since it has no competitors, the only promise to customers that it must deliver on is the promise to replace a worn piece of currency, with a new one. Since this currency is produced at virtually no cost, the issue of currency is not a liability of the issuer.[8] Thus, the owner's equity presented in Table 19.1 is grossly understated. In Table 19.2, this mischaracterization of Federal Reserve notes and bank reserves as liabilities, is corrected. This correction results in bringing the 2007 value of the Federal Reserve to $832 billion.

Tables 19.1 and 19.2 provide examples of the period before October 2008, the month the Federal Reserve began paying interest on bank reserves and thereby converting them into a genuine liability. Tables 19.1 and 19.2 are also representative of the period before the Federal Reserve's

---

[8] This issue was controversial in the 1960s and was resolved after considerable debate concerning what is the meaning of a liability. In that debate, simply calling something a liability does not make it a liability. For a thorough discussion of what makes something a liability see Pesek and Saving (1967, especially Chapters 3 and 4).

Table 19.3.   Federal Reserve System Balance Sheet January 3, 2018

Assets		Liabilities	
Gold Certificates	11,037	Reverse Repurchase Agreements	383,990
Special Drawing Rights	5,200	Bank Reserves	2,194,651
Coin	1,895	US Treasury Deposits	169,957
T-Bills	0	Foreign Official	5,253
Notes and Bonds, nominal	2,318,404	Other Deposits	71,402
Inflation Indexed	110,134		
Inflation Compensation	19,670		
Federal Agency Debt Securities	4,391		
Mortgage Backed Securities	1,764,929		
Net Unamortized Premiums	144,494		
Repurchase Agreements	0	Other Liabilities	5,806
Loans	44		
Maiden Lane LLC	1,713		
Items in Process of Collection	169	Total Liabilities	2,831,058
Bank Premises	2,203		
Central Bank Liquidity Swaps	12,067		
Foreign Currency Denominated Assets	41,440		
Other Assets	25,927		
Total Assets	4,443,718	Paid in Capital	31,387
		Surplus	10,000
		Owner's Equity	1,571,273

great asset expansion. To get a vision of the difference the great asset expansion made, Table 19.3 shows the Federal Reserve balance sheet for the close of 2017 (January 3, 2018). The table easily shows the tremendous change in the asset side of the balance sheet. Truly, this is not your parents' Federal Reserve. The correctly measured owner's equity increased from just over $830 billion to more than $1.5 trillion, an 82.6% increase. The two owners of the Federal Reserve are the member banks in each district, who own preferred stock and receive a fixed return, and the Treasury. The Treasury is the true residual claimant as it receives all Federal Reserve earnings after the fixed payment to the owner district banks and other costs. The public as the grantor of the system's legal tender monopoly is the dominant shareholder. Figure 19.1 shows the path of public equity and transfers to the Treasury. The rapid growth in public equity after 2008 is apparent in the figure and coincides with the growth of Federal Reserve net assets. Importantly, the decline in the transfers to the Treasury, in spite of a rising public equity, is the result of the flattening yield curve and the fact that the Federal Reserve holds long assets and issues short liabilities. As the interest rate on the principal Federal Reserve liability, bank reserves, has risen, net earnings have fallen. It is readily apparent that transfers as a percent of equity grew significantly after 2009, more than doubling from 3.4% in 2006 to an average of 7%.

Figure 19.2 illustrates the increase in rate of return on public equity. The significant increase in rate of return is due to the dramatic

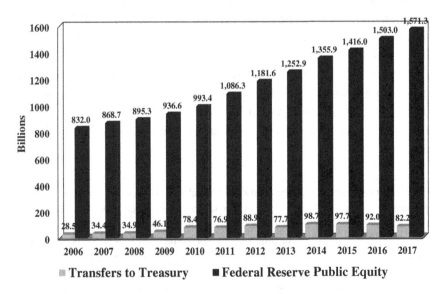

Figure 19.1. Federal Reserve Public Equity and Transfers to the Treasury

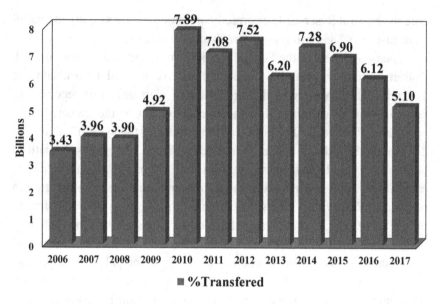

Figure 19.2.   Federal Reserve Treasury Transfers as a % of Public Equity

change in the composition of Federal Reserve assets as they moved from being 50% long to 100% long. Part of this lengthening of the duration of the Federal Reserve portfolio was the addition of MBSs that now comprise more than 40% of Federal Reserve assets. A second part of the duration lengthening, was an operation twist that replaced all short-term Treasury bills with longer-term notes and bonds. The falling differential between the rate of return on the Federal Reserve's long assets and the interest rate it is paying on its main liability, bank reserves, has caused and will continue to result in reduced transfers to the Treasury.[9]

---

[9] In contrast to the scale of public equity and Federal Reserve transfers to the Treasury, the member bank share of Federal Reserve net worth has remained about 2%. This is not surprising as the regional nature of member banks having shares of their regional Federal Reserve Bank is a vestige of the original nature of the regional Federal Reserve banks. In the beginning, these banks were largely independent as the country feared a centralized central bank. The Banking Act of 1935 removed the ability of the regional banks to conduct monetary policy independent of the Federal Reserve System. Essentially, that act made the Federal Reserve System a true "central" bank.

Conclusion

It is interesting that we rarely have discussions about the net worth of government institutions. However, the Federal Reserve as a central bank is on a different footing than most government agencies. Most importantly, it has over time been recognized as the monopoly producer of legal tender currency. Just as important is the fact that the grantor of this monopoly is the public, as represented by the Treasury.

The basic output of a central bank is currency and bank reserves. Traditionally, both of these monetary instruments are produced by the central bank at virtually no cost. Because both have full value, they can and are used by the central bank to acquire income producing assets. At the beginning, as a central bank replaces all prior currency with its new monopoly currency, it acquires assets as well.

Next, we come to the important part, and that is that the currency issued by the central bank is non-refundable and non-returnable in any real sense. This same currency can be used as currency or used as bank reserves by the commercial banking system. It is wealth in its own right. The assets acquired by its issue and by subsequent increases in its issue remain with the central bank. Since the monopoly status of the central bank is granted by the public, the assets acquired by the central bank are net worth, and that net worth belongs to the public.

Based on this analysis, the Federal Reserve System has a net worth of more than $1.5 trillion. Because it is owned by the people, it must transfer the earnings of this net worth to the Treasury as a representative of the people. All of this must be tempered with the realization that since October 2008, the Federal Reserve has been gambling with its owners' equity. This gambling is the result of playing on the differential between the earnings it receives from long-term investments and the interest it must pay on its short-term liabilities, bank reserves. In fact, if the yield curve were to become inverted, the Federal Reserve's payments to its ultimate owners, the public, as represented by the Treasury, could become negative. Then the Treasury could be in the position of subsidizing the Federal Reserve!

Finally, in an ideal world of balanced budget government, these transfers would be distributed to the people in the form of lower taxation. Even in a world of budget deficits, the transfers benefit the public by reducing the interest burden on the public debt.

Chapter 20

Is There a Path Back to Your Parents' Federal Reserve?

Introduction

It takes very little imagination to see that the Federal Reserve of today is very different than the one we knew before 2008. It is certainly different than what was imagined when the Act establishing the Federal Reserve was passed in 1913. Part of this difference is due to the delegation by Congress of certain regulatory duties that have expanded over the last half-century. But these regulatory duties are not the real source of the difference between today's Federal Reserve and the one we knew for most of the Federal Reserve's prior history. There are at least three major differences in this Federal Reserve and the traditional version of the Federal Reserve:

- First, this Federal Reserve has, as part of its permanent asset portfolio, private financial assets from a specific industry.
- Second, this Federal Reserve has issued financial liabilities in the form of bank reserves.
- Third, as a result of the Dodd-Frank legislation, this Federal Reserve is greatly involved in the regulation of a broad range of financial markets.

The important issue, however, is whether or not this Federal Reserve is still capable of doing its specified job of protecting the value of the currency? Or does the configuration of this Federal Reserve make it difficult, or perhaps impossible, to conduct monetary policy independent of the political part of the government?

In the summer of 2017, the Federal Reserve announced that beginning in October of 2017, it would begin a program designed to reduce its asset holdings. Such a reduction was to be conducted at a level consistent with its ability to conduct monetary policy. In their words, *The Committee intends to gradually reduce the Federal Reserve's securities holdings by decreasing its reinvestment of the principal payments it receives from securities held in the System Open Market Account. Specifically, such payments will be reinvested only to the extent that they exceed gradually rising caps.*[1]

Now that this asset reduction program is occurring, the question is how did we get to a level that requires unwinding? This chapter will document the ramping up of assets that led to the current level. To bring the extent of the expansion into perspective, we make comparisons between this ramp-up with what occurred during the only other significant rapid expansion of Federal Reserve assets, World War II.

How We Got Here

The Great Recession and even any lingering effects are now in the past. But have the unprecedented deficits of that era and the Federal Reserve's response to these deficits affected the future of the economy and the Federal Reserve? At the beginning of fiscal year 2009, immediately after the September 2008 financial crisis, the federal debt stood at $5.8 trillion, 39.3% of GDP, and by 2016, the federal debt was $14.2 trillion, 77% of GDP. During that 8-year period, the debt rose by 244%, and its share of national output almost doubled.

To get a perspective of the extent of the deficits that led to this unheard of increase in federal debt, consider only the first four post-meltdown fiscal years 2009–2012. During these four fiscal years the deficits were all in excess of $1 trillion. Note that the following years deficits

---

[1] See *FOMC issues addendum to the Policy Normalization Principles and Plans* (2017). The addendum is available at https://www.federalreserve.gov/newsevents/pressreleases/monetary20170614c.htm.

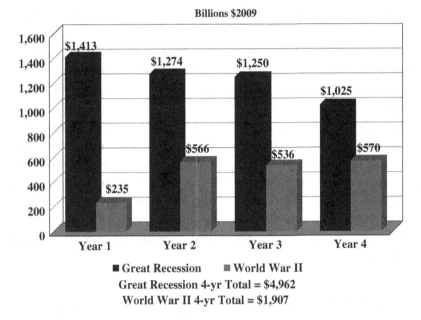

Billions $2009

Great Recession 4-yr Total = $4,962
World War II 4-yr Total = $1,907

Figure 20.1. Great Recession Deficits versus World War II Deficits

were small by historical standards, they were on the order of only half a trillion annually.

Before the onset of the Great Recession, we would have pointed to the financing of World War II as the largest deficit in our history. Figure 20.1 shows the first 4 years after the financial meltdown and World War II expressed in 2009 dollars. The comparison is striking!

The Roosevelt Administration incurred deficits over 4 years of World War II of more than $1.9 trillion 2009 dollars to finance and win the Second World War. Beginning in 2009, in the subsequent four fiscal years, the federal government spent almost three times that much, almost $5 trillion 2009 dollars. All that expenditure accomplished little, at least in terms of restoring economic growth to its pre Great Recession level. In the World War II case, the cause was just and the outcome victory. In the Great Recession case, whatever the cause, the outcome was modest at best.[2]

---

[2] Measured as a share of GDP, World War II deficits averaged 20% while deficits of the first 4 years of the Great Recession averaged 8%.

Another comparison immediately suggests itself: What did all of this debt accomplish?

For World War II, the deficit bought war materials (guns, tanks and planes) and paid personnel in our military services. Output rose as the wartime labor force grew with the addition of women, idealized by the "Rosie the Riveter" posters.

For the Great Recession, the federal deficits gave us an unprecedented expansion of income transfer programs. These programs resulted in a declining labor force. The labor force decline has resulted in a labor force participation rate that for the first time in our history did not start to rise with the beginning of the recovery. Lest we forget, the recovery began in July of 2009, a full four months before the beginning of fiscal year 2010. The bottom line is that the Great Recession deficits bought a smaller workforce and lower income growth.

World War II versus Great Recession and the Federal Reserve

An important distinction between these two federal debt explosion episodes is how they affected the nation's central bank, the Federal Reserve System. In spite of the fact that the Federal Reserve was required by the Treasury to support the market for federal debt during and briefly after World War II, the Federal Reserve's actual contribution as shown in Figure 20.2 to funding the war was relatively small.[3] From the beginning of fiscal year 1942 to fiscal year 1946, the monetary base grew 94%, at an annual rate of 14.2%.[4] During that war period, the federal debt grew 471%, an annual growth rate of just over 36%. For the entire war period, the Federal Reserve funded through purchases of Treasury securities only 11.3% of the deficits.

Once the necessity of helping finance World War II was over, the expectation was that a central bank would revert back to a normal level of

---

[3] The Federal Reserve was required to support an interest rate ceiling on Treasury Bills of 0.375% and on Treasury Bonds of 2.5%. Because of rationing and the general unavailability of durables goods and automobiles, these ceilings put little pressure on Federal Reserve policy.

[4] Fiscal years at that time began in July and ended in June. Thus, fiscal year 1942 in the above figure was from July 1, 1941 to June 30, 1942.

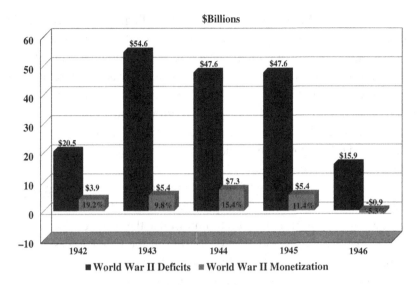

Figure 20.2. World War II Fiscal Year Deficits and Federal Reserve Monetization

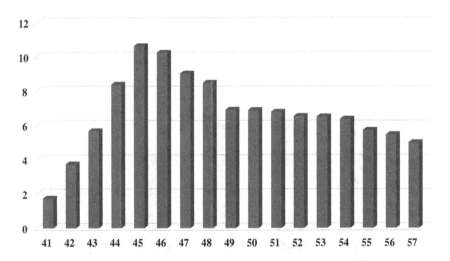

Figure 20.3. Federal Reserve Securities % of GDP 1941–1957

asset holdings. As Figure 20.3 shows, that is exactly what happened. US Treasuries, as a share of the nation's GDP rose rapidly during the early war years from their pre-war level of just under 2% of GDP at the close of 1941, to more than 10% in just 4 years. After the close of hostilities, the GDP share of Federal Reserve security holdings fell rapidly until by 1958, they were at levels that became the pre-Great Recession norm.

The rapid return to a normal Federal Reserve following World War II was due to two factors. First, the Federal Reserve was reducing its holdings of securities and had disposed of 25% of its war-time acquisitions by 1950. Second, both real and nominal GDP grew rapidly during the 1947–1957 period at 3.95% and 6.63%, respectively. The result of the combination of rapid GDP growth and Federal Reserve reductions in their security holdings is exhibited in Figure 19.3.

Now, we come to the first 5 years of the Great Recession. Figure 20.4 shows the Great Recession fiscal year deficits and the level of Federal Reserve involvement. In marked contrast to the role of the Federal Reserve in financing World War II, its role in the Great Recession was enormous. In three of the first five Great Recession years, the Federal Reserve covered over half of the federal deficit. After actually decreasing its holdings in fiscal 2012, it doubled down and increased assets by the largest amount for the entire period. In fiscal year 2013, the Federal Reserve increases assets by almost $900 billion, covering 131% of the $680 billion fiscal year 2013 federal deficit.

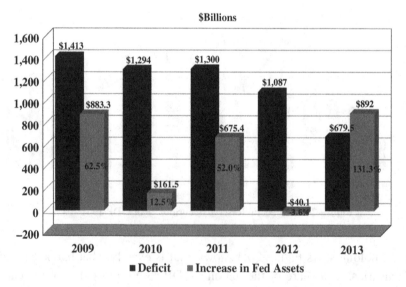

Figure 20.4.   Great Recession Fiscal Year Deficits and Federal Reserve Monetization

The Post-Great Recession Federal Reserve

Given the tremendous Great Recession increase in Federal Reserve assets and the concomitant increase in the traditional monetary base, inflation expectations abounded, especially among economists. But the expected inflation never happened, and the reason is another change in Federal Reserve policy. This change involves the Federal Reserve being an issuer of debt rather than solely a purchaser of debt. This debt is primarily due to the introduction of paying interest on bank reserves but also issuing reverse repurchase agreements. The combination of these two debt instruments offset the inflationary effect of the tremendous asset expansion. Instead of the pressure of a 51% annual growth of Federal Reserve assets on the money supply and inflation, we had a much smaller but still significant annual 25% growth in net assets. Truly, this is not your parents' central bank! Can it ever be the old Federal Reserve again?

During this same period, the Federal Reserve, in an effort to keep long-term (especially mortgage) rates low, engaged in what in the past was called "Operation Twist." The original Operation Twist involved replacing the normal Federal Reserve portfolio of short-term treasuries with long-term treasuries; that is, the Federal Reserve sold short-term treasuries to raise their interest rate and bought an equivalent quantity of long-term treasuries to lower the long-term rate.

This newer version of "Operation Twist" differed from the original in two ways. In the original twist, total Federal Reserve assets remained unchanged as only their term to maturity composition changed. In the new version of twist they bought long-term assets and actually issued short-term liabilities by making bank reserves the equivalent of short-term bonds. In addition, they increased net assets significantly.

The introduction of interest on reserves is essentially speculating in financial markets. Here, the Federal Reserve was buying long-term high yielding private financial assets, Mortgage-Backed Securities (MBSs), in addition to long-term treasuries and issuing on-demand short-term liabilities, bank reserves. The difference in interest rates is all profit that accrues to the Treasury. In 2014, that difference peaked at $98.7 billion, over 40% of the 2014 cost of servicing the national debt. This is a high risk strategy, as anyone familiar with the 1994 Orange County California bankruptcy is aware.[5] A flattening of the difference between the long-term and short-term rates of return can eliminate this subsidy to the Treasury. This began after 2014 so that by 2017, the Federal Reserve transfer to the Treasury had fallen to $82.2 billion, still over 30% of total debt servicing cost. In the Federal Reserve case, even a negative yield curve cannot result in bankruptcy or insolvency since they have the money printing press. However, such a yield curve reversal will impose a significant cost on taxpayers and result in increased inflation potential.

The biggest change, however, as shown in Chapter 17, is that this new Federal Reserve is now subject to being a victim, rather than a determiner, of interest rates. The fact is that the Federal Reserve determined interest rate on reserves is now more important to monetary policy than open-market operations. This fact is apparent in the relation between the Federal Reserve determined interest rate on reserves and the rate of return on 1-year treasuries, as shown in Figure 20.5.

For most of the interest on reserves period, the rate of return on excess reserves exceeded the yield on 1-year treasuries. That is not surprising since the reason for paying the banks to hold reserves rather than investing in financial assets, was to make the massive increase in Federal Reserve assets inflation proof. As the yield on 1-year treasuries has risen, the

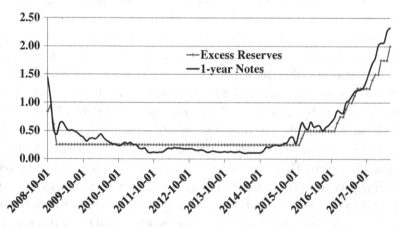

Figure 20.5.　Interest Rate on Reserves and 1–Year Treasuries

---

[5]The New York Times story of this bankruptcy is available at: https://www.nytimes.com/1994/.../orange-county-s-bankruptcy-the-overview-orange-co.

Federal Reserve has been forced to increase the interest rate on reserves. In a sense, the Federal Reserve is a captive of market interest rates. If they want to prevent the inflation that is pent up in the massive holdings of reserves, they must continue to make reserves superior to other short-term bank investments.

Currently, the Federal Reserve's long-term asset portfolio consists of roughly 60% long treasuries with a duration of 7 years and 40% MBSs with a duration of 25 years. The combination of these two assets means that the Federal Reserve's asset portfolio has a duration of almost 15 years, long by most financial standards.

Now, we come to Federal Reserve liabilities. Historically, Federal Reserve liabilities were easily rounded to zero. All that has changed since banking system's reserves are Federal Reserve liabilities, and their level is now significant. These liabilities consist primarily of bank excess reserves, essentially demand liabilities, and short-term reverse repos, either overnight or 15 days.

As the spread between the interest rate on long-term assets held by the Federal Reserve and their short-term liabilities (reserves) falls, the yield on its net assets will fall. Currently, that yield measured by the level of transfers to the Treasury is on the order of 5.1%.

Rising interest rates coupled with a return to the long-run spread between short-term and longer-term securities will dramatically affect the federal cost of servicing the ever-growing federal debt. Over the past 4 years, Federal Reserve transfers to the Treasury have fallen from almost $100 billion to just over $80 billion. Federal Reserve transfers in 2014 were financing over 40% of the total debt servicing cost. Now, the transfer share of total debt servicing cost has fallen to just over 30%. A return of interest rates to their long-run levels will increase the debt servicing cost and further reduce the transfers from the Federal Reserve.

In the interest on reserves world, once the Federal Reserve sets a desired level of money stock growth, it becomes a reserve interest rate taker. If market interest rates rise with no change in the reserve interest rate, banks will move away from reserves and into other assets. Consequently, the money supply will rise. If the Federal Reserve does not want the money supply to rise, it must raise the interest rate on reserves to meet the market. If market interest rates fall, banks will move away from investments in the economy and into reserves, and the money supply will fall. Once again, if the Federal Reserve does not want the money supply to fall, it must lower the interest rate on reserves to meet the market.

Eventually, the Federal Reserve must extricate itself from the asset and liability mix brought on by burgeoning federal deficits, and it has already begun this process. But this restoration will not be simple. Figure 20.6 shows Federal Reserve assets, liabilities and assets net of liabilities. Several things are apparent from the figure. First, the traditional Federal Reserve, that is the Federal Reserve before October 2008, had virtually zero liabilities. Second, the pre-crisis Federal Reserve had assets that kept pace with GDP, remaining virtually constant at about 6% of GDP. Third, the surge in liabilities began in October 2008, was principally bank reserves that now paid interest but also to a much smaller extent, reverse repos.

The result of the three quantitative easing (QEs) is very apparent in Figure 20.6, as gross Federal Reserve assets more than quadrupled as a share of GDP, rising from just over 6% to just under 25%. In order to stop the inflation pressure that would have existed with this dramatic increase in assets, the Federal Reserve began paying interest on bank reserves, essentially converting these reserves into short-term liabilities. The net effect was an increase in Federal Reserve net assets from their 2003 to 2008 average of roughly 6% of GDP to roughly 10% of GDP.

How, or even can, we return the Federal Reserve to its pre-Great Recession configuration? Before we can answer this question, we must

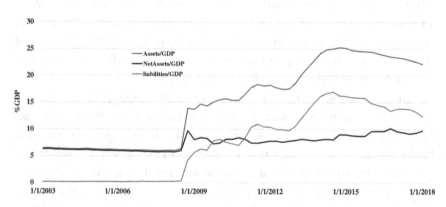

Figure 20.6.   Federal Reserve Assets, Liabilities and Net Assets Relative to GDP

first decide what we mean by such a return. We can begin by reiterating the goals of an independent central bank. The Federal Reserve Act indicates that these goals are maximum employment, stable prices and moderate long-term interest rates in the United States.

We might question these goals, especially the maximum employment and moderate long-term interest rates as relevant for a central bank. Certainly, the goal of maximum employment is admirable. However, in any long-run sense, the central bank is helpless in this arena.

The same should be said concerning the goal of moderate long-term interest rates. In fact, there is no real meaning to the adjective "moderate" in any real economic context. Interest rates are market determined. In a completely static world, the time preference of the population would determine the rate of interest, both the short-run and the long-run rate. In a dynamic world of changing technology, the marginal productivity of new capital would interact with the population's time preference to determine interest rates.

Returning to the Traditional Federal Reserve

Success in achieving the goal of returning the Federal Reserve to its traditional configuration requires two changes in its current configuration. First, traditionally Federal Reserve assets have been about 6% of GDP and are now over 20% of GDP. Second, the traditional Federal Reserve had virtually no liabilities and now has liabilities of over 12% of GDP. The path back to its former self can be a gradual one in which the Federal Reserve simply lets economic growth return its asset holdings to the long-run 6% share of GDP. Alternatively, the Federal Reserve can accelerate the return to its former self by actively pursuing reductions in its asset holdings.

The do-nothing approach

One path back to previous Federal Reserve normalcy is to stand pat on assets and let GDP growth absorb its liabilities. GDP growth with stable prices will require increases in the money stock. These money stock increases will gradually absorb the excess reserves as banking system expansion converts excess reserves into required reserves.

While the do-nothing approach sounds simple, it is anything but simple. For one thing the money supply will not expand just because GDP rises. What must happen during the period of reserve absorption and money expansion is that the spread between market interest rates and the interest rate on reserves must gradually rise. Just the right amount of interest rate difference will induce the banks to give up excess reserves until they return to their historic near zero level.[6] This reduction of excess reserves is actually a transition from "excess" to "required" as the reserves do not disappear.

In the end, this seemingly simple approach is mislabeled as a do-nothing approach. It requires continual monitoring by the Federal Reserve, as they are the setters of the interest rate on reserves. The rate of decline in bank holdings of excess reserves has to match the growth in GDP and will only do so with just the right difference between market interest rates and the Federal Reserve determined interest rate on reserves. In a simple sense to achieve the 2% inflation goal while reducing assets, bank desired reserve holdings must fall at a rate that makes Federal Reserve net assets, gross assets less reserve liabilities, rise 2% faster than real GDP.

Assuming that the Federal Reserve can implement just the right path for interest rates on reserves, the GDP growth approach will require a GDP of $68 trillion to restore the long-run ration of Federal Reserve assets to GDP ratio of 6%. Current dollar GDP in July of 2018 was $19.96 trillion. At the then current nominal GDP growth rate of 4%, it will take 31 years to restore the Federal Reserve assets to GDP ratio to its past level of just over 6% of GDP.

The asset reduction approach

While a do-nothing approach to returning the Federal Reserve to its traditional old self is possible, it will require many years and is fraught with uncertainty. One way to speed up the return to the old Federal Reserve is a continuation of the already in place asset reduction program. This planned sale of both treasuries and MBSs will help in the absorption of

---

[6] If market interest rates remained constant, this increase in the spread between market rates and the reserve interest rates would require a gradual reduction in the reserve interest rate.

reserves. But on the MBS front, the Federal Reserve holds a significant proportion of all MBSs so that their disposal must be done so as to not have large market effects.

Returning to Figure 20.6, the post-October 2008 balance sheet of the Federal Reserve showed the rapid increase in both assets and liabilities. After the initial jump in the fourth quarter of 2008, net assets remained about the same throughout this period. Federal Reserve gross assets peaked in 2015, at the close of QE3. An asset reduction approach that will return to the Federal Reserve asset portfolio to its traditional share of the economy involves two components.

First, the composition and scale of the Federal Reserve's investment in the economy's financial instruments is far from its normal asset portfolio. Traditionally, the Federal Reserve operated in the market for short-term treasuries. As such, their portfolio of assets was largely Treasury debt of less than 1 year. In contrast, the current Federal Reserve asset portfolio composition is largely long-term assets. In fact, the duration of its Treasury portfolio is greater than 7 years. Then, almost one-half of this asset portfolio consists of non-Treasury debt, MBSs, with an even longer duration.

Second, the traditional Federal Reserve financed its asset purchases by running the printing press to produce the required currency and reserves. Neither the currency nor reserves issued in this manner were liabilities of the Federal Reserve. The traditional Federal Reserve had no liabilities. The new Federal Reserve has introduced two forms of liabilities. One, by paying interest on bank reserves it converted these reserves into liabilities. Essentially, rather than running the printing press, it financed the acquisition of long-term assets by issuing short-term debt. Two, it sold short-term debt to the banking system in the form of reverse repurchase agreements. The sum of these new liabilities are now over $2 trillion.

The Federal Reserve began a transition back to the pre-2008 Federal Reserve in October 2017. Initially, they intended to proceed by not renewing assets in their portfolio as they matured. Traditionally, the principal payments for these assets are reinvested in new issues so that the Federal Reserve portfolio would remain constant or at most increase at the same rate as the nation's GDP.

The initial goal for the non-reinvestment program involved treasuries, agency debt and MBSs. For payments of principal that the Federal Reserve receives from maturing Treasury securities, it was anticipated that initially a maximum of $6 billion per month will not be reinvested, and that amount will increase in steps of $6 billion at 3-month intervals over 12 months until it reaches $30 billion per month. For payments received from non-treasury government agency debt and MBSs initially, no more than $4 billion per month will not be reinvested, and that amount will increase in steps of $4 billion at 3-month intervals until it reaches $20 billion per month.

The issuers of these securities regularly roll over these maturing securities, and some part of that rollover is purchased by the Federal Reserve. Now the Federal Reserve is reducing its participation in the rollover of this debt financing. The part that was repurchased by the Federal Reserve must now be purchased by the general public. As a result, the public's share of these securities will rise by an amount equal to the decline in Federal Reserve holdings.

As their assets mature, the Treasury and other agencies issue replacement securities. To the extent that the Federal Reserve does not reinvest the earnings, they turn these assets back to the issuer. As a result, Federal Reserve revenue falls. Further, the decline in assets is equivalent to an open-market sale of assets of that amount and immediately reduces reserves and the monetary base.

Figure 20.7 shows the weekly reduction in Federal Reserve assets and the cumulative total from the October 2017 beginning of the reduction program through mid-June 2018. The reduction proceeded at a slower rate than the maximum set by the Board but by the end of September of 2018, the Federal Reserve had reduced its asset holdings by $254 billion. By design, this initial reduction is small considering that total Federal Reserve holdings of these assets were $4.1 trillion in mid-July 2018. In what we might call the normal Federal Reserve world, this reduction in reserves would result in a reduction in bank loans, increase in interest rates and a reduction in the money stock. What actually happens will depend on the banking system's response to this reserve reduction. Further, these sales will result in a reduction in the public's wealth as Federal Reserve transfers to the Treasury fall so that taxes must rise.

Figure 20.7. Weekly and Cumulative Federal Reserve Securities Held Outright Sales

In this world of bank reserves being income earning assets for banks, the final effect of the Federal Reserve asset reductions on the money supply will depend on how the reduction in reserves affects the banking system's demand for reserves. Further, the banking system's response will depend on the spread between rate of return on investments in the economy, and the rate of interest on reserves. If banks simply restore their reserve holdings by reducing investments in the economy, then the money supply will decline, which is what would have happened following a Federal Reserve open-market sale of assets.

But the announced goal of the Federal Reserve is to conduct policy to achieve an inflation rate of approximate 2.0%. For this inflation goal to be met the net assets of the Federal Reserve must rise 2% faster than real GDP. Thus, for the asset reduction program to be consistent with an inflation target, banks must desire a reduction in their level of reserves that exceeds the reserve reduction implied by the net Federal Reserve asset sales. For this result to be achieved requires a virtual fine-tuning of the rate of asset reduction and the interest on reserves.

Figure 20.8 shows the path of Federal Reserve net assets over this first year of the asset reduction program. After an initial fall during the first phase of the asset reduction program, net assets began to rise. Over the entire first year of the program net assets rose 5.7%, clearly well in

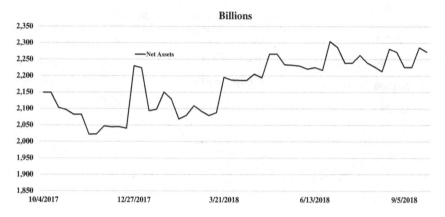

Figure 20.8.   Federal Reserve Net Assets

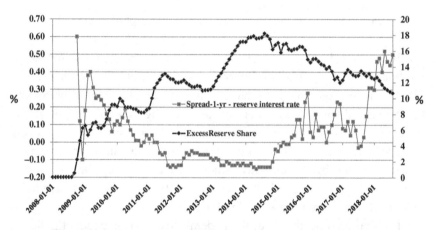

Figure 20.9.   Excess Reserve Share of Total Commercial Bank Assets

keeping with the 2% inflation goal. This first year of the planned return to a traditional Federal Reserve certainly indicates that it is possible to achieve both the inflation and asset reduction goals.

That the necessary fine-tuning is possible in the longer run is evidenced by the fact that bank investment in interest paying reserves as a share of their assets is related to the returns on reserves relative to other bank investments. Figure 20.9 shows the relation between the excess reserve share of bank assets and the spread between 1-year treasuries and the interest rate on reserves, from the onset of interest on reserves.

During the period of a negative spread between 1-year treasury interest rates and the interest rate on reserves, the excess reserve share of bank assets rose from about 9% in early 2011 to more than 18% in mid-2016. Then when the spread once again reached positive levels the share of excess reserves began to decline. By the end of August 2018, the share of excess reserves had fallen to less than 11% as the spread reached 50 basis points.

Figure 20.9 demonstrated the importance of the interest rate spread in the value of excess reserves as a part of an optimal bank portfolio. As the figure shows, the rapid growth in bank reserves occurred when the spread was negative, i.e., the yield on reserves exceeded the return on 1-year treasuries. The figure further shows that as the return on reserves relative to other assets has declined, so has the reserves share of bank assets.

As of the end of September 2018, the Federal Reserve had reduced its asset holdings by just over $254 billion, close to the maximum reduction set by the Board of $300 billion. Even if they achieved the projected maximum of $300 billion, how would that compare to the rate of asset growth when the portfolio was on the rise? For example, in 2013, the Federal Reserve added $1.090 trillion to its asset holdings, a 41% increase. They followed that up in 2014 by adding $482 billion, a 13% increase. In comparison, the $170 billion reduction is only a decrease of 4% of total assets and even a reduction of the projected maximum of $300 billion represents only 7% of total assets.

While a reduction of 4% of assets sounds small, any asset reduction is totally uncharted territory. We know that the rapid accumulation of assets was seamlessly associated with the absorption of these assets as bank reserves as evidenced by the slow rise in Federal Reserve net assets during this period. The asset absorption was facilitated by the fact that almost from the beginning of the massive accumulation of assets the rate of interest on reserves exceeded the 1-year treasury rate of return by an average of at least 10 basis points. Before the payment of interest on reserves, banks held zero excess reserves. Banks now hold $2.1 trillion in excess reserves and have total assets of $16.2 trillion so that excess reserves make up 12.5% of bank assets.

Figure 20.10 shows further evidence of the impact of the earning power of excess reserves by tracking the ratio of excess reserves to bank

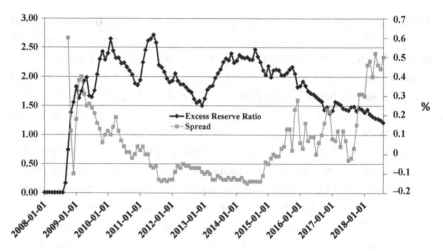

Figure 20.10.   Interest Rate Spread and Excess Reserves per Dollar of Demand Deposits

demand deposits. During the rapid Federal Reserve asset expansion period, the ratio of excess reserves to demand deposits, the excess reserve ratio rose dramatically. When the spread between 1-year treasuries was averaging 14 basis points in favor of reserves, the banks were holding $2.50 in excess reserves per dollar of demand deposits. Once the spread became positive banks began to reduce the level of reserves so that by August of 2018 the spread was 50 basis points and banks were holding only $1.21 in excess reserves per dollar of demand deposits.

    This effort was further aided by a fall in the velocity of money due to the fall in interest rates in general as shown in Figure 20.11. The simple theory is that higher interest rates make the public economize on money balances. That money balance economization is reflected in rising velocity. By the same token, falling interest rates make holding money balances less costly and results in falling velocity. During the 10-year period from the beginning of 2007 to the beginning of 2017, velocity fell in response to the falling interest rates at an annual rate of 3.31% or a monthly rate of 0.28%. But as we shall see as market interest rates rise, as they are now doing, this velocity effect will be reversed. Further to the Federal Reserve asset reductions will increase the level of securities in the economy. If this increase has an interest rate effect, it will contribute to the increase in the income velocity of money.

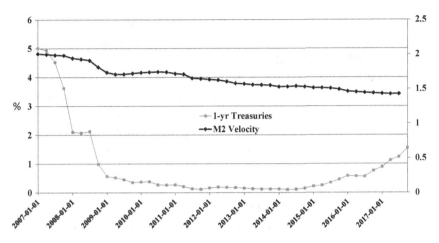

Figure 20.11. M2 Velocity and 1yr Treasury Yield

Issues in the Implementation of the Federal Reserve Asset Reduction Program

The Federal Reserve has set a course to reverse its Great Recession asset expansion. But can the Federal Reserve just reverse the asset and liability accumulation of the post-September 2008 period? Is it possible to reverse the excess reserve and velocity movements and reduce both assets and liabilities in unison just as they increased in unison?

The answer lies in an examination of the conditions that allowed the asset increase to be offset by an almost equal increase in excess reserves. The solution that a return to the old Federal Reserve is possible is clear from an examination of Figures 20.8 and 20.9. If we pay banks enough, they will hold any level of excess reserves we desire. That suggests the answer to our problem. We just set the interest rate on reserves such that bank investing in the economy is superior to holding reserves. But now what we want is just the right amount of substitution of market invest-ments for investment in reserves. Otherwise, we get more inflation than we bargained for or very much less inflation or perhaps even deflation.

The Federal Reserve asset reduction program is equivalent to a series of open-market sales of Federal Reserve assets. In a traditional open-market sale of Federal Reserve assets, once the public's resources used to purchase Federal Reserve assets reach the Federal Reserve, they are essentially sucked into the money printing press. Such a pure sale reduces the monetary base, currency plus reserves, makes banks search for reserves and reduces their loan portfolio. In addition, in a pure simple sale, the public in general is made poorer as the reduction in Federal Reserve earnings transferred to the Treasury results in higher taxes or increased public debt.

But the Federal Reserve asset reduction program is different from any past monetary policy as it is not intended to have any economic effect. In fact, the net result of the asset reduction program should be consistent with the Federal Reserve's goal of 2% inflation.

But how can the usual negative effect of Federal Reserve open-market asset sales be prevented? In the traditional central banking world, there would be no way to offset the negative effect of an open-market sale of assets. However, in the current world of interest on bank reserves, it is possible for the banking system to totally offset the open-market sale effect. What must happen is that the banking system must move investments in reserves to investments in the economy in response to the changes in the interest rate on reserves.

The fact that the Federal Reserve controls the interest rate on reserves gives it the power to control the relative value of reserves to the banking system, and offset any negative effect of its asset-reduction program. For the asset reduction goal and the inflation goal to both be met, the Federal Reserve's net assets must rise 2% faster than GDP growth assuming no change in velocity. Net asset growth with falling assets requires that liabilities fall faster than assets. What is required is just the right change in the interest on reserves to offset, or if the inflation goal to be met, more than offset the asset reductions.

But can the Federal Reserve achieve just the right rate of increase in the spread in the return bank market investment opportunities and excess reserves to offset the planned asset reduction? The issue is market return uncertainty. This uncertainty is the basis for the Federal Reserve Board directive that caps the non-reinvestment program at a relatively low level.

Assume that the Federal Reserve wants to restore its asset portfolio to pre-Great Recession levels as a share of GDP by the close of the next decade? Essentially this means that by the close of the decade, Federal Reserve liabilities in the form of excess reserves would return to their long-run level of virtually zero.

To address this process, assume that the Federal Reserve, in the process of this asset reduction program, meets its annual inflation goal of 2%. In addition, assume that real GDP grows at the same low 1.39% annual rate as the last decade so that nominal GDP in 10 years will be $27 trillion. In the 10 years up to 2007, the ratio of Federal Reserve securities held outright to GDP was 5.2%. Restoring the securities to GDP ratio sets the ultimate goal for Federal Reserve security holdings in 2027 at $1.3 trillion. It is the difference between current securities holdings of $4.2 trillion and this 10-year out goal of $1.3 trillion, $2.9 trillion that is the issue.

But, must it be assumed that real GDP growth will stay at the historically low level of the past decade? Faster real GDP growth is now happening and this growth will significantly reduce the difficulties in restoring Federal Reserve assets to their traditional share of GDP. For example, even with a modest real GDP growth of 3% and the Federal Reserve goal of 2% inflation, nominal GDP in 10 years will be $31 trillion. To be more optimistic, if real GDP growth equaled the 3.95% of the first 10 post-war years and the Federal Reserve achieves its 2% inflation goal, nominal GDP in a decade will be $34 trillion.

If the economy can achieve 3% real GDP growth, the 2% inflation target could within a decade restore the traditional Federal Reserve securities to GDP ratio of 5.2%. Such a restoration would require Federal Reserve security holdings in 2027 of $1.7 trillion. Even with this faster GDP growth, the task of getting back to the past is formidable. With current holdings of $4.2 trillion, the faster GDP growth scenario would still require that the Federal Reserve draw down their security holdings by $2.5 trillion.

What path is required to reduce the Federal Reserve asset portfolio to its historic share of GDP either with the slower 1.39% real GDP growth or a faster real GDP growth of 3.95%? The slow growth reduction of $2.9 trillion, or the fast growth reduction of $2.5 trillion that in a decade would return the Federal Reserve to its traditional size must be done in a way that leaves the Federal Reserve's 2% annual inflation goal in place. Even more importantly, the asset reduction must not have a negative effect on the economy.

The path to successfully giving us back the old Federal Reserve is composed of three parts. Part one is simply reversing the excess reserve growth that essentially financed the expansion. Part two involves accounting for the return of velocity to its pre-crisis level. Finally, part three accounts for the effect of growth in nominal GDP on the desired final level of Federal Reserve securities holdings.

Let's begin by seeing just how far the interest on reserves induced excess reserve growth can be used to offset the reduction in Federal Reserve securities holdings. Current excess reserve holdings are $2.1 trillion. But the Federal Reserve has also been selling reverse repos for the last several years. These sales reduce reserves dollar for dollar. Thus, the total amount of reserves available to offset security non-reinvestment is the $2.1 trillion of excess reserves plus $0.4 trillion of reverse repos, which brings the total available for asset reduction offset to $2.5 trillion.

For the low GDP growth of the last decade, the total asset reduction required is $2.9 trillion, and a simple reversal of excess reserve growth during the expansion can absorb $2.5 trillion of the open-market sales without affecting the economy. That leaves only $0.4 trillion of asset reduction that can have a negative effect on the economy. Importantly, for the higher GDP growth assumption, the level of excess reserves alone can suffice to allow the return to the past to be done without negative effects on the economy.

While the massive Great Recession asset acquisitions of the Federal Reserve did not result in significant increases in the price level, they did result in significant increases in the money supply. The money supply grew at a rate more than three times the inflation rate. The 18.4% per year growth in Federal Reserve assets resulted in only 6.5% annual growth in the M2 money supply. The difference between these growth rates was absorbed by the growth in excess reserves.

To get at the potential inflationary effect of a 6.5% rate of growth of the money supply, we must consider that real income was growing at 1.4% per year so that money growth in excess of output growth was 5% per year, still well above the CPI inflation rate of 1.7%. Why didn't the inflation rate match the money growth rate? The answer is the public's demand for money rose, as evidenced by the fact that M2 velocity was falling at 3.1% per year. The M2 money growth of 1.76% plus the rate of decline velocity (the increase in the public's willingness to hold money as interest rates declined) of 3.31% less the observed real GDP growth of 1.38% predicts an inflation rate of 1.76%.

The increase in the public's demand for money and the banking system's demand for reserves combined to allow the last decade's unprecedented increase in Federal Reserve assets to have little effect on the inflation rate. These factors also point to the possibility that the undoing of the past asset expansion can happen with little or no negative effect on inflation or the economy. If so, then what is the problem and why did the Board of Governors caution in instituting such an asset reduction?

The caution is the result of considerable uncertainty in what is happening to money velocity and how much and in which direction to change the interest rate on reserves to absorb each asset reduction. Bear in mind that every asset reduction is the equivalent to what is usually referred to as a Federal Reserve tightening of money markets. We know that some or all of this tightening can be untightened by banks reducing their demand for excess reserves, which increases their demand for market assets. The effect of the asset reduction on the economy can be offset by the public reducing its demand to hold money balances, an increase in velocity.

One uncertainty in all this is we do not know the exact relation between the demand for excess reserves and the spread between market interest rates, e.g., 1-year treasuries, and the interest rate on reserves. What is clear is that once the Federal Reserve has returned to an asset level consistent with their pre-Great Recession asset to GDP ratio that the interest rate on excess reserves should be zero, i.e., the banking system will hold virtually no excess reserves. The beginning and the end points of this new policy are known, but the path to that end point is important. Just as the last two QE periods were offset by banks increasing excess reserves, this new quantitative tightening event must be offset by banks decreasing excess reserves.[7]

Conclusion

As we enter this new era of the Federal Reserve reversing the series of QEs, is it possible to achieve a return to the past levels of Federal Reserve

---

[7] Chapter 21 contains a method of estimating the amount of change in the banking system's desire to hold reserves as part of their investment portfolio related to the speed that the Federal Reserve reduces assets.

assets without negatively affecting the economy? The impact of the last two QEs on the potential for inflation was avoided by the institution of interest on reserves so that the banking system absorbed the majority of the asset increase. Reversing this process will require that the banking system follow the asset reduction with reserve reduction.

It is making this seemingly simple solution of the asset draw down work that is the problem. The change in the banking system's desire to hold excess reserves must match the level of excess reserves reduction that is consistent with the level of non-reinvestment chosen by the Federal Reserve. The Federal Reserve asset expansion was absorbed by the economy in two ways. First, by initiating the payment of interest on reserves, the banking system absorbed a large part of the increase in assets. Second, the fact that interest rates were near historical lows increased the public's demand for money as evidenced by the fall in velocity. The combination of these two events allowed the virtually unprecedented expansion in Federal Reserve assets to have little effect on the inflation rate.

Can we reverse these events and draw down Federal Reserve assets to their historic share of GDP? Certainly, the Federal Reserve can induce the banks to hold fewer reserves by lowering the interest rate of reserves relative to other investment alternatives. Also, and almost certain is the fact that as market interest rates rise, a falling demand for money can offset the money reduction inherent in the series of open-market sales of Federal Reserve assets. It is the managing of these two factors that is perplexing. These conditions show why it makes sense for the Federal Reserve to begin small as they try to return to a world where excess reserves do not pay interest and the banking system reduces excess reserves by an amount equal to the Federal Reserve's reduction in assets.

We know that the banking system's response to the Federal Reserve's acquisition of assets was to increase reserves as the yield on excess reserves exceeded the rate of interest on 1-year treasuries by 10–15 basis points. To get the banks to give up reserves as an investment will require that reserves be inferior to non-reserve investments. The question is how much?

The Federal Reserve can manage two components of the equation that will allow them to reduce assets without harming the economy. These two components are the interest rate on reserves and the rate of asset reduction. The remaining two components, market interest rates and the velocity of money, are out of their control. It is these last two components that the Federal Reserve must counter if it hopes to succeed in a no-harm asset reduction program.

Chapter 21

Estimating a Path to Your Parents' Federal Reserve

Introduction

Beginning with the financial crisis of September 2008 and continuing for almost a decade, the Federal Reserve made a transition to become a very different entity than it was for most of its more than 100-year existence. The difference lies in three distinct areas.

One, the sheer level of Federal Reserve assets as a share of GDP dwarfs any previous period. From the period following World War II to the beginning of the Great Recession, Federal Reserve assets were about 6% of the nation's GDP. Assets at the close of 2017 were on the order of 25% of GDP.

Two, except for temporary responses to financial crises, the Federal Reserve asset portfolio was exclusively Treasury securities. In contrast, its current portfolio is more than 40% private market securities, MBSs.

Three, throughout its history, Federal Reserve liabilities were, for all practical purposes, zero. With the introduction of paying interest on bank reserves, Federal Reserve liabilities are on the order of 63% of its assets.

Chapter 20 outlined in a general way what would be required to return the Federal Reserve to its traditional role in the economy. Here, I will present a methodology for accomplishing this transition while allowing the policy to result in the Federal Reserve's announced goal of a steady 2% inflation.

Issues in Returning to the Traditional Federal Reserve

Assume that the Federal Reserve in its new policy to return to its roots leaves its annual inflation goal of 2% unchanged. The initial projected annual reduction in assets was $300 billion but was actually just over $200 billion. The $300 billion would have been just over 7% of its close of 2017 securities holdings. While a reduction of 7% of assets sounds small, Federal Reserve asset reduction is totally uncharted territory. As Figure 21.1 shows, the accumulation of assets was seamlessly associated with the absorption of the majority of the asset accumulations as bank liabilities, primarily excess reserves but also reverse repos. That absorption was facilitated by the fact that almost from the beginning of the asset accumulation, the rate of interest on reserves exceeded the 1-year treasury rate of return by an average of at least 10 basis points.[1]

Considering that the commencement of an asset reduction is new territory, for illustrative purposes, assume that the initial non-reinvestment by the Federal Reserve was $300 billion in the first year. To keep things simple, assume that rather than the gradual increase in asset reduction, the

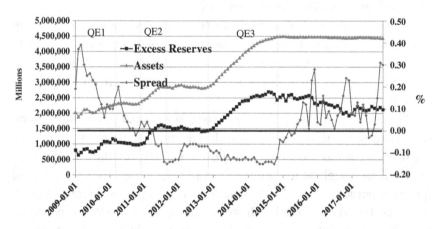

Figure 21.1. Asset and Liability Growth and the 1yr Treasury-Reserves Interest Rate Spread

---

[1] In Figure 21.1, beginning in 2015 as the 1-year treasury interest on reserves spread became positive, both total assets and reserves began to fall but reserves fell much faster. What happened was that reverse repos, another Federal Reserve liability, sales rose. Such sales reduce reserves by the amount of the sale so that net assets remained about the same.

rate of reduction remains constant at $25 billion per month. At this constant rate, the implied monthly % rate of reduction in the monetary base would be 0.657%. The problem for the Federal Reserve is to ensure that the monetary base reduction does not affect its goal of 2% inflation. For this to happen, as the Federal Reserve transitions to a smaller asset portfolio, the banking system must simultaneously reduce their demand for excess reserves by more than the asset reduction.

Understanding the rate of inflation

To understand this problem, let's reflect on just how a 2% rate of inflation happens. In the simplest terms, inflation comes from too much money chasing too few goods. Translating this simple adage into the real world, it means that the rate of growth in the money stock must exceed the rate of growth in real output by 2%. If the rate of growth in real GDP continues at the pace of the 2008–2018 period of 1.67%, then the money stock must grow at 3.67% consistently for inflation to be 2%.

Now, we come to the problem facing the Federal Reserve. As it reduces its asset portfolio, it reduces bank reserves. If the banks' response to the reduction in reserves is to restore the reserves lost, then they will reduce investments in the economy, and the money supply will fall. But a falling money supply will cause deflation and not the desired 2% inflation. Therefore, to insure that he banks will not want to restore the reserves lost, the Federal Reserve must make reserves less profitable for the banks. The profitability of reserves depends on the spread between the rate of interest on reserves and bank market opportunities. The Federal Reserve must allow the spread between the 1-year treasury interest rate and the interest rate on reserves spread to widen if it wants the banks to reduce excess reserves. But by how much?

If inflation is to be 2%, then the supply of money services must rise 2% faster than the nation's real output, real GDP. A measure of the change in the supply of money services is simply the sum of the change in the measured money stock and the change in the amount of money the public wants to hold per dollar of output. The latter is simply referred to as the velocity of money. Velocity might be viewed as the efficiency of money in the transactions process. It depends on the cost of holding money in that the more it costs to hold money, the more you will try to conserve on holding money. This cost is essentially what you give up by holding money, what you could have earned if you reduced on average the amount of money you hold.

Inflation is simply the rate of change in prices and is the result of the rate of money growth exceeding the rate of output growth. The rate of change in the public's desired money stock is the sum of the rate of change in any of the measures of the money stock and the rate of change in velocity. That is, actual inflation depends on the rate of change in the money supply adjusted for its efficiency compared to how fast the economy is growing. Often, this relation is expressed in a simple *equation of exchange* and is expressed in words in the following equation:

Rate of inflation = (money growth rate + velocity growth rate)
– real GDP growth rate

This equation simply expresses the idea that the rate of inflation will equal the difference between the rate at which the public's effective money stock is growing and the rate at which real output is growing. Despite the simplicity of the equation, it has great power to explain the rate of inflation. As proof of the power of simplicity, the following table indicates how well this simple equation does in explaining the rate of inflation for three common definitions of the money supply, M1, M2 and MZM, and the three common price level measures, CPI, Personal Consumption Expenditures Index (PCE) and the GDP deflator. Inspection of Table 21.1 shows that the simple equation of exchange is very successful in explaining the actual monthly rate of change for all three measures of inflation. The equation of exchange predictions is slightly below the actual CPI inflation and slightly above the PCE and GDP deflator inflation measures.

Table 21.1. Actual and Equation of Exchange Predicted Monthly Inflation Rates 2007–2017

Money Definition	Predicted Inflation	CPI Inflation	PCE Inflation	GDP Deflator
M1	0.130%	0.138%	0.124%	0.125%
M2	0.127%	0.138%	0.124%	0.125%
MZM	0.128%	0.138%	0.124%	0.125%

Understanding the rate of money growth

The Federal Reserve controls the monetary base, defined as the sum of the currency and reserves. There is a simple relation of the money supply to the monetary base. It recognizes that the users of the monetary base are the public in the form of currency and the banks when they hold reserves. When the Federal Reserve sells assets, as it is now planning on selling to reduce its assets, it reduces the monetary base, the sum of currency and bank reserves.

The public controls how much currency they want relative to other components of what we call money, the various kinds of deposits at financial institutions. To keep this simple, summarize the public's demand for currency in terms of their desired ratio of currency to other forms of money, bank deposits; *currency/deposits*.

Further, the deposits part of the money supply is affected by the Federal Reserve reserves required per dollar of deposits, rate at which banks hold reserves instead of economic assets. This reserve component of the monetary base before interest on bank reserves was simply the reserves the banks were required to hold by Federal Reserve regulations: *required reserves/deposits*. The bigger the required reserve component, the smaller are bank deposits and the smaller is the money supply.

Now, with interest on reserves, we have a new ratio that is important: *excess reserves/deposits*. Just as with required reserves, the greater the level of excess reserves the banks desire to hold, the smaller is the money supply. As is apparent in Figure 21.1, the level of excess reserves is closely linked to the spread between the rate of interest on 1-year treasuries and the interest rate paid on reserves.

While the Federal Reserve determines the level of the monetary base, choices of both the public and the banks affect the money supply that is associated with any given level of the monetary base. The following equation is shown to give the reader an idea of the complexity involved in the path back to your parents Federal Reserve. Without going into the detail of the derivation, the simplest version of the relation between the money supply and the monetary base can be expressed by the following equation. Importantly, only two of the factors in the equation are in control of the Federal Reserve: the level of the monetary base and the required ratio of reserves to deposits. All other factors in determining the money supply are determined by the public.

$$Money\ Supply = \left(\frac{\frac{currency}{deposits} + 1}{\frac{currency}{deposits} + \frac{required\ reserves}{deposits} + \frac{required\ reserves\ excess\ reserves}{deposits}} \right) Monetary\ Base$$

The proposed reduction schedule of Federal Reserve assets will reduce the monetary base. The goal during the reduction is to retain the policy goal of 2% annual inflation. Thus, the money supply must grow even though the fundamental input into the money supply, the monetary base, is falling. In the above equation, the only element of the multiplier of the monetary base that the Federal Reserve directly controls is the ratio of required reserves to deposits. However, the Federal Reserve can affect the ratio of excess reserves to deposits through the interest rate it pays on bank reserves. From the equation, the smaller the excess reserve ratio, the larger the money supply. Then, from Figure 21.1, we know that the lower the interest rate the Federal Reserve sets on reserves for any given interest rate on 1-year treasuries, the smaller the share of the banking system's assets that will be invested in reserves and the larger the money supply.

The problem for the Federal Reserve in returning to the traditional scale of assets relative to the size of the economy is that selling assets reduces the monetary base. Something must happen at the same time to allow the money supply to grow enough to meet the 2% inflation goal while the monetary base falls. How can this happen? Simple, just adjust the interest paid on reserves so that the rate of return on bank investments in the economy becomes better, relative to getting the interest that the Federal Reserve pays on reserves.

The goal is to reduce reserves and the monetary base, while at the same time letting the money supply grow to meet the 2% inflation goal. This can only happen if banks want to reduce excess reserves by more than the reserve reduction that results from Federal Reserve asset sales.

But for the banking system to desire to reduce excess reserves by more than the asset sale reserve reduction, the Federal Reserve must increase the spread between the 1-year treasury interest rate and the interest rate on reserves. In fact, it must increase the spread enough so that the banking system reduces its desired excess reserves per dollar of demand deposits. To aid the reader, Figure 21.2 is a reproduction of Figure 20.9.

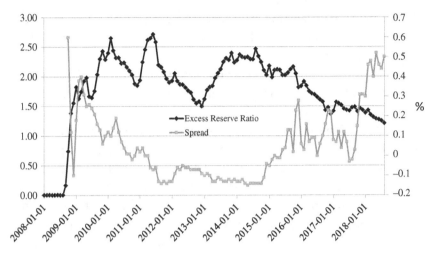

Figure 21.2.   Interest Rate Spread and Excess Reserves per Dollar of Demand Deposits

This figure shows that this it is possible by controlling the spread with appropriate changes in the interest rate on reserves to control the rate at which the banking system reduces reserves. Specifically, the figure shows that the smaller the benefit of holding reserves relative to 1-year treasuries, the smaller the dollars of reserves per dollar of bank deposits. What is also apparent from the figure is that once the spread became positive the excess reserve ratio began falling and has continued to fall as the spread rose.

Estimating the Interest Rate on Reserves to Achieve both Asset Reduction and 2% Inflation

The Federal Reserve policy necessary to achieve both the increase in the money supply consistent with their 2% inflation goal and the proposed asset reduction program is new territory. That both goals are possible is apparent from the observed relation of excess reserves per dollar of demand deposits to the interest rate spread. The problem is finding the path of the interest spread that is just right. What is required is that the asset reduction and the resulting reduction in bank reserves be consistent with the banking system's demand for excess reserves falling by more than the asset reduction induced reduction in reserves. As it turns out, we can use the simple equation of exchange to estimate how fast the spread must be increased to achieve the ultimate goal of returning to the Federal Reserve's traditional asset to GDP ratio.

First, as noted above, the Federal Reserve target for inflation of 2% per year implies a 0.165% monthly inflation rate. This is the inflation rate that becomes the left-hand side of the equation of exchange. For now, assume that the public demand for currency relative to other deposits will be unaffected by the asset reduction program. Then the rate of growth of the money supply will be equal to the difference between the rate of decline in bank excess reserves and the Federal Reserve determined rate of decline in the monetary base. The former depends on the difference between bank earning opportunities in the economy and the rate of interest the Federal Reserve pays on excess reserves. The latter is the rate at which the Federal Reserve chooses to reduce its asset portfolio. Put simply, the following equation is a representation of the determination of the money growth rate.

Money growth rate
    = excess reserve decline rate minus monetary base decline rate

The Federal Reserve asset reduction program makes the rate of growth in the monetary base negative. With a declining monetary base in order to make monetary growth positive, which is necessary to reach the inflation rate target, the rate of change in the banking system's desire to hold reserves must be negative and exceed the Federal Reserve determined rate of change in the monetary base. The following equation incorporates the above money growth equation and uses the fact that real GDP growth for the last decade has been about 2% annually, or 0.165% monthly, so that the equation of exchange is

0.165% = (Money growth rate + velocity growth rate) − 0.165%

The only parts of the above equation that are in the control of the Federal Reserve are the rate of decline in the monetary base resulting from non-reinvestment rate and the rate of interest on reserves that affects banks' desired excess reserve to deposit ratio. The monthly rate of change in the monetary base is projected to initially be −0.657%. Then, the current levels of the currency-deposit ratio, the required reserve ratio, and the excess reserve ratio are, respectively, 1.018, 0.081, and 1.436 so that the above equation can be written as

Required decline rate of excess reserve ratio
= –0.577% + 1.765 (rate of velocity growth)

If we don't have to worry about changes in velocity, then this indicates that the Federal Reserve must adjust the interest rate of reserves so that banks desire to hold excess reserves falls by 0.577% per month. Or, if velocity rises as interest rates rise at the same rate it fell as interest rates fell, 0.28% a month, then a smaller rate of change in the banking system's desire to hold excess reserves of 0.083% per month is required. But, without exact knowledge of the banking system's demand for reserves as a function of the spread and the fact that market interest rates are uncertain, suggests that the asset reduction program must proceed slowly so that Federal Reserve adjustments in the interest rate on reserves is to be consistent with their inflation goal.

The above attempt to estimate the rate at which banks desired excess reserves per dollar of deposit must decline to offset the projected reduction in Federal Reserve assets demonstrates that the approach bank to a normal Federal Reserve level of assets relative to GDP is filled with uncertainty. This analysis raises the question did we err on the side of paying too high an interest rate on reserves and, as a result, mitigated the monetary growth that would have allowed the Federal Reserve to reach its 2% inflation target? Further, did the policy followed of allowing the interest rate on reserves to exceed the rate of interest on 1-year treasuries for an extended period of time, slow or prevent a timely economic recovery? Finally, these same issues cloud the planned Federal Reserve return to a normal asset to GDP portfolio.

Conclusion

The above analysis shows that a return of the Federal Reserve to its traditional role in the economy is going to be as difficult as the path to its current position was easy. But perhaps easy is not the appropriate term. There is no doubt that most of the increase in Federal Reserve assets were offset by the banking system absorbing a significant portion of the federal deficit financing by holding excess reserves, essentially short-term Federal Reserve liabilities. Further, since the Treasury is the residual recipient of Federal Reserve earnings, this debt is for all intents and purposes the equivalent of short-term federal debt.

There is no doubt that after the fact, the effect on inflation of the huge federal deficits was minimal. At least two factors were responsible for the anticipated rampant inflation not happening.

First, in spite of each of the common definitions of the money supply growing significantly, although at a much slower rate than the monetary base, the velocity of all definitions of money declined. Such a decline in velocity is expected since velocity is related to the public economizing on money balances. However, the historically low interest rates made holding money less costly so that the ratio of GDP to money balances, velocity, fell.

Second, from the onset of the rapid expansion of Federal Reserve assets that began in October 2008, the Federal Reserve initiated the payment of interest on bank reserves. By making reserves an income earning asset, the banking system absorbed much of the increase in Federal Reserve assets. Moreover, these interest payments to banks on reserves made reserves a short-term liability of the Federal Reserve. The net assets of the Federal Reserve as a share of GDP rose very little over this entire period.

It is apparent from the above analysis that the path back to your parents' Federal Reserve will have many bumps. Thus, it is not surprising that the Board has decided to move slowly. As the economy develops and market interest rates change, the Federal Reserve must move the interest rate on reserves appropriately to ensure that the money supply continues to grow even as they reduce the monetary base. Even then, they must account for the effect of market interest rates on the velocity of money.

Chapter 22

Cryptocurrencies and Monetary Policy

Introduction

The rise of cryptocurrencies such as Bitcoin, Ethereum and Ripple has reopened an old debate concerning what constitutes money. The simplest definition of money is "money is what money does." But what does money do? Well, it facilitates transactions and trades, between and among individuals and businesses. What must this thing, money, be like to perform this function? It must have three characteristics:

- First, it must be readily recognizable in that when I have this item and want to trade it to someone else, they must immediately know what it is. More than that, any individual or business must be readily willing to exchange this thing for whatever they want to trade. With these characteristics, whatever is money will be the unit of account so that asset values will be expressed in terms of units of money.
- Second, it must be portable. This sounds simple, but this characteristic of money differentiates it from other assets that are recognizable, but fixed in location.
- Third, to be acceptable, something that is money must have a stable value. That is, when I accept it in trade and then present it the next day to someone else, its value must not have changed significantly. Money must also be a reliable store of value.

In summary, money must be easily recognizable as real, be portable and be a reasonable store of value. But all this sounds circular, doesn't it? So, what makes something a store of value? To be a store of value requires that its supply be controlled and that the demand for it not be overly volatile.

Transactions Technology and Money

Money is unique in that its productivity is proportional to its price. But, what is the price of money? In one sense, the price of a dollar is one dollar. But, in another sense, price of that dollar the number of real goods that a dollar can purchase. For all non-money goods, their real output is independent of their cost of the good, its price. An important implication of this attribute of money is that an increase in the quantity of money only reduces its price with no increase in national output. In contrast, an increase in the quantity of non-money goods increases welfare and national output. This difference is the reason for the critical importance of a stable quantity of money, at least a stable quantity of money relative to the quantity of real money transactions.

Once we solve the problem of a stable supply of whatever is money, is it necessary to have a central bank as the monopoly supplier of what is money? To answer this question, we must first determine what we want of the monetary system. For money to have a stable value, the supply of money relative to its uses must be controlled. But what are the uses of the money supply? First and foremost, having something that is money, makes transactions simpler because all traders will accept money. But trading does not require money. Indeed, in today's world, the internet makes it easier for individuals to trade with one another without using money. That said, however, the majority of trades are made with money, even internet trades.

There is no doubt that a stable money supply, or a stable existence of a supplier of this money, requires that potential competitors must be excluded or their output controlled by the money monopoly. In general, a competitor money supplier must also have adequate control over its supply. Such control has traditionally been the competitor making their money convertible into the central bank's money or a precious metal.[1]

Even with total control of the supply of what is money, can we be assured that the value will be stable? The issue is a simple one. The price

---

[1] For example, see Saving (1976, 1977).

of anything, including money, is determined by demand and supply. Even with supply fixed, in absolute amount or in a quantity relative to the aggregate amount of trading to be done, demand is not so fixed.

But how and why might the demand for a fixed quantity of money be changed? Any change in the available technology of transacting, has the potential to increase or reduce the demand for money. Let's consider some changes that have occurred in the last half-century that have affected the demand for money.

First, we have the rise in the consumer credit card as a way to consolidate monthly purchases. In its simplest form, the credit card did for everyone, what having a monthly account at the store did for individuals in the pre-credit card world. Specifically, such an account reduced the average quantity of money held over a specific period of time. It potentially reduced it to the minutes from receiving a pay envelope to paying your monthly store bill times the size of your bill.

The general use of credit cards allowed everyone to essentially have an account at every store that accepted these cards. However, the predictions that we were on the verge of a cashless society were certainly premature. It was true that this change in the frequency of payments for transactions reduced the demand for money and, as a result, increased the velocity of money.

Second, recent changes in the ability of individuals to make sale or purchase information available has decreased the cost of finding trading partners. This technological change has at least two effects on the demand for money. One, as with credit cards, it can reduce the necessity of keeping a cache of cash on hand as uncertainty in the timing of transactions is reduced. Two, it increases the ease of making trades that do not involve what we usually term money. Both of these effects reduce the demand for money and increase the velocity of money.

Can Cryptocurrencies be a Viable Competitor in the Money Industry?

In the entire developed world money, at least the money that serves as official legal tender is produced by a monopoly central bank. Legal tender simply means that this form of money is recognized and approved by the government for payment of taxes and has a legal status to repay debts or in exchange for goods and services. Importantly, however, legal tender does not preclude exchanges being conducted in other instruments. This is an important distinction since unless outlawed by law, any commodity or financial instrument can, at least theoretically, be money.[2]

In fact, most transactions are conducted using instruments that are not legal tender. That said, however, these transaction instruments are convertible into legal tender. Historically, various forms of paper scrip or even wooden nickels were used in transactions in areas where there was little or no legal money. The fact that when small units of legal tender were not available, things that could aid in transactions would be developed, shows the tremendous value of money.[3]

Another important characteristic of circulating money is that proof of ownership is by possession only. Therefore, transfer of ownership only requires the physical transfer of the item serving as money from one possessor to the next, without interference from any outside authenticator. Therefore, such transfers are anonymous.[4]

Since things that are used as money do not have to be official legal tender, this makes the control of the money supply by a central bank difficult, or in some cases impossible. The question is then as follows: given that a central bank is the monopoly producer of legal tender, what conditions must a competitor supplier of a circulating media meet? Then can the existing cryptocurrencies meet these conditions? Does the fact that cryptocurrencies do not represent the title to a real asset but only title to themselves preclude them from being money? The answer to this question is clearly no, as no current currency represents a title to anything other than itself.

---

[2] Given that anything can be money, countries that desire to raise revenue through having their central bank just print currency must worry about substitute forms of money arising. Not surprisingly, when a government intends to use inflation financing, they first outlaw contracts in other than legal tender. Such contracts can still be written but if violated cannot be enforced in the legal system.

[3] Two excellent pieces on the importance of small denominations of money are Sargent and Velde (2001) and Gramm and Gramm (2004).

[4] This possession as ownership aspect of currency or any other circulating media has resulted in efforts to control anonymity that usually fail. Further, it is this anonymity that is a principal driver of the rise of cryptocurrencies.

Any new currency competitor must meet conditions similar to money issued by the central bank. First, a currency competitor must be recognizable by all traders. Second, it must be portable. Third, it must be relatively stable in value. When you leave home to shop, you want to be assured that the instrument to pay for purchases will be accepted by any store where you shop. Then you want some assurance of how much of the so-called money you will need when you get to the store. This relative stability in value is especially important in executing contracts when the payment is to be made at a future date.

In general, when multiple monies circulate the successful non-legal tender currencies are convertible at a fixed rate into a legal tender currency. However, there are important conditions under which this fixed convertibility is not necessary. Almost always, when the legal tender issuer loses control of the currency issue, such as currently in Venezuela, the substitute for legal tender will not be convertible into the local legal tender at a fixed rate of exchange.

Examples of such failure in today's world are Venezuela and Zimbabwe where the legal tender currency is depreciating at rates that often exceed 1,000% per year. In cases such as this, the US dollar is often the non-legal tender currency used. When this happens, stores could display two prices: one in legal tender currency and one in the alternative currency.[5] However, when currencies are in distress the posting of alternative prices is usually illegal and occurs off the books, in what is essentially a black market.

Future contracts are especially difficult when the legal tender currency value is in distress. Such contracts will at least informally be done in terms of some alternative but can only be done when both parties are known to be reliable. This joint reliability is required because a breach of contract in a restricted currency is not enforceable in the legal system.

Leaving aside substitute currencies that arise as a result of a legal tender that has become dysfunctional, what is required for non-legal tender money to circulate? The most important requirement is that the users

---

[5] This display of multiple prices occurred during the Civil War when greenbacks were not convertible and gold still circulated.

must be assured that the value of the competitor money will be stable. The cheapest way to ensure this value stability is to make the substitute currency convertible into legal tender at a constant exchange rate. This convertibility allows contracts with future payment to be done assuring that the value of the substitute currency will be the same as the legal tender currency into which it is convertible.

The fact that a potential currency competitor can be converted to legal tender, while a requirement for circulation, is not sufficient to make the competitor generally acceptable. All digital currencies are traded, and in that sense are redeemable into legal tender currencies. The catch is that the exchange rate between digital currencies and legal tender is anything but constant.

Figure 22.1 shows the path of Bitcoin daily closing prices. The tremendous variability of value is a problem for contracts that specify future payment for future delivery. For current transactions the exchange of bitcoin can be done at any time a transaction is made. In that sense it is similar to the foreign exchange market. Theoretically, at least, you could walk into a local store and spend a 100 Euro note and get change in dollars. It would be a simple matter to determine the current exchange rate but in general such transactions do not occur.

Given the extreme volatility shown in Figure 22.1, coupled with the fact that Bitcoin is not the title to any income yielding asset, what explains

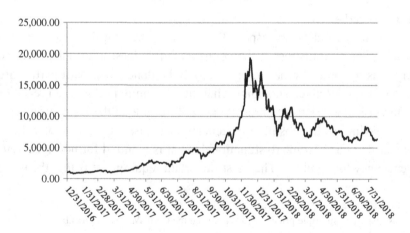

Figure 22.1.   Bitcoin Prices Daily 1/1/2017–8/15/2018

its position in the market? Put differentially, why have investors become so enchanted with trading in something with a zero yield that is a title to nothing except itself? Given that an active market exists, investors should be most interested in what a Bitcoin will be worth tomorrow. If ultimately, the interest in this type of asset goes away, as long as you are not holding it when that happens, you suffer no harm. This is similar to the classic "bubble" experiments that repeatedly show that assets of this type can trade at values that far exceed their final value, but then crash at some point.[6]

But in cryptocurrencies defense, no legal tender currency is title to any income yielding asset, but only title to itself. In that sense cryptocurrencies are on a par with legal tender currencies. The difference is that legal tender currencies are universally used in transactions, i.e., are generally accepted. The question is; are we headed to a future where acceptability of one or more cryptocurrencies will be on a par with legal tender currencies?

With today's technology, any financial asset with a continuous market could be used in transactions. You could conceivably take your ownership of a mutual fund to the store, shop, and at the close of the transaction, the store simply transfer the appropriate amount from that your shares in that fund to the store ownership in their fund. But even with today's advanced technology, we are still a long way from this kind of transfer of funds being a cost effective substitute for currency. What does work in today's world is the direct transfer of currency ownership using instruments such as debit and credit cards that transfer currency at fixed rates of exchange.

What is required for a digital currency to be generally used is a method of an instantaneous transfer from the digital currency spender to the digital currency receiver. While the market depicted in Figure 22.1 is at the close, the market is continuous, but ultimately the receiver wants dollars not digital currency. As technology keeps changing, that could change, but that the change would require that value fluctuations would have to be greatly reduced. One solution would be to make the digital currency convertible into dollars at a fixed exchange rate which would stabilize the digital currency's future value.

---

[6]This phenomenon is consistently demonstrated in simple economics experiments. See Lei *et al.* (2001).

Currency Substitutes and the Central Bank

From the perspective of a central bank, if digital transfer mechanisms become instantaneous, how will this competition affect the value of central bank ownership? The answer is simple and who owns the monopoly does not affect this answer. The production cost of legal tender is zero relative to the value of the currency since it is just the power to run the press and the cost of ink and paper. To simplify the discussion, let's begin by suggesting that the goal of the monopoly supplier of legal tender is to maintain the value of a unit of currency. Also, let's assume what is a fact for most nations, that legal tender is the unit of account for transactions. Further, assume that any competing monies are convertible into legal tender on a one-to-one basis, or at least instantly convertible at the then existing exchange rate.

With these assumptions, the owners of the legal tender monopoly, for most countries the owner is the government, receive assets equal in value to the issue of currency outstanding. The flow from these assets then accrues to the Treasury, as it does in the United States as Federal Reserve income is, by law, transferred to the US Treasury.

How does the existence and amount of competitive circulating media affect the value of the central bank and the flows it transfers to the Treasury? Importantly, all legal tender competitors must, to be viable, be convertible into legal tender at a fixed rate or at least instantly convertible at the current rate of exchange. Currently, there are two forms of central bank legal tender competitors, neither of which can be anonymous in transactions.

First, commercial banks are depositories of legal tender or titles to legal tender. Owners of these deposits can issue checks that transfer ownership of their deposits to others, but not without proof that the issuer of the check actually has on deposit with the bank, title to an adequate quantity of legal tender. Those banks that are members of the Federal Reserve are regulated by the central bank and must hold reserves of legal tender. Such reserve requirements could be viewed as a form of licensing fee for the privilege of competing with the monopoly legal tender issuer.

The necessity that these legal tender competitor instruments be convertible into legal tender on demand means that competitors must maintain a cache of legal tender even if not required to do so by the monopoly legal tender issuer. The level of required reserves may or may not be larger than these competitor issuers of money would hold for purposes of meeting a surge of redemptions of their money for legal tender.

Second, other legal tender competitors are issuers of circulating media that are not licensees of the monopoly legal tender issuer. Because the circulating media issued by these competitors must be convertible into legal tender, they must also hold reserves of legal tender.

How do these competitors affect the balance sheet of the central bank? The central bank controls the total issue of legal tender, but not the issue of competing monies. If the central bank does not control the competing issuers who does? Here, the answer is simple; it's the public who decides the form of money that they choose to use. What this means is that the public decides the composition of their money holdings in terms of the legal tender share of money holdings. The total demand for legal tender is the sum of the public's demand for legal tender plus the quantity of legal tender held by the competitor issuers of circulating media.

How does this competition affect the value of the central bank? Assume, for simplicity, that the cost of producing and maintaining the stock of legal tender is zero. Then, the value of the central bank is equal to the assets it acquires when it issues legal tender. When the public increases its use of competing money, it reduces the quantity of legal tender that can be issued, if the central bank wants to maintain the value of a unit of legal tender. Just as with any normal product and industry, market share matters.

This result does not depend on the assumption that the central bank wants to maintain the value of legal tender. All that is required is that the central bank acts to maintain a fixed rate of depreciation in the value of legal tender. The public's choice of circulating media still drives the bus. Thus, currency competition reduces the value of the central bank and reduces the transfers that the central bank makes to its owner, the Treasury.

How Will We Know that Cryptocurrencies Have Arrived?

This is the ultimate question with cryptocurrencies as a legitimate entry into the currency world. In one sense the answer is simple. We will know that a competing currency has arrived when most or all prices are expressed in terms of that currency. Importantly, prices may also be expressed also in terms of whatever the traditional currency is as well.

Current instances of multiple currency pricing are always in border cities where prices are expressed both in terms of that city's country's legal tender and the bordering country's legal tender. Other potential instances of multiple country legal tender pricing occur when one country's currency is subject to what is often called runaway inflation. As this was written, Venezuela was such a country.

Historically there have been multiple instances of distressed currencies. But even in instances of distressed currency, have prices in general been openly expressed in terms of multiple currencies? The answer is no. The country that is using money issue to finance its deficits invariably declares pricing in non-legal illegal. As a result in these countries non-legal currencies did circulate but the market for non-legal currencies while illegal, existed as what would be termed a "black market."

This does not mean that multiple currencies could not exist and open pricing in terms of these currencies be allowed. In fact, in the United States during the Civil War, both legal tender in the form of greenbacks and gold coins, both denominated in dollars, circulated and pricing in both was common. In general, however, nation's want to preserve the ability to generate the revenue by making the central bank the monopoly issuer of legal tender. To this end competitive issuers must be eliminated either through taxation, as in the elimination of State Bank issued Notes, or in the elimination of the special government bonds that were required for the issue of National Bank Notes in the United States.[7]

So, when will cryptocurrencies be real currencies? When prices are universally expressed in both legal tender and cryptocurrency. This is no more likely to happen than prices being expressed in shares in a mutual fund. In fact, once the first cryptocurrency declares itself to convertible into legal tender at a fixed exchange rate it will, for all practical purposes, be legal tender. Then what are now Bitcoins will become Bitdollars. Then these cryptocurrencies will have to hold reserves in order to honor their promise to exchange their currency for legal tender. Nonetheless, just as

---

[7] See Chapter 2 for a complete discussion of the path to a monopoly issuer of legal tender.

demand deposits are, any circulating cryptocurrency will be competitor of the Federal Reserve. As pointed out in Chapter 19, any Federal Reserve competitor reduces the net worth of the Federal Reserve.

Cryptocurrency: Is It a Threat to the Federal Reserve's Money Monopoly?

Perhaps the name cryptocurrency is a total misnomer, or at least the currency part is, at best, misleading.[8] The crypto part is on target, but for something to be currency, it must circulate in a general way. But, what does it mean to circulate in a general way? Essentially, all traders on both sides of a transaction must be willing to accept the asset in payment. Legal tender currency has that attribute and other circulating media convertible at a fixed rate into legal tender currency do as well. But, what about other financial assets?

Most, if not all, financial assets represent titles to an income flow or to a bank deposit that is convertible into legal tender. Then, there are titles to physical assets, such as precious metals or gems. Titles to precious metals are recorded somewhere so that transactions using precious metals titles are not anonymous. However, transactions using actual precious metals can be anonymous when the metals rather than titles to them are exchanged.

Cryptocurrency is unique from these titles to assets in that a cryptocurrency title represents only a title to itself. The innovation of cryptocurrency is that its' blockchain technology assures ownership and anonymity as long as there is no outside recording of ownership deeds. Mere digital possession proves your title to ownership just as physical possession does for standard paper currency. Is that all that is required for cryptocurrencies to really be money?

The cryptocurrencies assure the real and portable parts of the conditions required for something to be money through software, and seem to do it well. But to be a currency, that is be commonly used in transactions, they must be accepted by the majority of individuals in exchange for real resources, and must be viable in contracts involving future delivery.

---

[8] For an excellent summary of cryptocurrencies, see Berentsen and Fabian (2018).

Further, to be currency in fact, rather than in name, a user of a cryptocurrency has to be able to walk into a local fast food restaurant, buy a taco, and pay for said taco. Such a transaction requires that the cryptocurrency be sufficiently divisible. This divisibility has been a problem historically and has led to the issuance and circulation of many private issues of currency substitutes, especially in fractional denominations.[9]

What would make a "thin air" digital entity become universally traded? The past equivalent of a digital currency was the development of pure paper money that was not convertible into anything real but only into itself. This description fits most if not all legal tender money in the world. The issue with paper money has always been controlling its quantity and rate of growth. The same issue will be and is true for digital currencies that are not convertible into either a real resource or a legal tender currency.[10]

In one sense at least, the coming era of digital currencies is similar to the free banking era in the United States. Various state banks issued currency denominated on their face in dollars, the official currency of the United States. Just as with digital currency, the cost of producing notes relative to denominated value was minimal. When banks issued currency, they received real goods in return for currency. Each bank was identified on their notes so that bank notes that circulated had to control the value of the notes. That is, it had to convince the users that their bank was going to maintain the value of the notes issued. In equilibrium, that assurance was achieved by making the notes convertibility into gold or silver coins.

Now, we come to the "free" digital currency era with a large and growing number of digital entities hoping to become circulating currencies. Bitcoin controls the issue by the cost of solving the algorithm, referred to as mining, the solution of which generates a new Bitcoin. This mining cost is a natural control on the stock of cryptocurrencies just as gold mining costs control the world's stock of gold. And just as new

---

[9] See, for example, Timberlake (1974) and the previously cited Sargent and Velde (2001).

[10] As this was in press, at least two entities plan to issue convertible cryptocurrencies. The first is Sprott Global that was about introduce a cryptocurrency convertible into gold with reserves held in the Bank of Canada. The second is Venezuela that plans a cryptocurrency convertible into Venezuelan petroleum. Convertibility is a solution to the overissue problem provided it is honored. Historically whenever it became convenient issuers suspended convertibility.

discoveries or new technology changed the marginal cost of increasing the gold stock, the same holds true for cryptocurrencies. But the cost of real gold mining is determined by the existence of gold deposits. The cost of cryptocurrency mining is in the digital world and subject to manipulation. Thus, non-convertible cryptocurrencies have the same problem as non-convertible paper currency; namely, ultimately use and value depend on controlling the issue.

Imagine a world where all "money" is digital and you are a supplier of one of many digital currencies, Zaps, with Zips as fractional units where 100 Zips equals 1 Zap. As a money supplier, you sell Zaps for real resources. Once your digital money circulates, that is, it is accepted everywhere in commerce, what prevents you from issuing yourself a large quantity and using it to buy additional resources? Nothing, and therein lies the problem. Prices of goods expressed in Zaps will rise. But more importantly, digital money users will move away from Zaps and toward digital monies whose values are more stable.

Whenever the rate at which a money depreciates cannot be determined by simple costless examination of the money, brand name identification becomes a possible efficient method of supplying such information. Just the history of paper money demonstrates once the currency begins use as money, it is tempting for the issuer to surprise users by increasing its supply, just as in the early days of the stock exchange, issuers of shares "watered" their stock.

The fundamental issue is, in a world of competing digital currencies, how do you distinguish your digital currency from others? By ensuring against surprise increases in the quantity of your currency. In the early days of paper money, this was accomplished by making the paper notes convertible into a known resource, such as gold. Even this convertibility could only work so long as the issuer did not do a surprise cancel, called a suspension, of convertibility.

What is the mechanism that allows multiple digital currencies to exist? What is required is that each digital currency be convertible into the unit of account, "digits," at an announced fixed rate. But then who is the "digit" ruler?

In our current world, the "digit" ruler could be any of the major central banks. In some future world, it would be an independent of any government "digit" master.[11] Whomever is the keeper of the "digits," these "digits" are essentially what we now refer to as "high powered money." This increase in supply can only be accomplished by using the new issue to acquire assets.

Two things are clear concerning the future of the digital currency world. First, governments will not allow this expansion of the anonymity that now is almost the exclusive domain of paper currency. Second, the world's principal central banks have a comparative advantage in producing digital currency. That comparative advantage only holds for digital currency that is not convertible. Once a digital currency becomes convertible, it becomes similar to a debit card or a demand deposit. Digital currency issuers will have to hold reserves, although the level of these reserves will be a small fraction of the issue. As a result, any expansion in the use of digital currency will reduce the value of the central bank as an income source for the Treasury.

What is the nature of the comparative advantage of central banks, as new entrants in the world of digital currency? First, they have the long history of producing currency that is relatively stable in value. By this, I mean that, except in rare cases, they have resisted the temptation to introduce surprise increases in their currency to acquire resources from the public. Second, once one or more of the premiere central banks, US Federal Reserve, the European Central Bank, the Bank of England or the Bank of Japan, enter the digital currency world, all existing cryptocurrencies, to be competitive, will have to be convertible into one of these dominant currencies. This convertibility is the only way to ensure to their users that they will not water down their currency.

Conclusion

The rise of cryptocurrencies, such as Bitcoin, Ethereum and Ripple, has reopened an old debate concerning what constitutes money. The simplest definition of money is "money is what money does." But what does money do? Well it facilitates transactions, trades, between and among individuals and businesses. What must this thing, money, be like to

---

[11] Now, we really are getting into science fiction, but this approach is not far from the reality of cryptocurrency issuers.

perform this function? It must have three characteristics. It must first be readily recognizable in that when I have this item and want to trade it to someone else, they must immediately know what it is. More than that any individual or business must be readily willing to exchange this thing for whatever they want to trade. With these characteristics, whatever is money will be the unit of account, so that asset value will be expressed in terms units of money

While many odd things have served as money in a limited way, historically, it is survivorship that matters.[12] Money must be easily recognizable as real, be portable and be a reasonable store of value. The fact that others will be as ready to accept this thing in trade makes you willing to accept it. But this all sounds circular doesn't it? So what makes something have a reliable value, i.e., be a store of value? To be a store of value requires that its supply be controlled and that the demand for it not be overly volatile.

All this brings us to the latest entry in the money industry, cryptocurrency. Does such "currency" meet the criterion for being money? In one aspect, it does in that the blockchain technology possession is 100% of the law, just as it is with currencies that generally circulate. However, while ownership of a Bitcoin is not in dispute, Bitcoin has not exhibited stable value. So, if an individual accepts Bitcoin in exchange for a product, they must first find its current dollar, euro, pound or yen value. Even then, if they hope to use it for a subsequent trade, will they know what it will be worth? Clearly not! The way for a receiver of Bitcoin to ensure the future is to immediately convert the Bitcoin into dollars, euros, pounds or yen through one of the exchanges that exist. In contrast, if the trade is made using dollars, euros, pounds or yen at the next trade, these currencies will have experienced very little or no change in value.

If we accept the premise that for a currency to circulate, in general, it must have a relatively stable value, then cryptocurrencies as we know them will not replace currency. In fact, we can expect that the first cryptocurrency that can convincingly regulate its value will set the cryptocurrency standard.

Historically, it is convertibility into an accepted medium that has been required for a currency to survive as a circulating medium of exchange.

---

[12] For an excellent survey of primitive monies, that is things that have served a limited role in relatively primitive societies with minimal transactions, see Einzig (1966).

At least until the 1930s, this convertibility was in terms of gold. Even this hard standard could not ensure a stable value of any circulating medium of exchange since gold prices fluctuate and at times greatly so. Even so, the gold standard was more successful than relying on fiscal restraint at controlling monetary authorities from expanding the issue and creating inflation in prices expressed in terms of money. Indeed, when nations intended to expand government expenditures by running the money printing press, they suspended convertibility.

The bottom line is that the future of cryptocurrencies must be and will be convertibility into one of the major units of account, i.e., dollars, euros, pounds or yen. Only then will cryptocurrency begin to circulate in more than isolated transactions.

Chapter 23

Some Concluding Issues in the History and Future of the Federal Reserve

Introduction

Now that the Federal Reserve has concluded its first 100 years, it seems appropriate to ask a basic question: are we happy with what it has become? To answer this question requires a review of where it has been and how it transitioned to its current configuration. True central banking began in the United States as the result of repeated financial crises brought on by the fact that the money supply, currency plus bank deposits, was not flexible in terms of its form. Even assuming that all commercial banks in the country were solvent in that their assets equaled or exceeded their liabilities, the system was vulnerable to rapid changes in the public's desire to have money in their pocket rather than in their bank.

The problem was not bank insolvency, but the short-term illiquidity of bank assets. It was more than just value, the problem was instant value. Interestingly, these crises did not result in a shutting down of the banking system. Rather, what was done was a suspension of convertibility of deposits into currency. Not surprisingly then, one of the principal components of the Act establishing the Federal Reserves was to achieve currency elasticity. Currency elasticity means the ability of the system to respond quickly to the public's demand to change the way it holds its monetary assets. Put simply, a principal charge of the new Federal Reserve was to enhance the banking system's ability to supply currency whenever the public, for whatever reason, wanted to convert their bank deposits into currency.

This early Federal Reserve, as all major central banks, operated in a world in which currency was convertible into gold at a fixed rate of exchange. Such convertibility was designed to limit the ability of central bank to engage in an inflationary surge in its production of currency. That gold standard world is gone and most likely never to return. All major central banks are only constrained by their concern over their nation's economy.

The onset of the great recession brought major changes to the developed world's central banks as all expanded their holdings of both government and private assets. The level of that asset expansion if it had resulted in an equivalent change in the money supply would have led to levels of inflation not seen since 1980. That this outcome did not occur is a great tribute to the Federal Reserve. However, it did change the nature of the Federal Reserve. The question now is what does the future hold?

Four Significant Issues Facing the Federal Reserve

How much inflation?

As has been noted more than once in this manuscript, all the world's major central banks have a goal of keeping the rate of inflation near 2%. Although one might question why the goal of a monetary system should be a continued devaluation of its currency, a 2% devaluation rate is modest compared to actual results for most of the past century. The issue in the developed world over the past decade, has been a fear of falling prices and thus rising value of currencies.

The first question is: why or should a target inflation rate be a policy goal? Furthermore, it is important to realize that achieving a steady and constant inflation rate will not affect the equilibrium in the economy. This constant rate will simply be added to the economy's real interest rate and should have no effect on the real economy. That is not to say, however, that surprise inflations and deflations cannot have an effect.[1]

---

[1] The effect of inflation on the economy created considerable debate in the economics profession. The debate began with Phillips (1958), that showed that greater rates of inflation was associated with lower unemployment. The stand of the profession now is that the so-called Phillips curve is a short-run phenomenon. That is, once it is recognized that changes in prices are pure inflation the effect goes away.

The answer to the inflation goal mystery is that it provides some insurance against making a contractionary policy mistake. Just as insurance is designed to protect us against downside risk, this small inflation target reduces the probability of the Federal Reserve contributing to an economic downturn.

The federal reserve and the interest rate

Interest rates present a real dilemma. Borrowers want interest rates to be low, and lenders want them to be high. Market interest rates are the culmination of the battle between these two forces. Time preference, the desire to have something now rather than later, prompts individuals to enter the market as suppliers of their future income, i.e., demanders of current consumption. That something now may be pure consumption, as those in the early stage of their life-cycle earnings desire to smooth their consumption knowing that as they age their income will rise. Or, that something now may entail the belief that investment will yield returns greater than the cost of obtaining the funds.

Individuals saving for retirement are suppliers of current income as they consumption smooth for when their life earnings cycle turns down. In addition, individuals that essentially arbitrage between what they have to pay for current income and what the capital acquired by that current income will yield in the future. These forces together determine the equilibrium real rate of interest. Then, if both sides of the market have the same expectations concerning the real value of the money they receive or pay in the future, the nominal rate of interest, what we observe in the market, will be the sum of the equilibrium real rate of interest and the rate of inflation.

Put in this context, what is the role of the Federal Reserve in the determination of the equilibrium rate of interest? Historically, the fear of Wall Street determining interest rates led to the regional character of the original Federal Reserve System. That at least Congress believed that the Federal Reserve could influence interest rates was apparent in the imposition of the charge during World War II that the Federal Reserve operate to ensure that T-Bill interest rates do not exceed 0.375% and long-term treasury rates do not exceed 2.5%. While the 1950 Treasury–Federal Reserve Accord removed this constraint on the Federal Reserve, the 1977 amendment to the Federal Reserve Act explicitly made interest rates a factor in Federal Reserve policy.[2]

We know if we follow the monetary policy statements from the Federal Reserve, they are couched in terms of interest rate and inflation targets. But in reality, these markets are so huge relative to any potential Federal Reserve policy that, at least in the long run, the Federal Reserve is just a real interest rate taker. Thus, while the Federal Reserve can influence the money supply and, thus, the inflation rate, real interest rates are largely determined by market forces that are beyond the Federal Reserve's control.

How do we return to the old federal reserve?

As we enter this new era of the Federal Reserve reversing the series of quantitative easing (QE), is it possible to achieve a return to the past levels of Federal Reserve assets without negatively affecting the economy? The QE was aided by the institution of interest on reserves so that the banking system absorbed the majority of the asset increase. Reversing this process will require that the banking system follow the asset reduction with a reduction in their desired investments in reserves that counters the actions of the Federal Reserve.

But making certain that the banking system's is just the right size is the problem. The change in the banking system's desire to hold excess reserves must match the level of excess reserves reduction that is consistent with the level of non-reinvestment chosen by the Federal Reserve. Can we reverse the asset buildup and draw down Federal Reserve assets to their historic share of GDP? Certainly, the Federal Reserve can induce the banks to hold fewer reserves by lowering the interest rate of reserves relative to other bank investment alternatives. Also, and almost certain, is the fact that as market interest rates rise, a falling demand for money can offset the money reduction inherent in the series of open-market sales of Federal Reserve assets.

---

[2] In 1977, President Carter signed a Federal Reserve Reform Act that amended the original act by explicitly directing the Federal Reserve to maintain long-run growth of the monetary and credit aggregates commensurate with the economy's long-run potential to increase production, so as to promote the goals of maximum employment, stable prices, and moderate long-term interest rates.

Because interest on bank reserves has made a no action on the part of the Federal Reserve into an actual policy, changes in market interest rates can have significant effects on the economy. Of course, a vigilant Federal Reserve can offset these effects. However, such vigilance requires knowing when such changes will happen, or at least knowing if they are temporary or permanent.

The return to a Federal Reserve that existed in the past requires that the rate of disposition of assets and the path of interest on reserves are consistent with the rate of growth of the money supply that achieves the Federal Reserve's 2% inflation goal. Clearly, the management of these two components of the equation if done successfully will allow the restoration of the Federal Reserve to a portfolio that is consistent with zero interest on reserves. This configuration will return the Federal Reserve to having its principal policy being control of the money supply. Then we will be back in the world where total Federal Reserve inaction, leaves the quantity of money constant, i.e., is actually, no policy. In contrast, in the interest on reserves world, changes in market interest rates result in actual policy in that they affect the money supply without any action by the Federal Reserve.

Is digital currency the future of money?

There is little doubt that we are in an era of rapidly expanding methods of payment. A principal issue with non-cash payment is proof of ownership. The unique advantage of currency is the fact that possession is 100% of the law. You can spend currency without proving that you actually own it as mere possession is, in and of itself, proof of ownership. This is not true of any other asset, and that is perhaps why, in general, transactions trading financial assets does not occur. Although advances in digital technology, especially the blockchain technology, may bring us to the world where you can walk into a Walmart and use your mutual fund to pay for purchases. But, in today's world, trading financial assets in small every-day transactions remains out of reach.

To see this lack of general acceptance for titles to assets, just reflect on the three principal non-currency things used to conduct transactions: bank checks, credit cards and debit cards. In each of these, unlike currency, ownership must be established before transactions can occur. The claim of the digital currency contenders is that blockchain technology establishes ownership with certainty so that digital possession is proof of ownership.

Importantly, it is not just proof of ownership that is required for a user of a digital currency to be able to walk into a local fast food restaurant, buy a taco, and pay for said taco. What would make a "thin air" digital currency become universally traded? The entity that accepts a digital currency must be assured of its value in at least the near term, however defined. Further the digital currency must be divisible into small enough units to be useful in a typical consumer transaction. This usefulness in small transactions has been a problem with all things that have served as money, even things universally traded in the past, such as Spanish pieces of eight, were worth more than the annual income of a typical citizen.[3]

The past equivalent of a digital currency was the development of pure paper money that was not convertible into anything real but only into itself. This description fits most if not all legal tender money in the world. The issue with paper money has always been controlling its quantity and rate of growth. The same issue will be and is true for digital currencies that are not convertible into either a real resource or a legal tender currency.

Fundamentally, in a world of competing digital currencies, how do you distinguish your digital currency from others? One way is to ensure that there will be no surprise increases in the quantity of your currency. In the early days of paper money, this was accomplished by making the paper notes convertible into a known resource, such as gold. Even this convertibility could only work so long as the issuer did not do a surprise cancel, called a suspension, of convertibility.

Two things are clear concerning the future of the digital currency world. First, governments will not allow this expansion of the anonymity that now is almost the exclusive domain of paper currency. Second, the world's principal central banks have a comparative advantage in producing digital currency.

What is the nature of the comparative advantage of central banks if they were to enter as new digital currency entrants? First, they have the

---

[3] Once again see the past cited Sargent and Velde (2001).

long history of issuing money with a relatively stable value. By this, I mean that except in rare past cases, they have resisted the temptation to introduce surprise increases in their currency to acquire resources from the public. Second, once one or more of the premiere central banks, US Federal Reserve, the European Central Bank, the Bank of England or the Bank of Japan, introduce a digital currency that is convertible into a traditional currency, all digital currencies will have to be convertible into one of these dominant currencies. This convertibility is the only way an issuer of digital currency can ensure to the users of that digital currency that they will not water down their currency.

The bottom line is that while some form of digital currency may, at some time in the future, totally eliminate physical paper currency, that time is not in the lifetime of anyone alive when this manuscript is published. That said, however, digital currency, convertible into major central bank money will become a significant player in the payment world. These digital currencies convertible into, say Federal Reserve issued legal tender, will only require small reserves of legal tender. As they replace legal tender in transactions, they will reduce the net worth of the Federal Reserve.

Where Should We Go from Here?

As we reflect on this 100 years of Federal Reserve monetary policy history, can it suggest what institution might have made the mistakes of the past less costly, or prevented them entirely? This question is not new and is reflected in the "rules versus authority" controversy of the past. The initial rule was simple, just increase the money supply at a constant rate. The test of such a policy would be its behavior compared to actual Federal Reserve policy. Early work suggested that relative to actual Federal Reserve policy the constant rate of monetary growth was counter cyclical. Subsequent rules have been more complex, but the idea behind all these rules is to remove the discretion of the Federal Reserve from its conduct of monetary policy.

The rules versus authority is a way of tackling the issue of an independent central bank. That is, a central bank that is not controlled by the political party in power will conduct monetary policy for the general welfare and not to enhance the electability of members of any political party. Here, the rules versus authority is just as relevant. It is just who establishes the rule. If the rule can be changed at will by the authority then there is no rule.

Fundamentally, the issue is: should the central bank be independent? If so, then independent of whom? A rule driven central bank is independent of those in the political arena. But then who determines the rule? Is the rule invariant with economic conditions? Then is in times of a liquidity crisis, should the policy rule be abandoned, at least for the duration of the crisis? Then who makes the crisis call?

To decide any of this we must understand what a central bank can do to affect the economy. While we all want faster GDP growth and low unemployment, both are outside the ability of the central bank to control, at least in the long-run. What is in the central bank's purview is a stable value for the dollar. Indeed, the central bank can honor Section 8 of Article 1 of the constitution by being the agent that can coin money and regulate the value thereof. And as we know from our history and the history of other countries, this is no mean task.

Conclusion

Once uniform paper currency began to establish dominance over hard coinage and various titles to assets in conducting transactions, ensuring the value of costless to produce money became important for commerce. Not surprisingly, successful issues of paper currency required that the notes be convertible into "hard" currency or fixed weights of precious metals. This necessity was a characteristic of both privately and central bank-issued paper money. The reason was simple, the public required that "funny" money be stable in value, before they would take it in exchange for goods and services. This means that when you took in paper money you had to believe that when you presented it to someone else for something of value, they would take it and not say, "I don't accept anything but gold or silver."

From the start, central banks produced currency that was redeemable into hard currency. Importantly, the redeemable requirement still allowed the owners of the central bank, almost always the government, to profit from the issue. The profit margin was the difference between the total currency issued and the level of gold or silver that the bank had to keep to ensure that it would be able to redeem returned currency with metal on the demand of currency users. It is important to recognize that both bank owners and the public benefited from the issue of paper currency. Costless paper money does the same work as the resource intensive metal money did, thus saving the resources for other uses.

That was the world that existed when the Federal Reserve came into existence. The redeemable paper currency of the time, a combination of National Bank Notes and Treasury notes, was relatively fixed in size. This not-very-flexible stock of currency resulted in periodic liquidity crises, the last of which occurred in 1908. The establishment of the Federal Reserve System was to counter these liquidity crises by providing an "elastic" money supply so that when a sudden increase in the demand for currency at the expense of bank deposits, a system was there to satisfy that demand. Importantly, this early version of a central bank issued currency that was redeemable into metal, namely gold, and both paper currency and gold coins circulated.

Now, no central bank money is redeemable into anything except itself. It is this era of central banking that has been the essential topic of this manuscript. The first 100 years of Federal Reserve monetary policy is heavily concentrated post the demise of the gold standard in the 1930s. Through the history of central banking, governments have relied on these banks to support war financing. In fact, as the Federal Reserve first began operations, it was faced with what has been termed the Great War, World War I. While the nations in Europe abandoned the gold standard, that did not happen in the United States. However, the influx of gold resulted in considerable inflation as the money supply expanded.

The decades of Federal Reserve freedom from the gold standard were, to a different extent, subject to pressure from the Treasury to respond to financing federal government budget deficits. The latest of these issues resulted in the tremendous increase in the scale of the Federal Reserve that we find ourselves in at the present.

So, what does the future hold? Will we return to the Federal Reserve as we once knew it? Will this new world be one of a central bank directly engaging in the private sector of the economy or returning to traditional central banking? Will currency as we know it disappear? This volume has explored all of these issues, but we all must await the ultimate outcome.

References

Arias, Maria A. and Yi Wen, "The Liquidity Trap: An Alternative Explanation for Today's Low Inflation", *Regional Economist*, Federal Reserve Bank of St. Louis, April 2014.

Auernheimer, Leonardo, "The Honest Government's Guide to the Revenue from the Creation of Money," *Journal of Political Economy*, 1974: 598–606.

Auernheimer, Leonardo, "The Revenue Maximizing Inflation Rate and the Treatment of the Transition to Equilibrium," *Journal of Money, Credit and Banking*, 1983, 15: 368–376.

Balke, Nathan S. and Robert J. Gordon, *The American Business Cycle: Continuity and Change*, Robert J. Gordon, editor, University of Chicago Press, 1986, pp. 781–850.

Berentsen, Aleksander and Fabian Schär, "A Short Introduction to the World of Cryptocurrencies," Federal Reserve Bank of St. Louis *Review*, First Quarter 2018, 100(1): 1–16. https://doi.org/10.20955/r.2018.1-16.

Cochrane, John H., "Monetary Policy with Interest on Reserves." *Journal of Economic Dynamics & Control*, 2014, 49: 74–108.

Dwyer, Gerald P. Jr. and Thomas R. Saving, "Government Revenue From Money Creation with Government and Private Money," *Journal of Monetary Economics*, 1986, 7: 239–249.

Einzig, Paul, *Primitive Money*, 2nd edition, Pergamon Press (June 1966).

Fama, Eugene F., "Does the Fed Control Interest Rates?" *Review of Asset Pricing Studies*, 2013, 3: 180–199.

FOMC issues addendum to the Policy Normalization Principles and Plans, June 14, 2017. https://www.federalreserve.gov/newsevents/pressreleases/monetary20170614c.htm.

Friedman, Milton and Anna J. Schwartz, *A Monetary History of the United States 1967-1960*, Princeton University Press, 1964.

Gara Afonso, Alex Entz, and Eric LeSueur, "Who's Lending in the Fed Funds Market," *Liberty Street Economics*, Federal Reserve Bank of New York, December 2, 2013a.

Gara Afonso, Alex Entz, and Eric LeSueur, "Who's Borrowing in the Fed Funds Market," *Liberty Street Economics*, Federal Reserve Bank of New York, December 9, 2013b.

Gramm, Marshall and Gramm, Phil, "The Free Silver Movement in America: A Reinterpretation," *Journal of Economic History*, 2004, 64(4): 1108–1129.

Gust, Christopher *et al.*, "The Empirical Implications of the Interest-Rate Lower Bound," *American Economic Review*, 2017, 107(7): 1971–2006.

Henderson, Stephen W., "Consumer spending in World War II: the forgotten consumer expenditure surveys," *BLS Monthly Labor Review*, August 2015.

Hetzel, Robert L. and Ralph F. Leach, The Federal Bank of Richmond *Economic Quarterly*, Winter 2001.

Humphrey, Thomas H. and Richard H. Timberlake, *Gold, the Real Bills Doctrine, and the Fed: Sources of Monetary Disorder, 1922–1938*, Cato Institute, 2018.

Lei, Vivian, Charles N. Noussair and Charles R. Plott, "Non-speculative Bubbles in Experimental Asset Markets: Lack of Common Knowledge of Rationality vs. Actual Irrationality," *Econometrica*, 2001, 69(4): 831–859.

Meltzer, Allan H. *A History of the Federal Reserve*, The University of Chicago Press, 2003.

Pesek, Boris P. and Thomas R. Saving, "Monetary Policy, Taxes, and the Rate of Interest," *Journal of Political Economy*, 1963, LXXL(4): 347–362.

Pesek, Boris P. and Thomas R. Saving, *Money, Wealth and Economic Theory*, Macmillan, 1966.

Pesek, Boris P. and Thomas R. Saving, *The Foundations of Money and Banking*, Macmillan, 1968.

Phillips, A. W., "The Relationship between Unemployment and the Rate of Change of Money Wages in the United Kingdom 1861–1957". *Economica*. 1958, 25(100): 283–299.

P.L. 507, 77th Congress, 2d Session (S2208), Approved March 27, 1942. An Act to further expedite the prosecution of the war.

Saving, Thomas R., "Monetary Policy Targets and Indicators," *Journal of Political Economy*, August 1967: 446–456.

Saving, Thomas R., "Outside Money, Inside Money, and the Real Balance Effect," *Journal of Money, Credit and Banking*, February 1970: 83–100.

Saving, Thomas R., "Competitive Money Production and Price Level Determinacy," *Southern Economic Journal*, October 1976: 987–995.

Saving, Thomas R., "A Theory of the Money Supply With Competitive Banking," *Journal of Monetary Economics*, July 1977: 289–303.

Saving, Thomas R., *The Federal Reserve, the Great Recession and the Lost Inflation*, Private Enterprise Research Center Study, No. 1604, July 2016, available at http://perc.tamu.edu/perc/Publication/policybrief/study_no1604_07_2016.pdf.

Saving, Thomas R., "Rethinking Federal Debt: What Do We Really Owe?" Private Enterprise Research Center Study, No. 1607, August 2016.

Sargent, Thomas J. and Francois R. Velde, *The Big Problem of Small Change*, Princeton University Press, 2001.

Timberlake, R. H., "Denominational Factors in Nineteenth-Century Currency Experience." *Journal of Economic History*, 1974, 34(4): 835–850.

United States Treasury, Financial Report of the United States Government, Fiscal Year 2015, Department of Treasury, Washington District of Columbia.

Walker, Michael, *Why Are Interest Rates so Low?*, Fraser Institute, February 2016.

Index